COMPU MADE S

GW00319358

NEW
AOL 4.0
Keith Brindley
0 7506 4626 8   1999

NEW
Access 2000
Moira Stephen
0 7506 4182 7   1999

NEW
Access 2000 in Business
Moira Stephen   1999
7506 4611 X   £11.99

Access 97 for Windows
Moira Stephen
0 7506 3800 1   1997

Access for Windows 95 (V.7)
Moira Stephen
0 7506 2818 9   1996

Access for Windows 3.1 (V.2)
Moira Stephen
0 7506 2309 8   1995

NEW
Adobe Acrobat & PDF
Graham Douglas
0 7506 4220 3   1999

NEW
Compuserve 2000
Keith Brindley
0 7506 4524 5   1999

Compuserve (V.3)
Keith Brindley
0 7506 3512 6   1998

NEW
Designing Internet Home Pages Second Edition
Lilian Hobbs
0 7506 4476 1   1999

NEW
Excel 2000
Stephen Morris
0 7506 4180 0   1999

NEW
Excel 2000 in Business
Stephen Morris   1999
0 7506 4609 8   £11.99

Excel 97 for Windows
Stephen Morris
0 7506 3802 8   1997

Excel for Windows 95 (V.7)
Stephen Morris
0 7506 2816 2   1996

Excel for Windows 3.1 (V.5)
Stephen Morris
0 7506 2070 6   1994

NEW
Explorer 5.0
P K McBride
0 7506 4627 6   1999

Explorer 4.0
Sam Kennington
0 7506 3796 X   1998

Explorer 3.0
Sam Kennington
0 7506 3513 4   1997

NEW
Internet In Colour .
P K McBride
0 7506 4576 8   £14.99

NEW
Internet for Windows 98
P K McBride
0 7506 4563 6   1999

Internet for Windows 95
P K McBride
0 7506 3846 X   1997

NEW
FrontPage 2000
Nat McBride
0 7506 4598 9   1999

FrontPage 97
Nat McBride
0 7506 3941 5   1998

NEW
The iMac Made Simple
Keith Brindley
0 7506 4608 X   1999

NEW
Microsoft Money 99
Moira Stephen
0 7506 4305 6   1999

NEW
Publisher 2000
Moira Stephen
0 7506 4597 0   1999

Publisher 97
Moira Stephen
0 7506 3943 1   1998

MS-DOS
Ian Sinclair
0 7506 2069 2   1994

Multimedia for Windows 95
Simon Collin
0 7506 3397 2   1997

Netscape Communicator 4.0
Sam Kennington
0 7506 4040 5   1998

Netscape Navigator (V.3)
P K McBride
0 7506 3514 2   1997

NEW
Office 2000
P K McBride
0 7506 4179 7   1999

Office 97
P K McBride
0 7506 3798 6   1997

NEW
Outlook 2000
P K McBride
0 7506 4414 1   1999

NEW
Pagemaker (V.6.5)
Steve Heath
0 7506 4050 2   1999

NEW
Photoshop 5
Martin Evening
Rod Wynne-Powell
0 7506 4334 X   1999

.point 2000
Moira Stephen
0 7506 4177 0   1999

Powerpoint 97 for Windows
Moira Stephen
0 7506 3799 4   1997

Powerpoint for Windows 95 (V.7)
Moira Stephen
0 7506 2817 0   1996

NEW
Sage Accounts
P K McBride
0 7506 4413 3   1999

Searching the Internet
P K McBride
0 7506 3794 3   1998

Windows 98
P K McBride
0 7506 4039 1   1998

Windows 95
P K McBride
0 7506 2306 3   1995

Windows 3.1
P K McBride
0 7506 2072 2   1994

NEW
Windows CE
Craig Peacock
0 7506 4335 8   1999

Windows NT (V4.0)
Lilian Hobbs
0 7506 3511 8   1997

NEW
Word 2000
Keith Brindley
0 7506 4181 9   1999

NEW
Word 2000 in Business
Keith Brindley   1999
0 7506 4610 1   £11.99

Word 97 for Windows
Keith Brindley
0 7506 3801 X   1997

Word for Windows 95 (V.7)
Keith Brindley
0 7506 2815 4   1996

Word for Windows 3.1 (V.6)
Keith Brindley
0 7506 2071 4   1994

Word Pro (4.0) for Windows 3.1
Moira Stephen
0 7506 2626 7   1995

Works for Windows 95 (V.4)
P K McBride
0 7506 3396 4   1996

Works for Windows 3.1 (V.3)
P K McBride
0 7506 2065 X   1994

Includes New Titles for 1999

The Internet
Made Simple

Second edition

The Internet
Made Simple
Second Edition

P.K.McBride

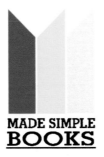

MADE SIMPLE
BOOKS

OXFORD • AUCKLAND • BOSTON • JOHANNESBURG • MELBOURNE • NEW DELHI

Made Simple
An imprint of Butterworth-Heinemann
Linacre House, Jordan Hill, Oxford OX2 8DP
225 Wildwood Avenue, Woburn MA 01801-2041
A division of Reed Educational and Professional Publishing Ltd

ꞅ A member of the Reed Elsevier plc group

First published 1998
Second Edition published 1999

© P.K.McBride, 1998, 1999

TRADEMARKS/REGISTERED TRADEMARKS
Computer hardware and software brand names mentioned in this book are protected
by their respective trademarks and are acknowledged.

British Library Cataloguing in Publication Data
A catalogue record for this book is available from the British Library

ISBN 0 7506 4576 8

Typeset by P.K.McBride, Southampton
Icons designed by Sarah Ward © 1994

PLANT A TREE

British Trust for Conservation Volunteers

FOR EVERY TITLE THAT WE PUBLISH, BUTTERWORTH-HEINEMANN
WILL PAY FOR BTCV TO PLANT AND CARE FOR A TREE.

Contents

Preface

The Internet is vast, varied and changing fast. Some parts of it are designed for very specialist audiences, some of its facilities are complex to use. Other parts are of general interest and some services are simple to access. This book concentrates on those aspects that will be of interest to most people – browsing and searching the World Wide Web, using electronic mail, reading newsgroups, downloading files and creating Web pages.

The best way to get to grips with the Internet is to explore it. But exploration, Livingstone-style, can take you into a lot of dead ends, or round in circles. While this is fascinating, it can also be frustrating – I speak from experience. This book aims to provide you with a map, and some of the basic tools that you need, so that you don't get (too) lost.

The first four chapters cover the preparations to be made while at the base camp. They provide a crash course in the native language of the Internet, its key concepts and jargon, and setting up the equipment that you will need for your expedition.

The next four chapters explore the World Wide Web, trying out a number of routes into it and seeing what you can do while you are there.

From the Web, we strike out into other areas of the Internet – e-mail, newsgroups and the stores of files for downloading.

Towards the end of the book, we take a brief look at creating Web pages, introducing the basics of HTML – HyperText Markup Language – and sampling the possibilities of the HTML editors that can be found in the Netscape and Internet Explorer packages.

The final chapter contains lists of sites to see and some useful sources of shareware and other files.

Tip

If you are a new computer user and need to know more about Windows 98 or 95, there are *Made Simple* books on these – and many more – topics.

Many thanks to my local Internet access providers, Total Connectivity Providers for their excellent service over these last four years; to fellow authors Sam Kennington and Nat McBride for sharing their enthusiasms; and to Catherine Fear, my copy-editor, for going over the text with her fine-tooth comb!

I've found both entertainment and challenge in researching this second edition of the book. I hope that you find the same pleasure in your travels around the Internet!

P.K. McBride

Take note

The information in this book was up to date as it went to press, but any-thing you read anywhere about the Internet may be out of date. It changes so rapidly, and there are so many people creating new services and devising new uses for the Internet, that by the time any book or magazine has been printed, some of the things de-scribed in it may well have been overtaken by events.

If you want to know what's happening **NOW** get onto the Net and watch the changes from the inside.

1 Instant Internet

The Net and the Web

Let's start by clearing up a common confusion – the Internet and the World Wide Web are not the same thing.

The Internet is the basis of hardware, software and data and the connections that join it all together. It consists of millions of computers – of all shapes and sizes – in tens of thousands of computer networks, throughout the world. They are joined through a mixture of special high-speed cables, microwave links and ordinary public and private telephone lines.

The World Wide Web is one of the ways of organising and looking at the information held on the Internet. It is probably the most important way – and certainly the simplest – but there are others (see page 10).

What's in it for me?

If you have access to the Internet, you have access to:

- **16 million host computers**. These are the ones that provide services and information, any of which could be useful to you in your work, your travelling, your academic research or your hobbies.

- **100+ million people.** You probably already know of some friends and relations who are on the Internet, and you will almost certainly discover more once you start using it – and you could find new friends, customers, fellow enthusiasts, problem-solvers.

- **gigabytes of files** containing programs – including the software that you need for working on the Internet – books, articles, pictures, video, sounds and much else.

- **a whole raft of services**, such as financial advice, stock market information, airline times and reservations, weather reports, small-ads and electronic shopping malls.

Who owns the Net?

The computers, networks and connections that make up the Internet are owned and run by thousands of separate businesses, government agencies, universities and individuals but no-one owns the Internet as a whole.

Take note

There will be even more computers and people on-line by the time you read this! The Internet is growing at a phenomenal rate – if the number of users continues to grow at its current rate, everyone in the World will be on the Internet in about six years. I don't quite think so...

The Internet is truly international, linking people in every country in the World, and it is open to all. This screenshot is from the Web site of Amanaka'a – a group campaigning for the rights of Amazon indians.

Where do I start?

Here, of course. Read on to get an idea of what's going on out there, then learn how to set up your hardware and get on-line with an access provider. You can then start to explore the World Wide Web, e-mail and the other services available through the Internet.

The World Wide Web

This is the fastest-growing aspect of the Internet. It consists of hundreds of millions of pages, held in millions of computers, joined together by *hypertext* links and viewed through a *Web browser*, such as Internet Explorer or Communicator (Chapters 3 and 4). The links allow you to jump from one page to another, which may be on the same machine or on one far, far away! The sheer number of pages, and the fact that thousands are added or changed every day, mean that there can be no comprehensive index to the Web, but there are *directories* and *search engines* (Chapters 6 and 7) to help you to find what you want.

Most pages are illustrated with still or animated graphics, though some keep to simple – but fast – text-only displays. Some have video or sound clips that you can enjoy on-line; other have links to files – programs, documents, pictures or multimedia clips – that you can *download* into your computer. Some pages work interactively with the reader, or act as places where users can meet and 'chat' – usually via the keyboard, but increasingly by really talking.

Take note

In the 20 years since the Internet started, people have developed a number of different ways of using it. The ones covered in this book are those that most people find the most useful – and the easiest to handle!

Take note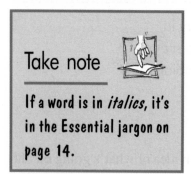

If a word is in *italics*, it's in the Essential jargon on page 14.

The old meets the old. The National Trust runs one of the most popular Web site in the UK, with thousands of visitors every day.

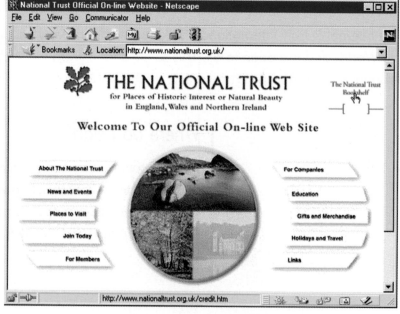

National Trust Official On-line Website - Netscape

File Edit View Go Communicator Help

Bookmarks   Location: http://www.nationaltrust.org.uk/

THE NATIONAL TRUST
for Places of Historic Interest or Natural Beauty
in England, Wales and Northern Ireland

The National Trust Bookshelf

Welcome To Our Official On-line Web Site

About The National Trust
News and Events
Places to Visit
Join Today
For Members

For Companies
Education
Gifts and Merchandise
Holidays and Travel
Links

http://www.nationaltrust.org.uk/credit.htm

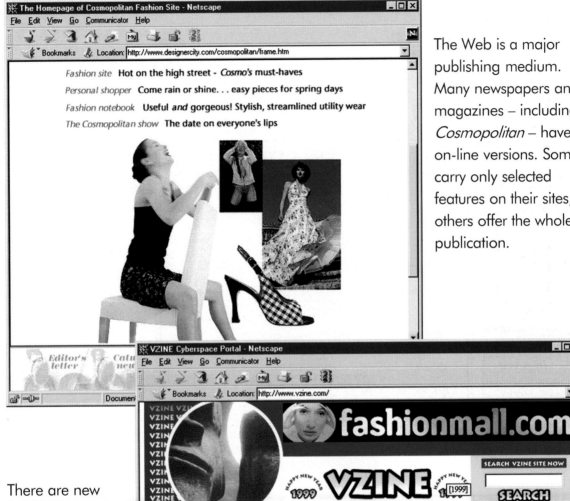

The Web is a major publishing medium. Many newspapers and magazines – including *Cosmopolitan* – have on-line versions. Some carry only selected features on their sites, others offer the whole publication.

There are new 'electronic magazines', such as *Vzine*, which exist only on the Web.

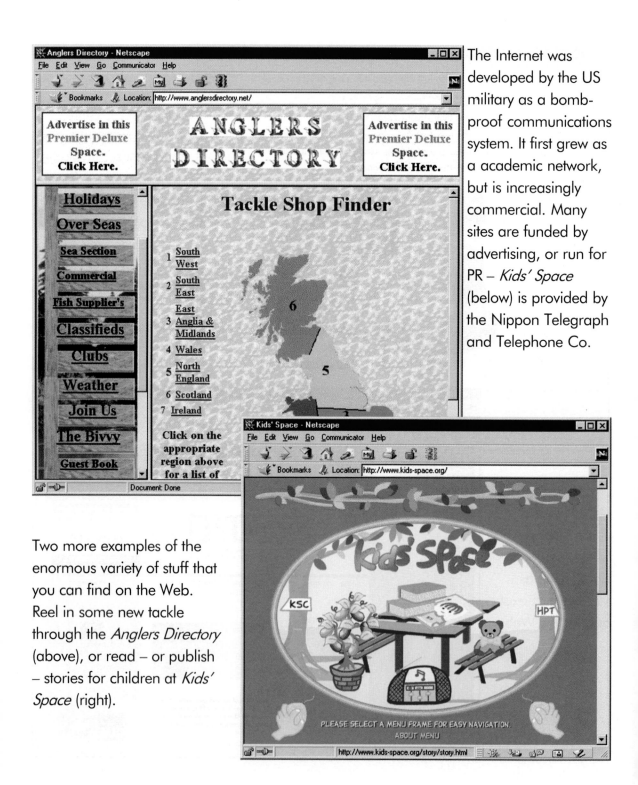

The Internet was developed by the US military as a bomb-proof communications system. It first grew as a academic network, but is increasingly commercial. Many sites are funded by advertising, or run for PR – *Kids' Space* (below) is provided by the Nippon Telegraph and Telephone Co.

Two more examples of the enormous variety of stuff that you can find on the Web. Reel in some new tackle through the *Anglers Directory* (above), or read – or publish – stories for children at *Kids' Space* (right).

The Web is a wonderful equaliser. Here are two sites, both based around animations and both excellent, but one is produced by the mighty Disney Corporation, the other by a fan.

Anyone can publish their own pages on the Web to tell the world about themselves, their enthusiasms or their products.

Tip

If you want to visit any of the sites shown in this book the addresses are in Chapter 15.

Almost all computer hardware and software firms make great use of the Web to provide technical support, upgrades and beta tests, as well as to advertise and sell their products.

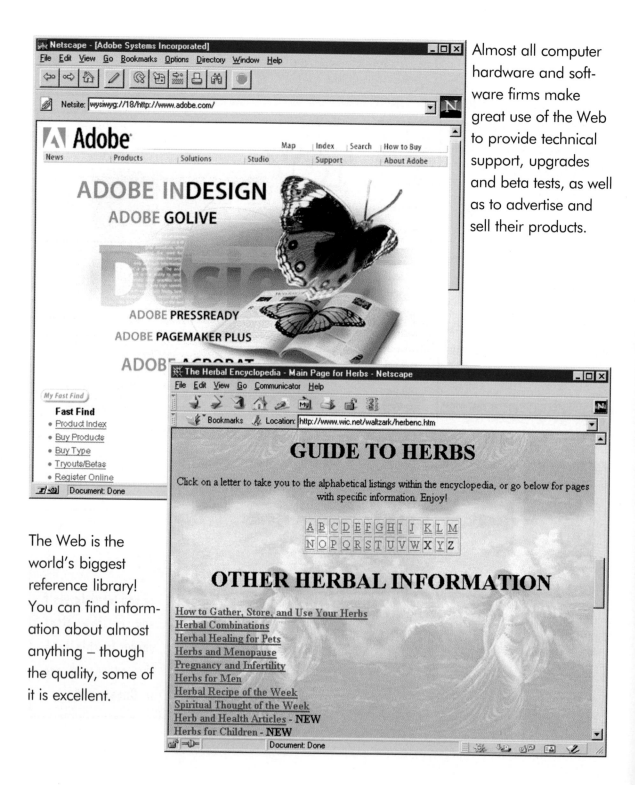

The Web is the world's biggest reference library! You can find information about almost anything – though the quality, some of it is excellent.

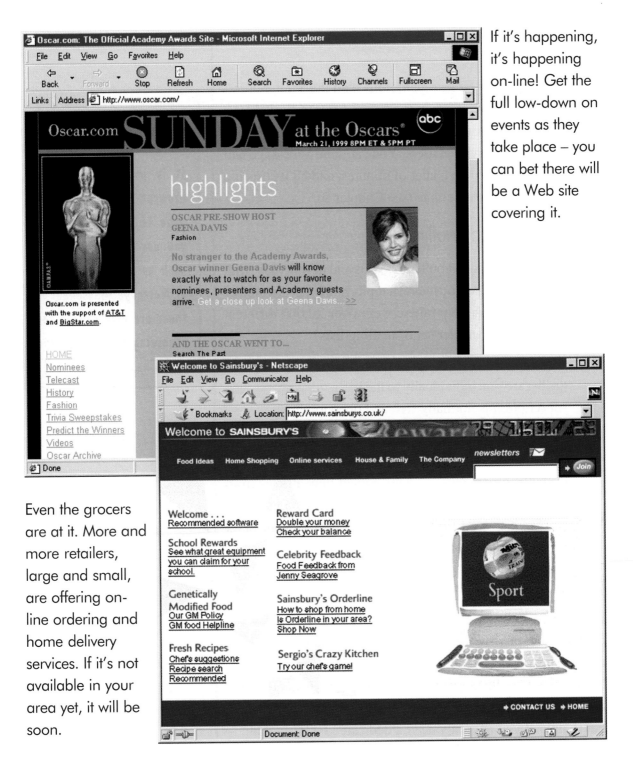

If it's happening, it's happening on-line! Get the full low-down on events as they take place – you can bet there will be a Web site covering it.

Even the grocers are at it. More and more retailers, large and small, are offering on-line ordering and home delivery services. If it's not available in your area yet, it will be soon.

9

Other uses of the Net

E-mail

Electronic mail may be less glamorous than the Web, but it is arguably more useful. Simple to use, and (pretty) reliable, it allows you to communicate and exchange files quickly and cheaply with other Internet users. You can send a message half way round the world in a matter of minutes, and all it costs is a few seconds of telephone time (see Chapter 9).

Newsgroups and mailing lists

They are a combination of bulletin boards and newsletters, with each dedicated to a specific interest, topic, hobby, profession or obsession. At the last count there were over 20,000 different newsgroups, plus a smaller set of mailing lists.

- A mailing list is a direct extension of e-mail. Messages to the list are sent individually to the list's subscribers – and subscription is normally free and open to all.

- Newsgroups are more centralised. The messages – here called articles – are initially sent to the computer that hosts the group. News servers collect new articles from the groups several times a day and hold them in store. If you want to read the news, you connect to your *news server* and download articles from there.

FTP

FTP – File Transfer Protocol – is the standard method for copying files across the Internet. FTP *host computers* hold archives, open to anyone to search and *download* files from. Some hosts have directories into which you can *upload* files, for others to share. You can download files through a Web browser, but to upload you normally need a dedicated FTP program.

Take note

It is possible to use a browser for e-mail (see page 166), but normally you use special software such as Outlook Express or Netscape Messenger – these are also needed for accessing the newsgroups (see Chapters 9 and 10).

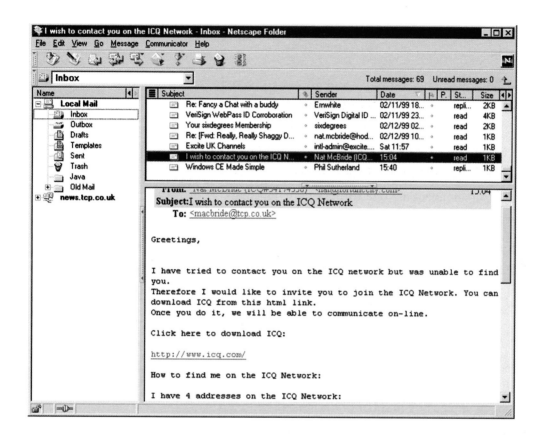

E-mail and news are text-based though files can be sent with messages. The same software can handle mail and newsgroups – and the two most popular applications, Messenger and Outlook Express are almost identical.

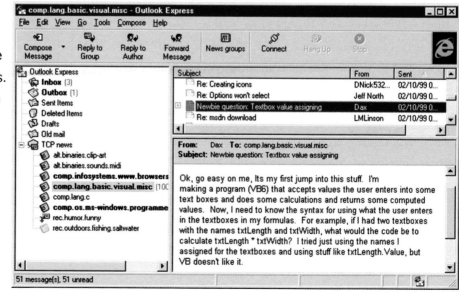

What will it cost me?

Setting up costs

Of course, if you do not have a computer and a modem, you must buy those before you can do anything. Bottom of the range multimedia PCs – fine for Internet use – are selling for around £750 at the time of writing, and could well be cheaper by the time you read this. A good fast *modem* should cost under £150, though you can pick up an adequate one for less than half that price. We'll return to modems in the next chapter.

The essential software is free and most of the more useful extras are low-priced *shareware* – £100 should be more than enough.

Running costs

You must sign up with an Internet *access provider*. Charges are typically around £12 a month for unlimited access or £6 a month for 20 hours, with a surcharge for extra time – but prices are dropping. There are an increasing number of organisations that offering free access – no subscription and no surcharge. How do they do it? Advertising and on-line sales can make it worthwhile. Advertisers are willing to pay well for space on sites that have lots of visitors, and firms that sell on-line will pay commision to those sites that direct buyers towards them. Be aware – with a free service, you will probably spend more of your time online waiting for adverts to download and display!

Don't forget that you will normally also be paying the standard phone charges at the same time, but even so you shouldn't expect the total cost to be more than £20 to £30 per month – and BT users can make their access provider one of their 'Friends and Family' to help keep the cost down. (After the initial 'new toy' phase, most households find that their on-line time settles down to a significantly lower level!)

Tip

E-mail is cheaper than snail mail (i.e. the post), and finding information on the Web is cheaper than travelling down to the library, so you could even save money!!

Take note

There's more on finding and choosing an access provider on pages 22.

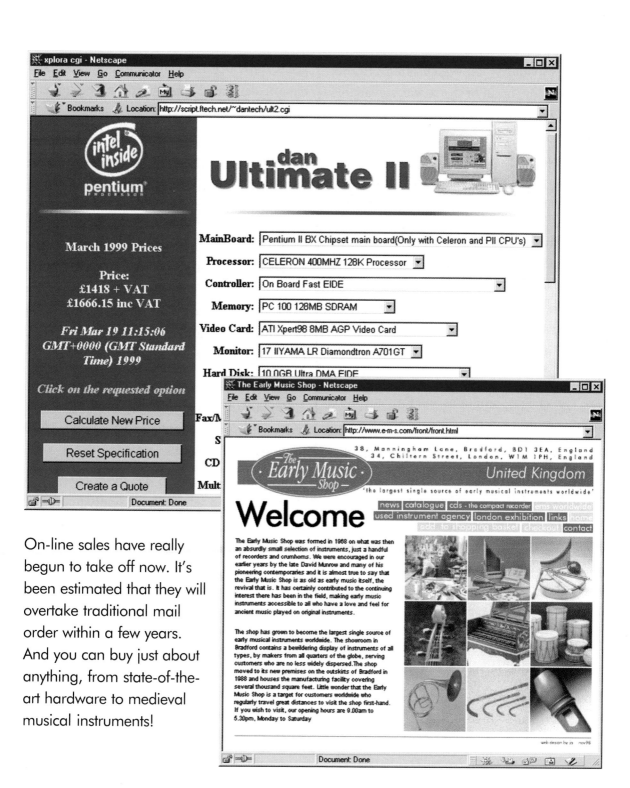

On-line sales have really begun to take off now. It's been estimated that they will overtake traditional mail order within a few years. And you can buy just about anything, from state-of-the-art hardware to medieval musical instruments!

Jargon

Access provider – an organisation offering access to some or all of the services available over the Internet.

ASCII – the American Standard Code for Information Interchange. The ASCII code is a set of characters – letters, digits and symbols. ASCII text is plain, unformatted text.

Bandwidth – strictly refers to the capacity of the phone line, but is also used to refer to other transmission and storage resources. If some-one refers to your e-mail or your Web site as being a 'waste of bandwidth', they didn't think much of it!

Binary files – any that are not plain ASCII text, e.g. images, programs and formatted text from word processors.

Browsing – moving from one site to another on the World Wide Web, enjoying the scenery and following up interesting leads. Also called *surfing*.

Byte – the basic unit of data. One byte can hold one character or a number in the range 0 to 255. A byte is made up of 8 **bits**, each of which can be 0 or 1, or an on/off electrical signal.

Content Provider – organisation providing information and/or services to Web users.

Dial-up connection – the method used by most home and small business users, where you get on-line to the Internet by dialling your access provider. Large organisations normally have a dedicated line, giving a permament, high-speed connection.

Directory – Web site holding an organised set of links (thousands of them!). The better ones only have links to reviewed and selected sites.

Download – copy a file from the Internet to your own computer.

FAQs (Frequently Asked Questions) – at almost every place on the Internet where you can ask for help, you will find a FAQ list – a set of common questions, and their answers. Check the FAQs first, before asking a question.

Gigabyte – a thousand megabytes or 1,000,000,000 bytes. Taking each byte as a letter, this is the equivalent of around 2,000 thick paperback books.

Home page – on a Web site, the home page is the top one of a set, or a user's only published page. On a browser, the home page is the one that the browser will go to when it first starts.

Host computer – one that provides a service for Internet users. The service may be simple pages of information, access to files for downloading, a place to meet and chat with other users, or a complex interactive service.

Hypertext – documents linked so that clicking on a button, icon or keyword takes you into the related document – wherever it may be. Web pages are written in **HTML** (HyperText Markup Language) which handles links in a standardised way.

ISP (Internet Service Provider) – alternative name for Access Provider.

LAN (Local Area Network) – network operating within one site or organisation.

Log on – connect to the Internet. This gives grammar purists a headache. As a noun, 'logon' – the act of connection – is one word. So, to match, the verb should also be one word, but that leaves you with 'logonned' and 'logonning' (aargh!!) instead of 'logged on' and 'logging on'. Just to make life really interesting, some people talk of 'log **in**'. Don't let it get to you.

Modem – (**mo**dulator-**dem**odulator) a device which translates digital computer signals into an analog form for transmission down the ordinary phone lines.

Newbie – someone new to the Internet. Just remember, everybody was a newbie once.

News server – a computer at an Internet access provider's site that collects newsgroup articles for the benefit of its users.

Network – a collection of linked computers. On a LAN, users can share printers and other networked resources. On any network – including the Internet – users can communicate and share data with each other.

Offline – using your e-mail software or browser while not connected to the Internet. Mail can be more conveniently be read or written offline.

Online – connected to the Internet (and clocking up phone charges!).

Portal – an Internet site which offers a range of services, including organised links into the Web. Portals aim to encourage as many users as possible to come through their site on their way into the Internet – and to read the adverts that pay for it all!

Search engines – Web sites that hold searchable indexes to Web pages and other Internet resources.

Shareware – software that you can try for freely, but for which you should pay a (small) fee to continue to use.

Site – set of Web pages run by one individual or organisation. The site may occupy one or more computers all by itself, or be one of many in a shared space.

Upload – copy a file from your computer onto an Internet host computer.

Web browser – program that lets you leap between hypertext links to read text, view graphics and videos, and hear sounds. The two leading browsers are **Netscape Navigator** and **Microsoft's Internet Explorer.**

Summary

◆ The World Wide Web is only one of many aspects of the Internet – though a very important part of it.

◆ The Internet gives you access to people, information, files and a vast range of services – and the number of people, quantity of information and range of service are all increasingly faster than anyone can measure.

◆ The World Wide Web consists of an uncountable number of pages, held together by hypertext links. The pages are published by individuals and by all kinds of commercial and non-commercial organisations.

◆ E-mail is the second most widely used Internet service, offering cheap, fast communication world wide.

◆ Newsgroups are places where people can share special interests – and with over 20,000 to choose from, there should be at least one that you will find interesting!

◆ Once you have paid for the hardware, Internet access is cheap to run.

2 Getting on-line

Hardware

To get on-line, you need:

- **Hardware** – a computer, modem and telephone line;
- **Software** – for surfing the Web, downloading files and handling the mail and news.
- **An access provider** – to connect you to the Internet.

If you have Windows 98, then you have all the software that you need to get started – you can pick up other stuff off the Internet as and when you want it. And a Windows 98 PC is more than powerful enough to handle anything the Internet can throw at it. If your computer does not already have a modem in it, or attached to it, you will need one.

The modem

The quality of the modem dictates the maximum speed at which it can transfer data. Speed is measured in Baud – bits per second. There are 8 bits to a *byte*, but all transmissions have extra addressing and error-checking information attached to them, so divide by 10 to get the approximate bytes per second speed, or by 10,000 to get the Kilobyte rate. A 56.6k modem can move data at 56,600 Baud, or 5.6Kb per second – around 1Mb in 3 minutes. They cost around £100, but if you are on a tight budget, you can still get 28.8k modems for less than half that price. Fast modems help to make browsing more enjoyable and keep the phone bills down, but even with the fastest, you may find that data trickles in from busy sites at busy times of day. When it's really bad, the rate can drop below 500 bytes per second.

Modern modems use compression to push data through faster. There are standards, MNP and V.42bis, and most newer modems can handle both. Data compression does not always give faster throughput. It basically works by replacing repeated

Jargon

Modem – MOdulator/ DEModulator. A device that converts digital signals from a computer into analog ones for transmission over the phone lines (and vice versa).

MNP – Microcom Network Protocol. Microcom is one of the leading data communications companies.

Zip – extension given to files that have been compressed by WinZip. You need WinZip to restore these to their proper state.

Port – connection between the PC and other hardware. Normally a socket on the back of the PC, but expansion slots can also be ports.

Serial port – transmits data one bit after another down a single line. Data communications are almost always done via a serial port.

Phone connection

□ You connect to your access provider through the normal phone lines. The only extra kit you may need is an extension kit and wall-mounted socket to put a socket within reach of your desktop.

Tip

Don't leave the modem switched on and plugged into the phone, when you are not on-line, as incoming calls may be answered by the modem, making lots of noise — so the caller will get an ear-bashing!

patterns of bytes by one copy plus a count of the repetitions. It works best with text files, where blocks of spaces and repeated patterns are common. It does not work well with executable files, where repetition is rare, and if the file is already compressed, further 'compression' can make it bigger! Most picture formats use some sort of compression, and many of the files you can download over the Internet are Zipped.

Serial ports

All computers have one or more serial ports for getting data into and out of the machine. On a PC there are four, called COM1, COM2, COM3 and COM4. (COM is short for COMunications.)

A port may be a socket at the back of the main case, or reached through an expansion slot inside the case. If your modem is on a card, plugging it into any slot will give it access to the port, though you may have to tell it which one.

● Most PCs have a serial port at the back of the machine. This is COM1, and may have a mouse plugged into it.

● Some PCs have two external serial ports, COM1 and COM2.

An external modem must be allocated the port number that it is plugged into; a card modem can be allocated any internal port that is not already in use.

Buying a modem

● Card modems are easy to install and leave the serial port free.

● With an external modem, you must have a free serial port.

● If you are connecting to the normal public telephone lines, you can only legally use BABT approved modems.

● Most modems now are fax modems, which you can also use to send and receive faxes from your PC.

Modem settings

With the modem, as with much else in Windows 98, you can generally leave it to the system to find the best settings for it. However, it doesn't always get things right, so it might be as well to check the modem settings.

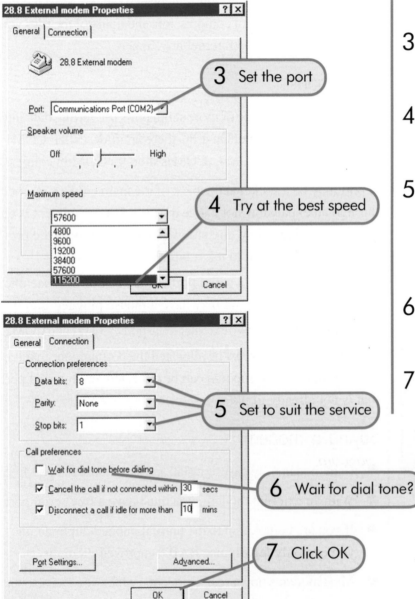

1 Open the Control Panel and double-click 🕮 Modems.

2 Click the Properties button.

3 On the General panel, check the COM port – normally COM 2.

4 Set the Speed to the fastest – reduce it later if this doesn't work.

5 Switch to Connection and set the Preferences to suit the access provider. If in doubt, try 8 – None – 1.

6 If other people use the phone line, tick Wait for dial tone.

7 Click OK and close the Modem dialog box.

Basic steps

1 Open the Modem Properties/ Connection panel and click on
[Port Settings...].

2 Move the Buffer sliders down a notch.

3 Click OK.

4 Back at the Properties panel click [Advanced...].

5 Tick Record a log file.

6 Click OK then close the Properties panel.

Take note

The modem's pre-set con-figuration should work with your PC. If it does, you will only have to worry about COM ports when setting it up. If you have to change the COM port, you will also have to change the IRQ (Inter-rupt ReQuest) setting. See the modem's manual for details.

Trouble shooting

If you find that you have difficulty in making the connection to your service – or in keeping the connection intact – these things might help:

● Take the maximum speed down a notch;

● Reduce the Buffer sizes on the Port Settings panel;

● Turn on the Record Log file option on the Advanced Connections Setting panel – this won't cure anything, but when you ring your provider for help, you will be able to tell them what has been happening.

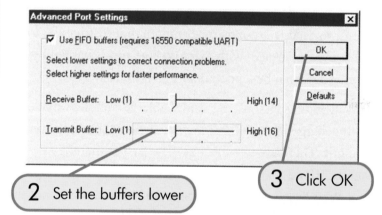

2 Set the buffers lower

3 Click OK

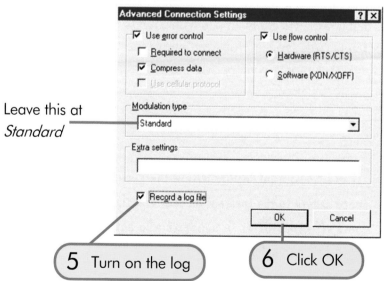

Leave this at *Standard*

5 Turn on the log

6 Click OK

Internet access providers

These vary from international organisations such as AOL, MSN (MicroSoft Network) and Compuserve, through national ones like Demon Internet and UUnet Pipex, to small firms operating mainly within one town – though many of these also offer a national network of local dial-in points.

Most providers charge between £10 and £15 per month for a *dial-up account*. This normally gives you unlimited time on-line, up to five or so e-mail addresses (so everyone in the family can have their own) and 5Mb of storage space on their computer for your home page.

Some firms charge around £6 per month, but restrict you to 10 or 20 hours free usage, with extra on-line time charged by the minute. These can be a good deal for light users.

Some, including Dixons, BT and Cable & Wireless make no monthly charge, though there may be a slight surcharge on the phone bill. There are two catches. The first is that they do not normally offer e-mail, so if you want to use it you must sign up with a Web-based service (see page 162) – and this is not the most convenient way to handle your e-mail. The second catch is that you tend to get swamped with adverts when you go online through a free service. However, one of these may be a sensible choice if you only want occasional access to the Internet.

Tip

CompuServe and AOL both offer a free trial membership and often put their software on the disks and CD-ROMs of computing magazines. Take up the offers and explore their services and the Internet beyond. See which works best, and whether you want any member services.

Dial-up account – one where you connect to your provider (and through them to the Internet) through the public phone lines. This is the way most home and small business users get onto the Net.

Tip

If you travel a lot, either within the country or abroad, and need access to the Internet on your travels, you are probably best off with AOL or CompuServe who both have local dial-up points throughout the world.

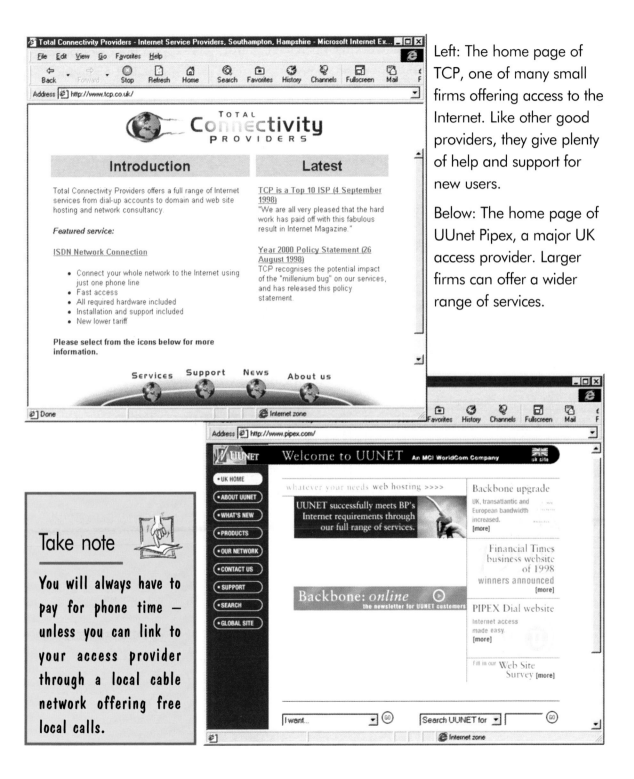

Left: The home page of TCP, one of many small firms offering access to the Internet. Like other good providers, they give plenty of help and support for new users.

Below: The home page of UUnet Pipex, a major UK access provider. Larger firms can offer a wider range of services.

Take note

You will always have to pay for phone time — unless you can link to your access provider through a local cable network offering free local calls.

Dial-Up Networking

If you have not installed Dial-up networking, open the Control Panel and use Add/Remove Programs to do so now.

There are two aspects to configuring a new connection:

● the network software within your computer.

● the connection to the service provider.

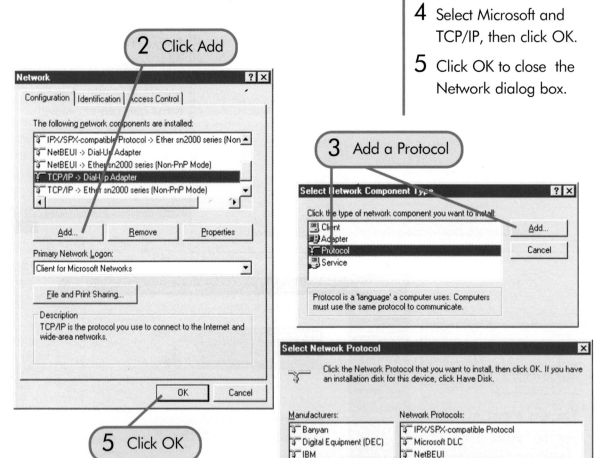

2 Click Add

Network

Configuration | Identification | Access Control

The following network components are installed:

- IPX/SPX-compatible Protocol -> Ether sn2000 series (Non ▲
- NetBEUI -> Dial-Up Adapter
- NetBEUI -> Ether sn2000 series (Non-PnP Mode)
- TCP/IP -> Dial-Up Adapter
- TCP/IP -> Ether sn2000 series (Non-PnP Mode) ▼

Add...   Remove   Properties

Primary Network Logon:

Client for Microsoft Networks

File and Print Sharing...

Description
TCP/IP is the protocol you use to connect to the Internet and wide-area networks.

OK   Cancel

5 Click OK

3 Add a Protocol

Select Network Component Type

Click the type of network component you want to install:

- Client
- Adapter
- Protocol
- Service

Add...   Cancel

Protocol is a 'language' a computer uses. Computers must use the same protocol to communicate.

Select Network Protocol

Click the Network Protocol that you want to install, then click OK. If you have an installation disk for this device, click Have Disk.

Manufacturers:
- Banyan
- Digital Equipment (DEC)
- IBM
- Microsoft
- Novell
- SunSoft

Network Protocols:
- IPX/SPX-compatible Protocol
- Microsoft DLC
- NetBEUI
- TCP/IP

Have Disk...

4 Select Microsoft and TCP/IP

OK   Cancel

24

Making a connection

1 Open the Dial-Up folder and click Make New Connection.

2 In the Wizard enter a name – this will be the label on the icon – then click Next.

3 Enter the phone number – the Area and Country code must also be given unless it is a local number.

4 Click Next, and Finish at the summary screen which follows.

Once the Network software is in place, you can set up the connection. Here's how to connect to BT Click – one of the better free services. (They make money simply on your phone calls.) You might like to use this while you have a look around the Internet to see what services are on offer and decide which access provider you would like to sign up with.

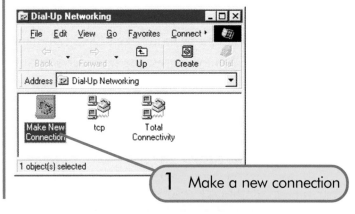

1 Make a new connection

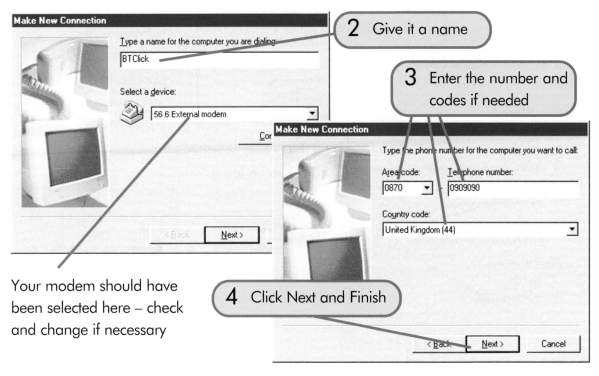

2 Give it a name

3 Enter the number and codes if needed

Your modem should have been selected here – check and change if necessary

4 Click Next and Finish

Setting Properties

The Make New Connection wizard only tells the computer how to reach the access provider. To tell it how to behave when it gets there, you have to set the options on the Properties panel. The key options are on the **Server Types** tab, and determine how data is transmitted between you and the access provider. The **TCP/IP settings** mainly relate to Internet addresses. With some providers you will have a fixed IP (Internet Protocol) address, and the provider may have one or more fixed DNS (Domain Name Server) addresses. In most cases, the provider's server will tell you these addresses when you log on.

Here are the settings for BT Click – your access provider will tell you what are needed to work with them.

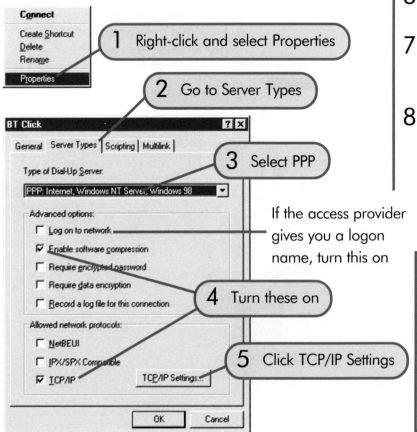

If the access provider gives you a logon name, turn this on

1 Right-click on the new connection and select Properties.

2 Switch to the Server Types tab.

3 For the Type, select *PPP:Internet...*

4 Check *Enable software compression* and *TCP/IP* – clearing all others.

5 Click TCP/IP Settings.

6 Select Server assigned IP address.

7 Set Specify name server and enter the Primary DNS address.

8 Click OK to close the panel and again when you get back to the Properties dialog box.

Take note

Some access providers have self-installing software which will do all this for you!

6 Leave it to the server

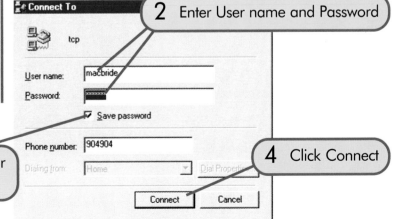

Some providers give you a fixed IP address

With many providers, the server assigns addresses at logon

Take note

IP and DNS addresses have four sets of numbers, each between 0 and 255, separated by dots.

TCP/IP Settings

- ○ Server assigned IP address
- ○ Specify an IP address

  IP address: [0 . 0 . 0 . 0]

- ○ Server assigned name server addresses
- ● Specify name server addresses

  Primary DNS: [194 . 73 . 82 . 242]

  Secondary DNS: [0 . 0 . 0 . 0]

  Primary WINS: [0 . 0 . 0 . 0]

  Secondary WINS: [0 . 0 . 0 . 0]

- ☑ Use IP header compression
- ☑ Use default gateway on remote network

  [OK] [Cancel]

7 Enter the DNS address

8 Click OK

Basic steps

1 Click (or double-click) the connection's icon.

2 Enter your User name (only needed the first time) and Password.

3 Turn on Save Password if you are the only one who has access to the PC.

4 Click Connect.

Logging on

Plug in the phone line, turn on the modem and try to log on to your service. These steps just connect you to the Internet. To do anything useful, you must also run your browser – either before or after you log on.

Connect To

tcp

User name: macbride
Password: xxxxxx
☑ Save password

Phone number: 904904
Dialing from: Home ▼ [Dial Properties]

[Connect] [Cancel]

2 Enter User name and Password

3 Save it if your PC is secure

4 Click Connect

27

Summary

◆ To get on-line, you need a computer, a modem and a
telephone socket, Internet software and an account with
an access provider.

◆ Modems may be fitted internally or externally, and must
be connected to a COM port. Most will simply plug in
and go; some may need configuring to your machine.

◆ The Baud rate describes the speed of a modem. The
faster your modem, the lower your phone bills!

◆ If you have not installed the Dial-Up Networking, you
must do so before you can go any further.

◆ To set up your PC to link to an access provider, you first
use the Make New Connection wizard, then configure
the properties of the Server Types.

Tip

Some access providers supply their
customers with special software
packages which install themselves
and handle all the details of
setting up the connection.

3 Internet Explorer

The browser

To view and travel through the World Wide Web you need a browser, and Internet Explorer 4.0 (IE 4.0) is the browser currently supplied with Windows 98. Let's have a look at it.

The main part of the window is used for the display of Web pages. Above this are the control elements. The **Menu bar** contains the full command set, with the most commonly used ones duplicated in the **Standard Toolbar**.

● The **Address** shows you where you are. You can type a URL (page 70) here to open a page. Up to 20 URLs are stored and can be selected from here, for easy revisiting.

● The **Links** offer an easy way to connect to selected places. Initially, they connect to pages on Microsoft's site, but you can replace them or add your own.

The Toolbars can be turned on or off as needed, but if you want the maximum viewing area click the **Fullscreen** icon.

The **Explorer Bar** can be opened on the left of the screen to give simpler navigation when searching the Internet (page 120), or when using the Favorites (page 74), History (page 76) or Channels (page 40).

The **Status Bar** at the bottom of the page shows how much of an incoming file has been loaded. This can also be turned off if you don't want it.

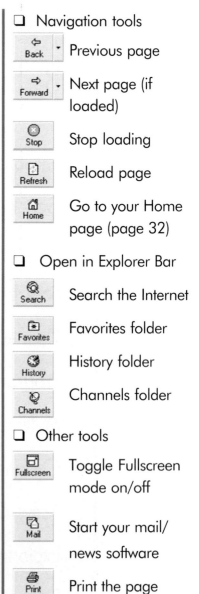

❏ Navigation tools

Back   Previous page

Forward   Next page (if loaded)

Stop   Stop loading

Refresh   Reload page

Home   Go to your Home page (page 32)

❏ Open in Explorer Bar

Search   Search the Internet

Favorites   Favorites folder

History   History folder

Channels   Channels folder

❏ Other tools

Fullscreen   Toggle Fullscreen mode on/off

Mail   Start your mail/ news software

Print   Print the page

Basic steps

❑ Display options

1 Click on View.

2 Point to Toolbar and turn them on (✔) or off from the submenu.

3 Click on Status Bar to turn it on or off.

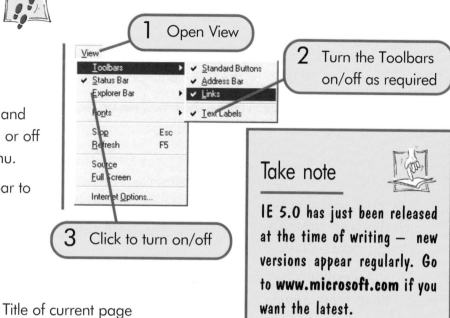

1 Open View

2 Turn the Toolbars on/off as required

3 Click to turn on/off

Take note

IE 5.0 has just been released at the time of writing — new versions appear regularly. Go to **www.microsoft.com** if you want the latest.

Title of current page

Menu bar

Standard Toolbar

Drag here to resize or move a toolbar

Links buttons

Address

Explorer Bar

Open folder

Status bar

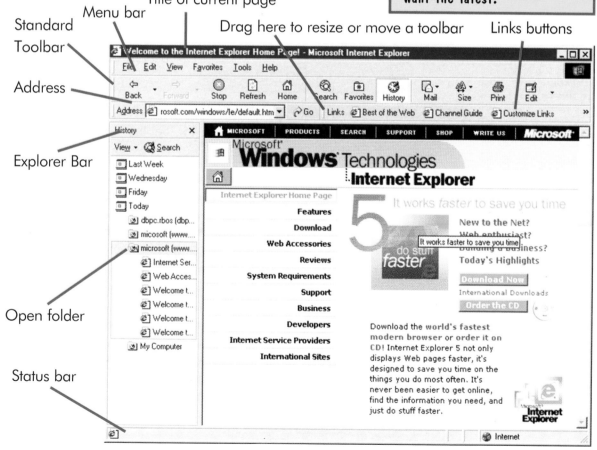

General options

The Internet Options control many aspects of Explorer's display and of how it works. Start on the General panel:

- Choose your **Home page**. This can be left blank or you can always start your browsing at the same place (such as a Net directory – see Chapter 6).

- Set the disk space for storing files of visited pages. When you revisit, Explorer will use these and only download new files if the pages have changed – allocate as much as you can spare for faster browsing.

- Set the **Accessibility** options and choose your own **Colors** and **Fonts** for maximum visibility, if needed.

Basic steps

1 Open the View menu and select Internet Options...

2 Go to General.

3 For the Home page, type the URL (or click Use Current if you are on that page), or click Use Blank.

4 Click Settings.

5 Select when to check for new versions of stored pages – Every visit is usually best.

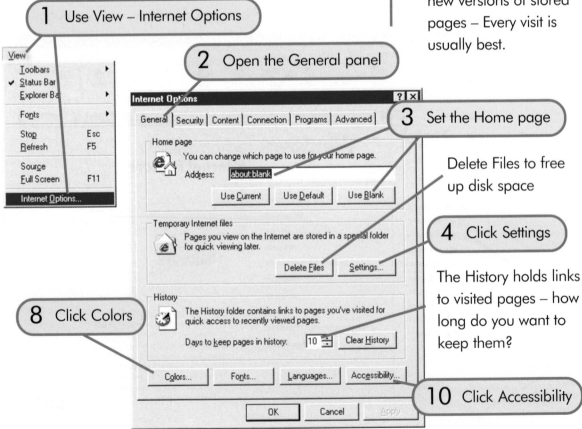

1 Use View – Internet Options

2 Open the General panel

3 Set the Home page

Delete Files to free up disk space

4 Click Settings

The History holds links to visited pages – how long do you want to keep them?

8 Click Colors

10 Click Accessibility

6 Set the amount of space for storage.

7 Click OK.

❑ High visibility

8 Click Colors... .

9 Set the colours for high contrast and click OK. Set Fonts in the same way.

10 Click Accessibility... .

11 Set Explorer to ignore the pages' own colours and fonts – so that yours are used instead.

12 Click OK.

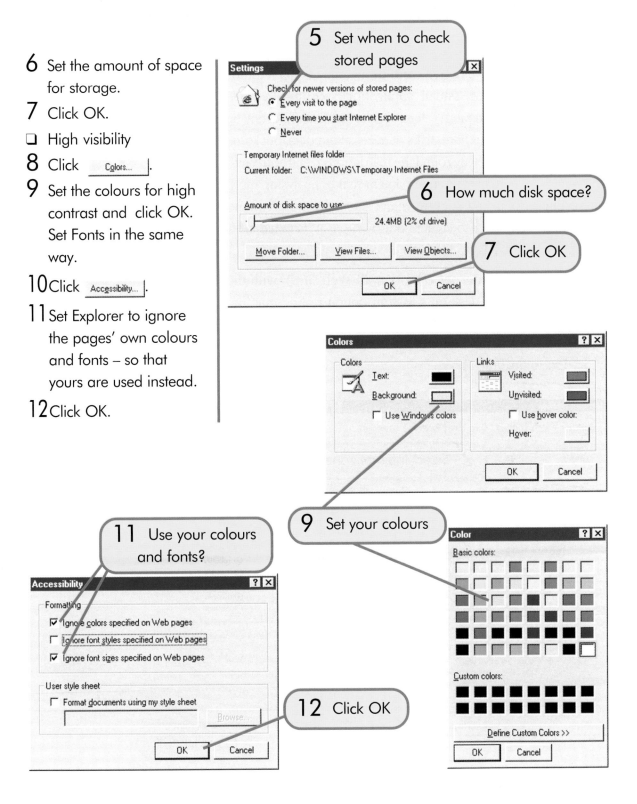

5 Set when to check stored pages

6 How much disk space?

7 Click OK

9 Set your colours

11 Use your colours and fonts?

12 Click OK

Security

Many Web pages have **active content**, i.e. they contain multi-media files or applets (small applications) written in Java, ActiveX or other interactive languages. These should not be able to mess with your hard disks or access your data, but some hackers have found a way round the restrictions – and anti-virus software is no help here. Active content makes browsing more interesting, and if you stick to major sites, should create no problems. (You can also create your own set of **Trusted sites** by adding their URLs to the list.)

At first, select the **Internet zone** (i.e. all Web sites), with the security set to **High**. Use the **Custom** option to fine-tune the settings later, when you have more experience.

Basic steps

1 Go to the Security panel.

2 Pick the Internet zone.

3 Select High security.

or

4 Select Custom and click
  Settings... .

5 Tell Explorer how to deal with each type.

6 Click OK.

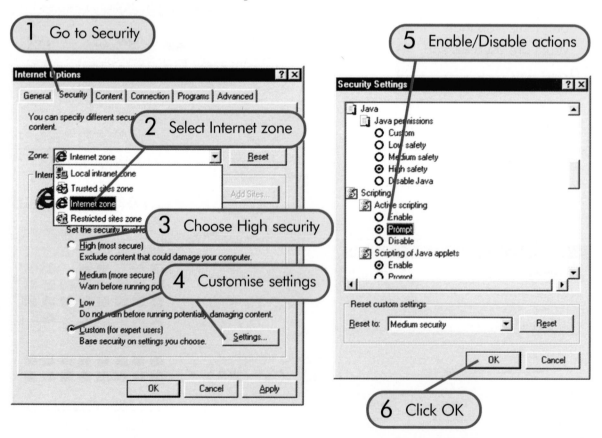

1 Go to Security

5 Enable/Disable actions

2 Select Internet zone

3 Choose High security

4 Customise settings

6 Click OK

Basic steps

1 Go to the Content panel.

2 Click Enable...

3 Decide on a Password and enter it – twice.

4 On the Ratings panel, set the limit for each Category – moving the slider to the right permits higher levels of sex'n'violence.

5 On the General panel, tick the options if you want to allow people to see unrated sites, or to use the password to view restricted sites.

6 Click OK.

With Explorer you can protect younger users – or anyone else who might be offended – from the unacceptable material that lurks in various corners of the Net.

The settings on the Content panel allows you to restrict the browser to sites rated by the (RSAC) Recreational Standards Advisory Council – over 50,000 at the time of writing – and to control the levels of sex'n'violence that can be viewed.

If a site's ratings are beyond the limits you have set, access is denied. This can be overriden by the use of the password, should you decide a site has been overrated and is suitable for viewing.

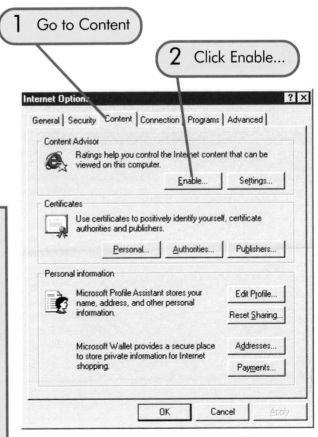

1 Go to Content

2 Click Enable...

Tip

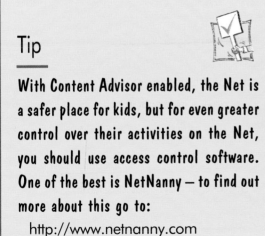

With Content Advisor enabled, the Net is a safer place for kids, but for even greater control over their activities on the Net, you should use access control software. One of the best is NetNanny – to find out more about this go to:
http://www.netnanny.com

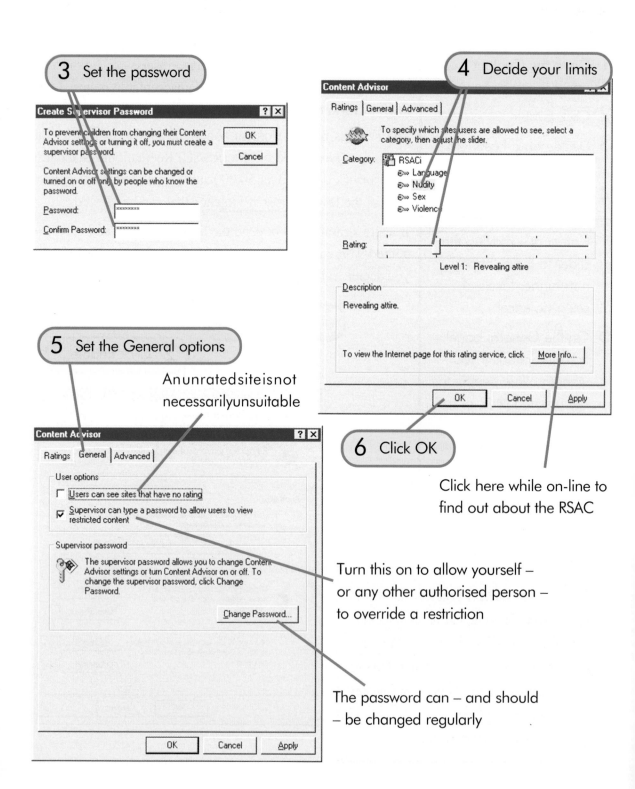

3 Set the password

Create Supervisor Password `? X`

To prevent children from changing their Content Advisor settings or turning it off, you must create a supervisor password.

Content Advisor settings can be changed or turned on or off only by people who know the password.

Password: `xxxxxxxx`

Confirm Password: `xxxxxxxx`

`OK` `Cancel`

4 Decide your limits

Content Advisor

Ratings | General | Advanced

To specify which sites users are allowed to see, select a category, then adjust the slider.

Category: RSACi
  Language
  Nudity
  Sex
  Violence

Rating:

Level 1: Revealing attire

Description

Revealing attire.

To view the Internet page for this rating service, click `More Info...`

`OK` `Cancel` `Apply`

5 Set the General options

Anunratedsiteisnot necessarilyunsuitable

Content Advisor `? X`

Ratings | General | Advanced

User options

☐ Users can see sites that have no rating

☑ Supervisor can type a password to allow users to view restricted content

Supervisor password

The supervisor password allows you to change Content Advisor settings or turn Content Advisor on or off. To change the supervisor password, click Change Password.

`Change Password...`

`OK` `Cancel` `Apply`

6 Click OK

Click here while on-line to find out about the RSAC

Turn this on to allow yourself – or any other authorised person – to override a restriction

The password can – and should – be changed regularly

Basic steps

1 Open the Internet Options panel and go to the Connection tab.

2 Click Settings... .

3 Set the number of redial attempts, and the delay between.

4 Turn on Disconnect if idle and set the time limit.

5 Turn the automatic update of subscriptions on or off as needed.

6 Turn on the security check if needed.

7 Click OK.

Connection options

The Connection options fine-tune the way that you connect to your service provider. As with most of the options, you might want to adjust these from time to time in the light of experience. The key options are on the **Dial-Up Settings** dialog box.

● Set the number of times to try to connect, and how long to wait before retrying.

● Turning on **Disconnect if idle...** will stop you running up phone bills should you forget to disconnect. Don't set too short a time. Explorer thinks it is idle if it is not transferring data, and could cut you off while reading a long page!

● Some Web sites run channels (see page 40) which send out news, views and other information. If you have subscribed to any, Explorer will normally get the updates automatically. You may prefer to switch this off, and pick up your subscribed pages when you want them.

● Turn on the **system security check** if you want to ensure that the password is given before going online.

If you change your service provider, use Add... to set up the connection

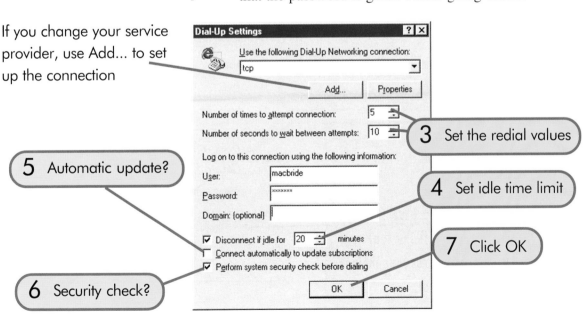

5 Automatic update?

3 Set the redial values

4 Set idle time limit

7 Click OK

6 Security check?

37

Programs

While you are surfing the Web with Internet Explorer, you may want to send an e-mail to someone – perhaps the person who runs a Web site that interests you – or come across a link to a newsgroup, and want to read its articles. Explorer cannot handle mail and news, but it can link to other applications to do so and to handle other activities. The **Programs** tab is where you select the applications.

The choices that you are given depend upon what software is installed on your computer. The Windows 98 and Explorer packages include:

●   Outlook Express, for mail and news;

●   NetMeeting, for Internet call (voice communications);

●   Address Book, for Contacts list.

If you want an interactive Calendar, you need Microsoft Outlook or similar personal/group organiser software.

1   Open the Internet Options panel and go to the Programs tab.

2   Click the arrow beside each box and select the application.

3   Click Apply.

1   Go to Programs

2   Select from the drop-down lists

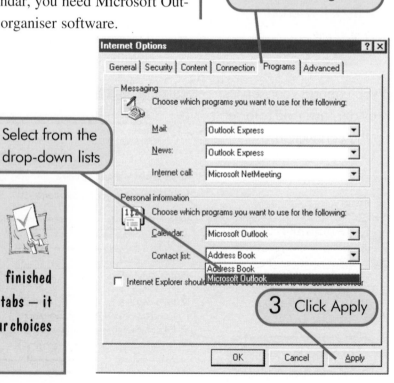

Tip

Don't click OK until you have finished setting the options on all the tabs – it closes the panel. Apply fixes your choices without closing the panel.

3   Click Apply

Basic steps

1 Open the View menu and select Internet Options...

2 Go to Advanced.

3 Scroll down to the Multimedia section.

4 Click to turn the options on or off as required.

5 Click Apply or OK to save and close the panel.

Multimedia options

The Advanced tab contains loads of options, most of which should be left at their defaults until you have been surfing for a while. You will then have a better idea of how you want to handle them. However, there is one section that is worth dealing with now – multimedia. Pictures, audio and video files are sometimes essential, often merely decorative and always slow to load. Turn them off for faster browsing but pictures often contain links – if you can't see them, you may not be able to navigate some sites. You can turn them back on and reload a page to view the files, or simply click on a non-displayed image (it will appear as [ ]) to load it.

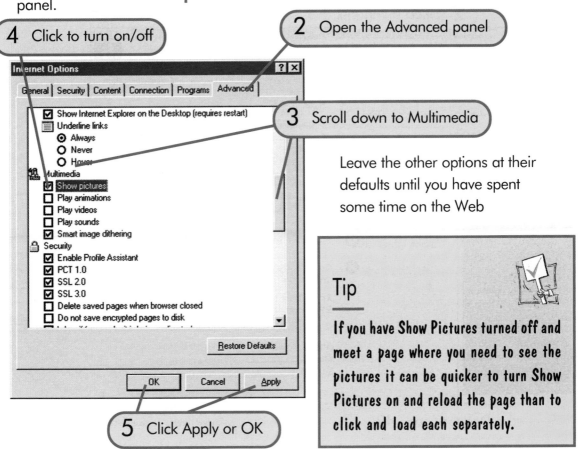

4 Click to turn on/off

2 Open the Advanced panel

3 Scroll down to Multimedia

Leave the other options at their defaults until you have spent some time on the Web

5 Click Apply or OK

Tip

If you have Show Pictures turned off and meet a page where you need to see the pictures it can be quicker to turn Show Pictures on and reload the page than to click and load each separately.

39

Channels

The theory behind channels is this: instead of you having to go to sites to see what's happening, you get them to send you updates of new material, which you can then read offline. It works well if you are in an organisation with a permanently open connection, as the updates can be scheduled to come in while you are doing other things. If you connect through a dial-up line, the approach is not so good. It is more efficient to go to a site to collect the material you want than to have a channel pour in stuff that may or may not be of interest.

Microsoft seem to have realised this – the Channel Bar has been dropped from Internet Explorer 5.0.

Basic steps

❑ Adding a channel

1 Go on-line.

2 Click the Channel Guide button or a link in the Channel Bar.

3 When the page loads, view the preview if there is one.

4 Click Add Channel.

5 Choose how to handle its update.

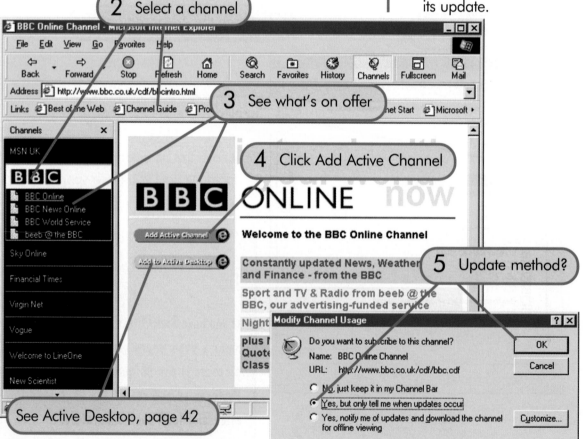

2 Select a channel

3 See what's on offer

4 Click Add Active Channel

5 Update method?

See Active Desktop, page 42

Basic steps

❑ Updating a channel

1 Go online.

2 Open a Favorites menu and select Manage Subscriptions.

3 Right-click on the channel and select Update Now.

4 Wait – the first download may be very slow!

5 Browse the channel, going online if you want to follow up links.

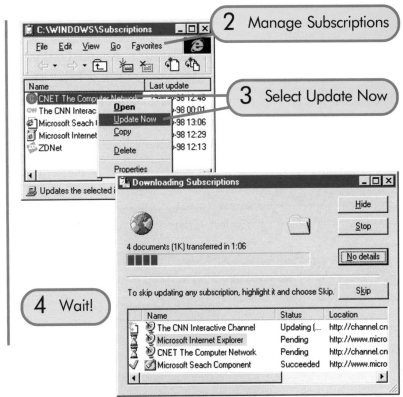

2 Manage Subscriptions

3 Select Update Now

4 Wait!

5 Browse the new pages

Channels usually download just the top pages and headlines – to follow the stories you must go online

Active Desktop

The Active Desktop can hold interactive links to sites. There are a range of items available at Microsoft's Active Desktop Gallery – including the Search Component shown here. This gives you a simple way to hunt through dozens of the different search engines (see Chapter 7) – sites that have indexes to Web pages, newsgroups and other Net resources.

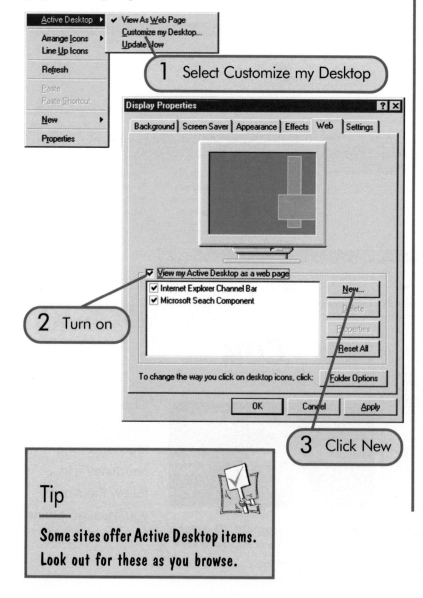

1 Select Customize my Desktop

2 Turn on

3 Click New

Tip

Some sites offer Active Desktop items. Look out for these as you browse.

Basic steps

❑ Adding a channel

1 Right-click on the Desktop, point to Active Desktop and select Customize...

2 Turn on View ... as a Web page.

3 Click ▢New...▢ and wait for the Gallery to download.

4 Select an item and click ▢Add to Active Desktop▢ 🅔 and wait for it to download.

❑ Using the Search component

5 Go online.

6 Select a search engine.

7 Type in one or more words to define what you are looking for.

8 Click 🔘Go▶. Internet Explorer will open, link to Microsoft, then on to the search engine, to find and display the results.

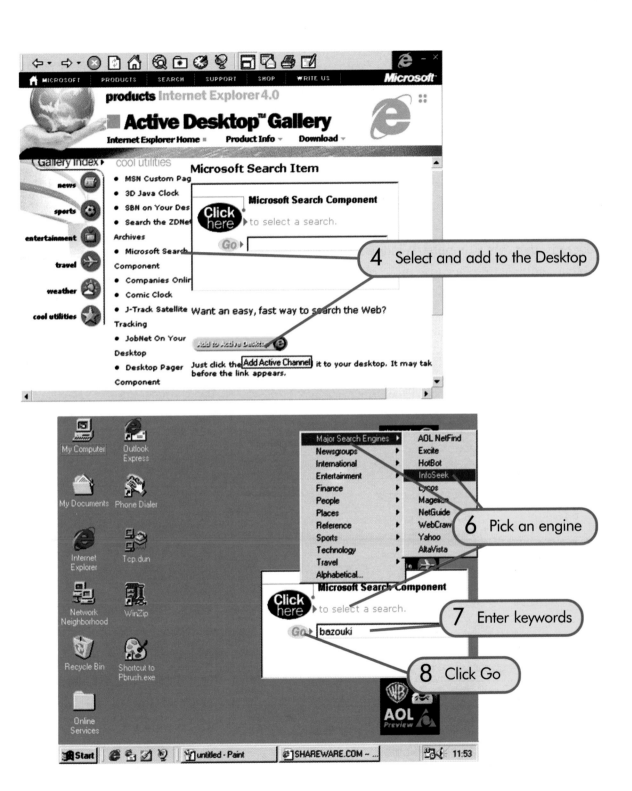

4 Select and add to the Desktop

6 Pick an engine

7 Enter keywords

8 Click Go

Exploring in Windows 98

Internet access is built into Windows Explorer and My Computer in Windows 98. In theory you can open a page on the Web as easily as you can open a file on your hard disk or from within your local network. In practice, of course, getting stuff off the Internet is always far slower and less reliable.

In Windows 98, My Computer and Windows Explorer both have an **Address** box. If you type an Internet address into here, the system will attempt to go online to pick up the link. If it succeeds, then My Computer/Windows Explorer will have its toolbar and menu replaced by those of Internet Explorer.

1 Run My Computer or Windows Explorer.

2 Enter an Address (see page 70).

3 After the page has loaded and you have finished with it, you can use the Back button to return to My Computer or Windows Explorer.

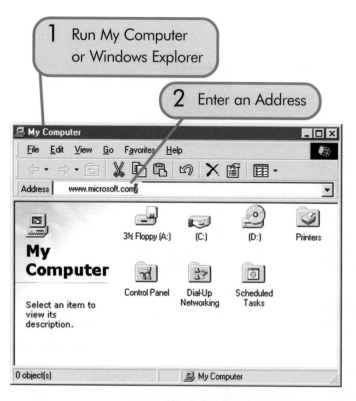

My Computer is seen here in Web page view – Internet access is still there in the alternative 'Classic' (Windows 95 style) display.

Take note

Web/desktop integration has advantages in an organisation with an intranet (Web for internal use only) and a fast ISDN connection to the Internet. The approach offers far less to home/small business users.

If you work through a dial-up connection and pay by the minute for your online time, exploring the Internet and working with your local files will normally be two separate activities.

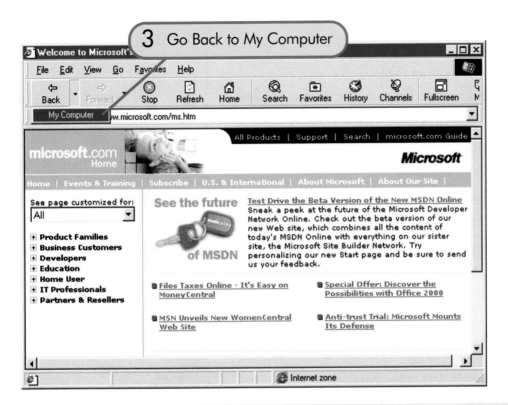

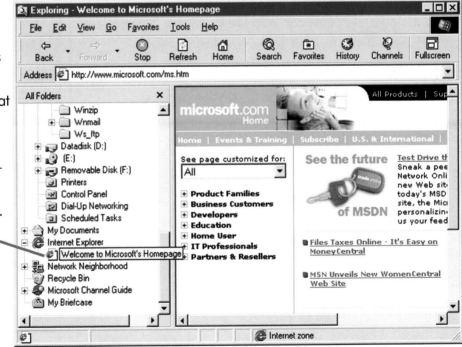

In Windows 98, Internet Explorer is in the All Folders list. Web pages that have been visited during the session can be called up – offline – through Windows Explorer.

Summary

◆ Internet Explorer 4.0 is the browser currently supplied with Windows 98. Internet Explorer 5.0 was released in Spring 1999 and new versions are produced regularly. Visit the Microsoft site if you want the latest version.

◆ The toolbars and other controls can be removed to create a larger viewing area.

◆ To get your browser working the way you want it, spend some time on the Options panels.

◆ ActiveX, Java and other applets in Web pages can be fun and useful, but there is a very slight danger that they could carry viruses or otherwise attack your system.

◆ If children have access to your system, you might want to turn on Content Advisor and set some restrictions.

◆ Use the Programs tab to select the applications to use for handling Mail and News.

◆ Multimedia elements can add life to pages, but you can surf faster if you turn off some or all of them.

◆ If you subscribe to channels, you can have the latest material from sites sent directly to your desktop.

◆ Items added to your Active Desktop will give you interactive links to sites.

◆ You can go to an Internet address from My Computer or Windows Explorer – they will then work like Internet Explorer.

Take note

Internet Explorer 5.0 is little different from IE4.0. A Radio toolbar has been added, the Channels button and Bar removed and the Internet Options moved from the View menu to the Tools menu. Otherwise, the windows and dialog boxes covered in this chapter are virtually identical on both versions.

4 Communicator

Navigator

Netscape Communicator is a full Internet suite – and we'll look at most of its components during the course of this book – but let's start with its central program, Navigator. It is similar to Internet Explorer, which is not surprising as they have a common root and do the same job!

The main part of the window is used for the display of Web pages. Above this are the control elements.

- The **Menu bar** is always present. The most commonly used commands are duplicated in the next three bars – any of which can be turned off if not wanted.

- The **Navigation** toolbar should be kept visible. Its tools make browsing much simpler.

- The **Location** toolbar shows you where you are, and lets you go places.

  Bookmarks (page 72) make it easier to return to a site.

  You can type a URL (page 70) into the **Go to** box to open a page, and typed URLs are stored in its drop-down list for ease of revisiting.

- The Personal toolbar is where you can add your own buttons to give you quick links to favourite places.

The toolbars can be slimmed down, or hidden completely, if you want a larger viewing area.

The Toolbar

![]	Back to previous page
![]	Next page (if visited already)
![]	Reload current page
![]	Home page
![]	Find text within page
![]	Load images (if image loading is turned off – see page 54)
![]	Print current page
![]	Security information
![]	Stop loading
![]	Start page at Netcenter – personalise this and the icon becomes …
![]	Personal start page

Take note

The other Communicator programs can be called up from the Taskbar. This can be dragged off and 'floated' anywhere on the screen. The floating Taskbar has larger icons.

Basic steps

- ❑ Toolbar display
1 Open the View menu.
2 Click on a Hide … or
   Show … option to turn
   a toolbar on or off.

Toolbars

Navigation

Location

Personal

Click to shrink
the toolbar

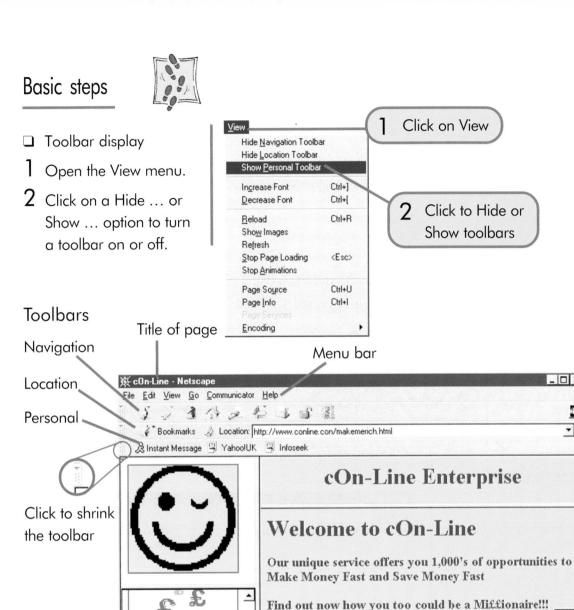

1 Click on View

2 Click to Hide or
Show toolbars

Title of page

Menu bar

cOn-Line Enterprise

Welcome to cOn-Line

**Our unique service offers you 1,000's of opportunities to
Make Money Fast and Save Money Fast**

Find out now how you too could be a Mi££ionaire!!!

Fill in this simple form now, and make me rich.

Name: O U Mugg

Address:

Credit Card No: 1234 0230 4312 1203

Submit Query

Make Money Fast

Pyramid Sales

Status bar – shows progress of incoming page

Taskbar – fixed or floating

Appearance Preferences

Basic steps

1 Open the Edit menu and select Preferences.

2 Select Appearance.

3 Tick the applications to launch at start up.

4 Select the button style.

5 Click on another Category heading to set more preferences.

Before you start to use Communicator in earnest, check the Preferences to make sure that they are right for you.

The Preferences can be changed at any point and the new settings take effect immediately.

Appearance

In this area you choose which applications to run when you start Communicator, and the style of the buttons on the Toolbars.

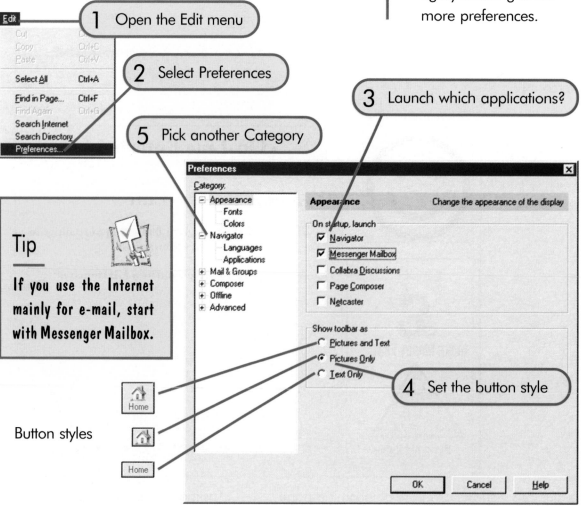

1 Open the Edit menu

2 Select Preferences

3 Launch which applications?

5 Pick another Category

Tip

If you use the Internet mainly for e-mail, start with Messenger Mailbox.

Button styles

4 Set the button style

Fonts

1 Select Fonts – if you can't see this, click ⊞ beside Appearance to open the folder.

2 Set the fonts and sizes as required.

3 Choose what to do when a page specifies its own fonts.

4 Click OK – you must do this to fix your choices on this panel.

Colours may be set and fixed in the same way if you need a high-visibility display

On most Web pages, the text will be displayed in the fonts defined in this panel. Some specify their own fonts which can be downloaded when you load the page. Disabling **Dynamic Fonts** will speed up browsing by preventing this download, but you will then only see the page in its proper fonts if you happen to have them on your system.

For high-visiblity display, set the fonts and sizes to suit your needs and insist that they are always used.

Take note

Some choices are kept if you move onto another Preferences Panel without clicking OK. Fonts – and a few others – aren't. Play safe and click OK after each set of options.

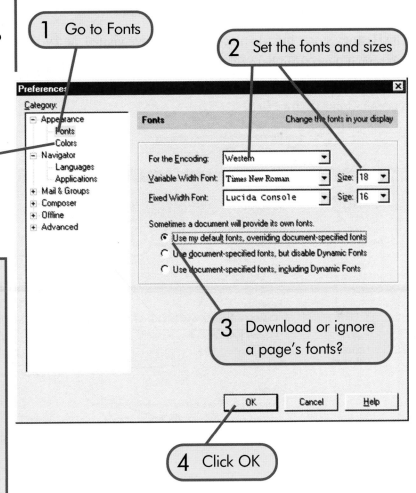

1 Go to Fonts

2 Set the fonts and sizes

3 Download or ignore a page's fonts?

4 Click OK

Navigator Preferences

Where do you want to go when Navigator starts? Select:

- **Blank page**, if you intend to go off in a new direction every browsing session.

- **Home page**, to set a regular starting place. This might be your own home page, Netcenter (page 68), Yahoo (page 82) or anywhere. To use this, you must enter the URL (page 70) or set this preference when you are at that page.

- The **Last page visited** option will let you pick up from where you left off in the previous session.

The **History** stores links to places that you have visited, and you can revisit them from here (page 77). You can set how long to keep the links – a few days is usually enough, as it's hard to find places in long History lists.

Basic steps

1 Open the Edit menu and select Preferences.

2 Select Navigator.

3 Choose your start with option.

4 If you choose Home page, enter its URL – or set this when you are at the site.

5 Set the number of days to keep links in the History list.

6 Click OK.

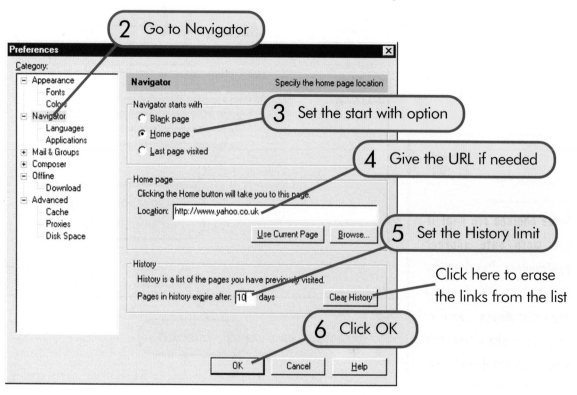

2 Go to Navigator

3 Set the start with option

4 Give the URL if needed

5 Set the History limit

Click here to erase the links from the list

6 Click OK

Basic steps

1 Select Offline.
2 Pick a Startup option.
3 Click OK.

The Offline panel

The choice depends upon how you connect to the Internet.

● **Online Work Mode** is for people in organisations where there is a permanent connection to the Internet.

● **Offline Work Mode** is for home users or others who reach the Internet through a dial-up connection.

● If in doubt, or if your connection mode can vary – e.g. a laptop user might connect through the network in the office and by dial-up at home – choose **Ask Me**.

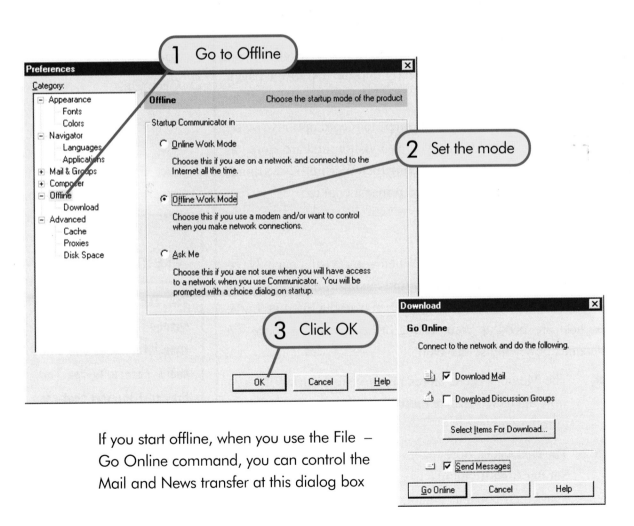

If you start offline, when you use the File – Go Online command, you can control the Mail and News transfer at this dialog box

Advanced Preferences

I'm not sure why these are called 'Advanced' as they include some basic preferences. The main set control the loading of the images and other enhancements that may be on a Web page – you may not want them all.

- Turning off **Automatically load images** will speed up your browsing. When you reach a page where you need to see the images, click the button to load them in.

- Disabling **Java** will also speed up downloading. Java applets (small programs embedded in Web pages) can be entertaining or useful, but are rarely essential.

- Disabling **JavaScript** has no effect on download times as the scripts are written directly into the text of the pages. This and the other 'enable' options may as well be left on.

Cookies are generated by some sites, to record options you set while visiting or to identify you as a visitor, and are stored as small files on your hard disk. Asking for a Warning slows things down, but gives you a chance to refuse a cookie.

The Cache panel

Caches are temporary storage. When you revisit a page, Navigator checks the caches, and if it finds an up-to-date copy of the page, will load it from there rather than over the Internet. Large caches can speed up your surfing or be a waste of space – it depends how you use the Web.

- The Memory cache stores pages visited during the session. Set this to 1Mb or more if you like to return to pages to follow up leads.

- The Disk cache stores pages from one session to the next. Set this high if you like to go regularly to the same sites – and their contents do not change much.

Basic steps

1 Open the Preferences dialog box and select Advanced.

2 Set the options to suit yourself, balancing speed against the richness of Web pages.

3 Go to the Cache panel.

4 Set the Memory and Disk cache sizes to suit your needs.

5 Click OK.

Take note

You can come back and change the settings at any time later, when you have had a chance to see how they suit the way that you like to work.

When in doubt, leave the settings at their defaults.

At FTP sites (page 190) you give your e-mail address as the password

Proxies are relevant only if you are on a local area network. Check with your LAN manager.

Disk Space controls the storage of messages and newsgroup articles

1 Go to Advanced

2 Enable/disable as required

3 Go to Cache

4 Set the cache sizes

Frees up memory or disk space instantly

Once per session makes good use of cached pages

5 Click OK

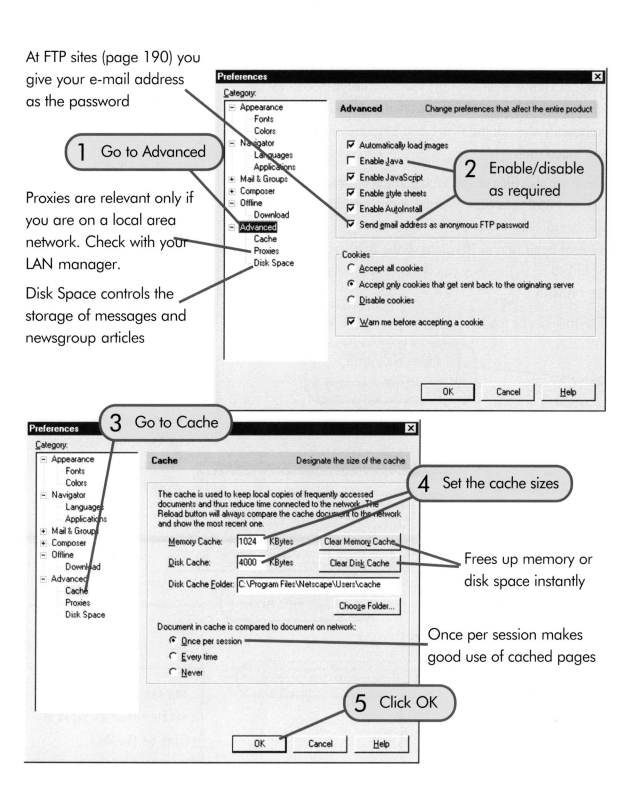

Applications

Much of the material that is on Web pages can be viewed through a browser without any special configuration. Navigator can handle GIF and JPEG files – the graphics formats most commonly used on the Web – and plug-ins (page 58) for audio and video files.

There are also files on the Web that the browser cannot handle. TIF and BMP graphics, Word documents, PDF and PostScript files are all quite common. To view these types, you have to turn to other applications. If you have the right programs, they can be linked in, so that they can be launched and used from within the browser.

The link can be made when you meet a file in a page.

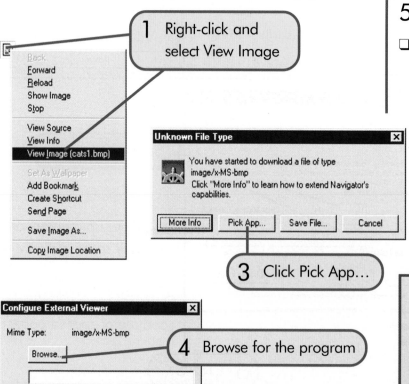

Basic steps

1 Right-click an image icon and select View Image from the menu.

or

2 Click the link to a file.

3 At the Unknown File Type dialog box, click Pick App…

4 Click Browse and locate the program file on your hard disk.

5 Click OK.

❑ The application will run and display the file. Next time it meets a file of the same type, Netscape will know what to do.

Tip

You can find programs to handle almost all types of files on the Web.

Basic steps

1 Open the Applications panel.

2 Select a file type that is not handled already, for which you have suitable software.

3 Click Edit.

4 Browse for the program and open it.

5 Click OK to return to the main Preferences panel.

For postscript files, you need Ghostview (see page 204)

Linking in applications

You can also set up applications before you start browsing. Check the file types listed in the Applications panel. If you find any with a blank Handled By: line, and you have applications to handle them on your system, link them in.

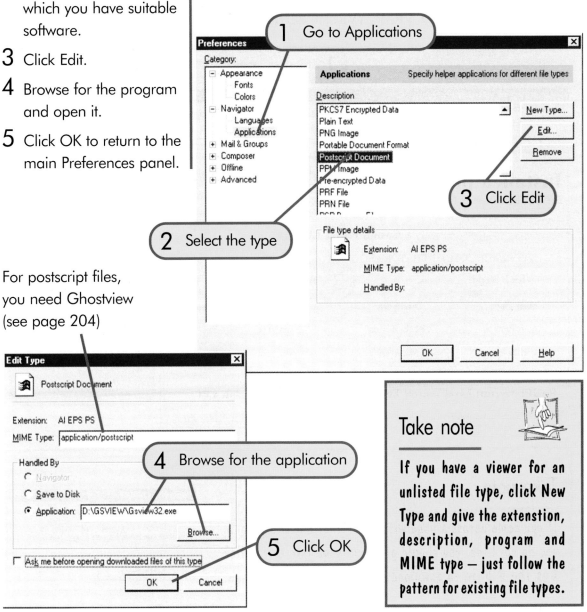

Preferences

Category:
- Appearance
  - Fonts
  - Colors
- Navigator
  - Languages
  - Applications
- Mail & Groups
- Composer
- Offline
- Advanced

Applications   Specify helper applications for different file types

Description
PKCS7 Encrypted Data
Plain Text
PNG Image
Portable Document Format
Postscript Document
PPM Image
Pre-encrypted Data
PRF File
PRN File

New Type...
Edit...
Remove

File type details

Extension: AI EPS PS
MIME Type: application/postscript
Handled By:

OK   Cancel   Help

1 Go to Applications

3 Click Edit

2 Select the type

Edit Type

Postscript Document

Extension: AI EPS PS
MIME Type: application/postscript

Handled By
- Navigator
- Save to Disk
- Application: D:\GSVIEW\Gsview32.exe

Browse...

☐ Ask me before opening downloaded files of this type

OK   Cancel

4 Browse for the application

5 Click OK

Take note

If you have a viewer for an unlisted file type, click New Type and give the extenstion, description, program and MIME type — just follow the pattern for existing file types.

Plug-ins

Plug-ins enable Navigator to cope with different types of files. You will have some installed already, and there are nearly 200 on offer at Netcenter – have a browse. Ones that you might like to download and install include RealPlayer, for 'streaming' (real time) audio and video; QuickTime, for video files; and Cosmo for viewing 3D VRML (Virtual Reality Modelling Language) 'worlds'.

Basic steps

1 Go on-line.

2 Select About Plug-ins from the Help menu.

3 Look through to see what's installed.

4 Click on the link.

5 See what's there, and download as required.

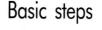
1 Go on-line

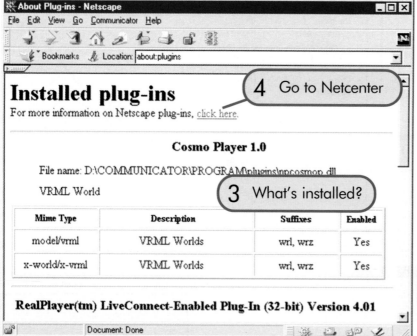

Installed plug-ins

For more information on Netscape plug-ins, click here.

4 Go to Netcenter

Cosmo Player 1.0

File name: D:\COMMUNICATOR\PROGRAM\plugins\npcosmop.dll

VRML World

3 What's installed?

Mime Type	Description	Suffixes	Enabled
model/vrml	VRML Worlds	wrl, wrz	Yes
x-world/x-vrml	VRML Worlds	wrl, wrz	Yes

RealPlayer(tm) LiveConnect-Enabled Plug-In (32-bit) Version 4.01

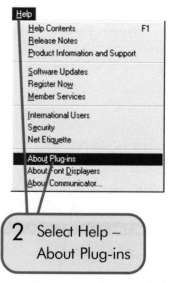

Help
Help Contents	F1
Release Notes	
Product Information and Support	
Software Updates	
Register Now	
Member Services	
International Users	
Security	
Net Etiquette	
About Plug-ins	
About Font Displayers	
About Communicator...	

2 Select Help – About Plug-ins

Take note

If you come across a page with a file that needs a plug-in you do not have, you should get a message like this. Click **Get the Plugin** to download it, then return to the page.

Plugin Not Loaded ✕

This page contains information of type "application/futuresplash" that can only be viewed with the appropriate Plug-in. What do you want to do?

| Get the Plugin | Cancel |

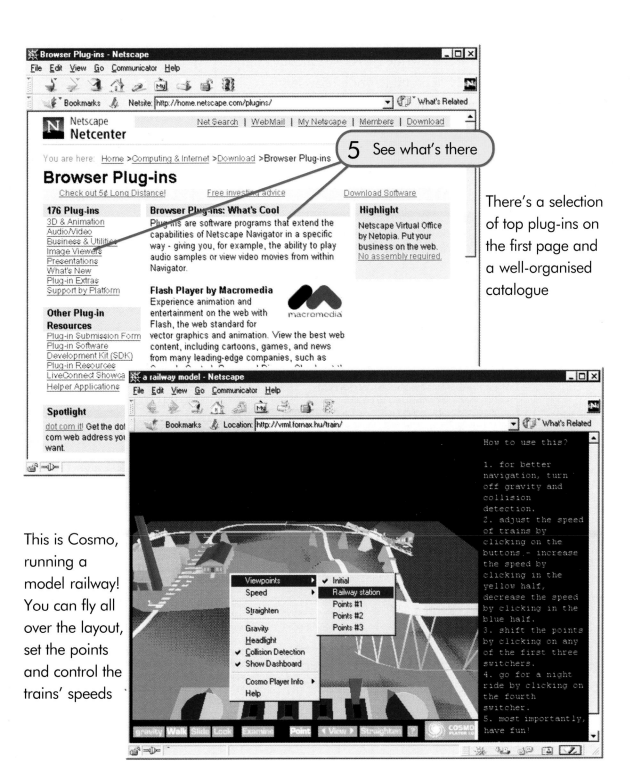

There's a selection of top plug-ins on the first page and a well-organised catalogue

This is Cosmo, running a model railway! You can fly all over the layout, set the points and control the trains' speeds

Getting Help

Communicator's Help files are written in HTML and JavaScript. While this may be highly appropriate for a browser, it is also significantly slower to use than a standard Windows Help system. Still, there's a lot of useful stuff in it, and finding Help is not difficult.

1 From the Help menu, select Help Contents.

❑ Browsing Help

2 Click on a heading to open its list of topics.

3 Select a topic, following up any relevant links.

❑ Help Index

4 Click the Index icon.

5 Type a word into the Look for: box.

6 Click on a heading.

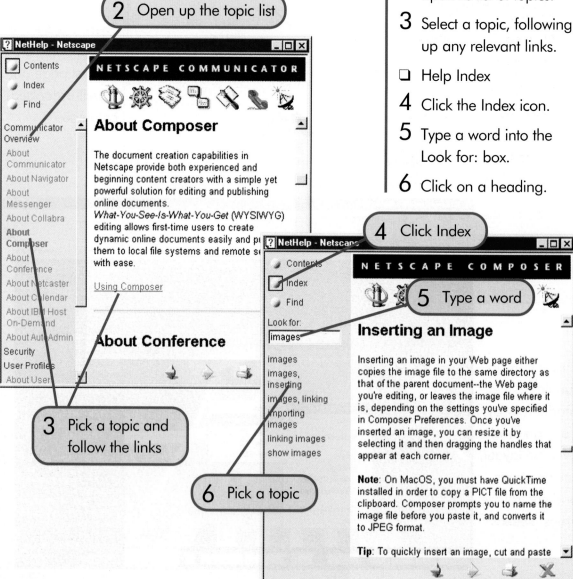

2 Open up the topic list

NetHelp - Netscape

Contents
Index
Find

NETSCAPE COMMUNICATOR

About Composer

Communicator Overview
About Communicator
About Navigator
About Messenger
About Collabra
About Composer
About Conference
About Netcaster
About Calendar
About IBM Host On-Demand
About Auto Admin
Security
User Profiles
About User

The document creation capabilities in Netscape provide both experienced and beginning content creators with a simple yet powerful solution for editing and publishing online documents. *What-You-See-Is-What-You-Get* (WYSIWYG) editing allows first-time users to create dynamic online documents easily and put them to local file systems and remote se with ease.

Using Composer

About Conference

3 Pick a topic and follow the links

4 Click Index

NetHelp - Netscape

Contents
Index
Find

Look for:
images

images
images, inserting
images, linking
importing images
linking images
show images

NETSCAPE COMPOSER

5 Type a word

Inserting an Image

Inserting an image in your Web page either copies the image file to the same directory as that of the parent document--the Web page you're editing, or leaves the image file where it is, depending on the settings you've specified in Composer Preferences. Once you've inserted an image, you can resize it by selecting it and then dragging the handles that appear at each corner.

Note: On MacOS, you must have QuickTime installed in order to copy a PICT file from the clipboard. Composer prompts you to name the image file before you paste it, and converts it to JPEG format.

Tip: To quickly insert an image, cut and paste

6 Pick a topic

❑ Finding Help

1 Click the Find icon.

2 Type a word into the Find what: box.

3 Click Find Next – if necessary, click Find Next again to find other references.

4 Switch to Up and click Find Next if you want to return to an earlier reference.

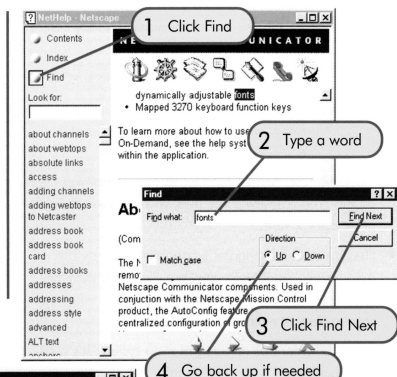

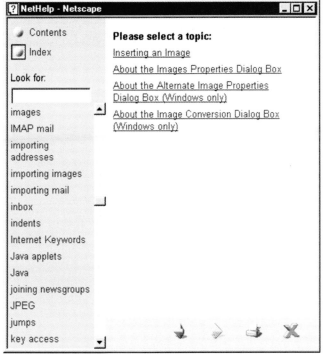

Take note

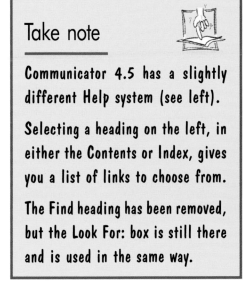

Communicator 4.5 has a slightly different Help system (see left).

Selecting a heading on the left, in either the Contents or Index, gives you a list of links to choose from.

The Find heading has been removed, but the Look For: box is still there and is used in the same way.

Summary

◆ Navigator is Communicator's browser, and the central application of the suite.

◆ The toolbars can be removed or reduced in size, to create a larger viewing area.

◆ To get Navigator working just the way you want it, spend some time on the Preferences panels.

◆ Navigator can handle most types of files that you meet on the Web. To view some files, you will have to link in other applications.

◆ Plug-ins extend Navigator's capabilities. There are many available at Netcenter, but you will usually be offered the chance to download the plug-in when you meet a file that needs one.

◆ Communicator has an integral Help system. It's a bit slow, but there's a lot of good information in it.

5 Navigating the Web

Hypertext links

The World Wide Web is held together by millions of hypertext links. These may take you from one page to another within a site or off to a far-distant site – though some pages are dead-ends, which is when the Back button comes in handy!

The links may be underlined words embedded in the text or presented as a list, or may be built into pictures. They are always easy to spot. When you point to a link, the cursor changes to 🖑 and the Status line shows the address of the linked page.

❑ When you find a useful page, you can often follow links from there to related pages on the same topic. The trick is to find a good place to start browsing – you'll meet some later in this chapter.

There's a link on this image

If you point at an image, you often get a pop-up label

Hypertext links are usually underlined and coloured blue

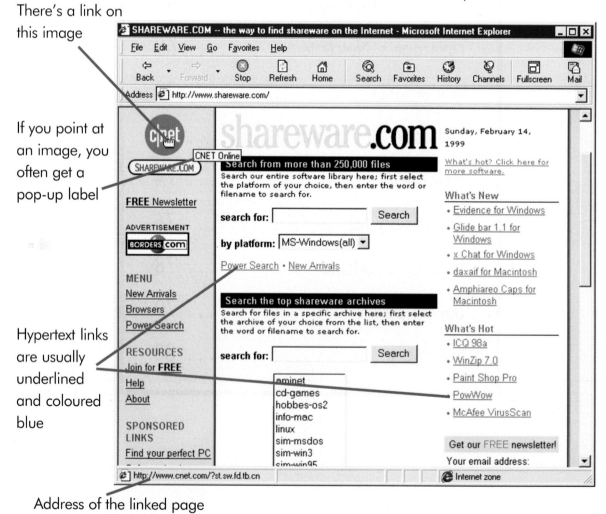

Address of the linked page

Image maps

Tip

If you want to include image maps in your page, you can create them easily using MapEdit. Find it at: http://www.boutell.com

Image maps are a special type of hypertext linked graphic. These can have any number of links embedded into them, each in its own area of the image.

In some image maps, like this map of Internet resources in Finland, it is quite clear what each part links to. In other more graphic ones, look for the hand icon. When you see it, you are pointing to a link.

Look for the hand

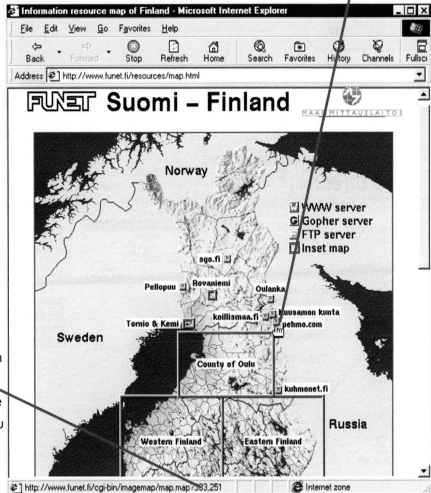

With image maps, the status bar usually shows the coordinates (in pixels measured across then down from the top left) of the cursor position, not the URL of the link that you are pointing to.

Starting to Explore

The Internet is a huge place. Where do you start browsing? Internet Explorer is supplied with a number of starting point links built into it. You'll find these on the **Links** buttons and the **Microsoft on the Web** menu, and all lead to places within Microsoft or at MSN (MicroSoft Network). A good place to start a browsing session is at the Best of the Web – is a directory of selected links, grouped under topic headings.

1 If you are not online, connect now.

2 Open the Help menu, point to Microsoft on the Web and select Best of the Web.

Or

3 Click the Best of the Web button.

4 Click a topic in the panel at the left.

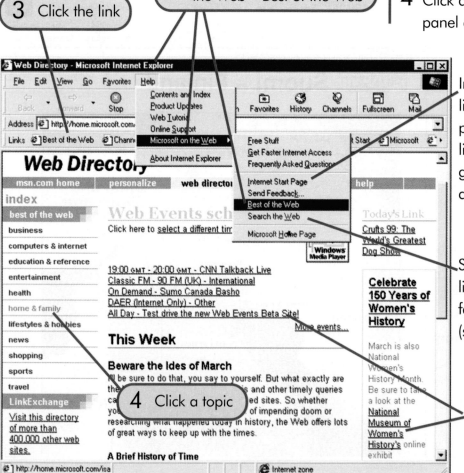

2 Select Help – Microsoft on the Web – Best of the Web

3 Click the link

4 Click a topic

Internet Start Page links to the top page at MSN with links, news, sport, games, shopping, and more.

Search the Web links to the search facility at MSN (see page 119)

Click the links to go to the feature pages

66

5 When the new page has loaded, click a category.

6 Read the reviews and click a title to jump to the linked site

Or

7 Click a subcategory and follow the links from there.

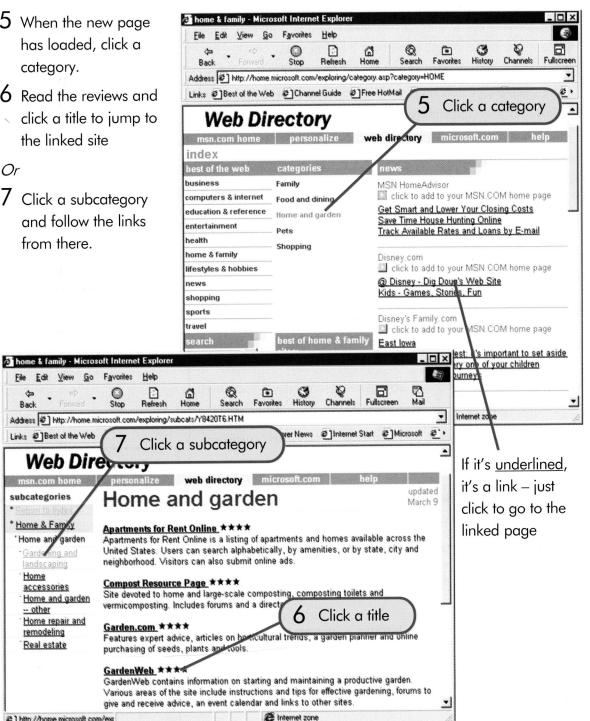

5 Click a category

7 Click a subcategory

6 Click a title

If it's <u>underlined</u>, it's a link – just click to go to the linked page

Netscape's Netcenter

Navigator also has a number of starting points built into it. In this case, the links all lead to parts of Netcenter, the 'portal' run by Netscape. Portals are sites offering doorways into the Net, where people can start their surfing sessions. But they are not not just doorways. Netcenter, like most other portals, offers free e-mail, free Web space, news, weather, sports and business information services, and many other activities all designed to encourage visitors to stay within the site for as long as possible. The longer people stay, the more adverts they will see, and the more the portal can charge for advertising space.

Netcenter's services include:

WebMail: free e-mail through the Web (see page 166);

Personal Home Page: select the information you want to see and the facilities you want to have to hand when you first reach Netcenter;

Instant Messenger: instant communication with friends and colleagues (if they are on-line at the same time);

SmartUpdate: automatic updates to your Netscape software;

In-Box Direct: free subscriptions to over 100 e-zines and other e-mailed publications (see page 147);

Search: access to six different search engines (see page 118);

What's New: a selection of the best of the new stuff on the Web.

Contact: address book with fax, messaging, and conference calling facilities;

Channels: from some of the Internet's best and most popular content providers.

Take note

Netcenter isn't just for Navigator users — anyone can join, or use its public services without even becoming a member. Just point your browser to: http://www.netcenter.com — see page 70 for more on going to addresses.

Take note

Other good portals include Yahoo, Excite, Infoseek and AltaVista, which all started out as directories or search engine sites. Microsoft is developing MSN, its access provider service, as a portal.

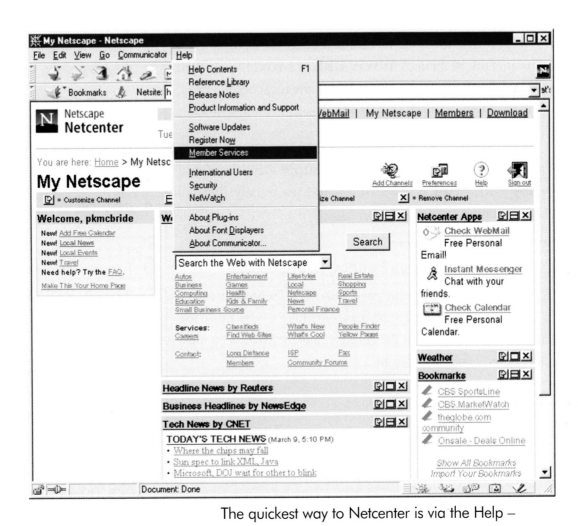

The quickest way to Netcenter is via the Help – Member Services command. You must register as a member to get the full benefits, but many of the services are also open to non-members.

The Communicator – Bookmarks – Guide menu leads to some great places, including People (see page 168) and What's Cool.

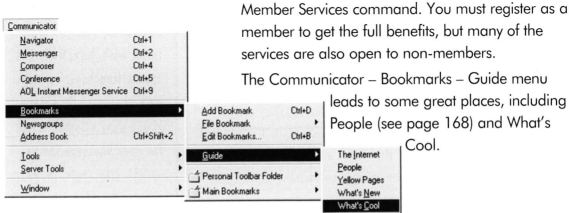

WWW URLs

Don't you just love TLAs (Three Letter Acronyms)? The Internet is full of them. A **WWW URL** is a World Wide Web Uniform Resource Locator and it gives the location of a page.

The URL may be a simple name:

http://www.cnet.com

This is the top page of the clnet site. **http://** identifies it as a WWW URL. **www** is how Web addresses usually (but not always) start.

Some URLs are more complex:

http://www.shareware.com/SW/Search/Popular

This takes us to the **Popular** page in the **/SW/Search** directory at **shareware.com**. URLs are case-sensitive – you must use capitals and lower case as they are given in the URL. You must also get the punctuation right!

Using URLs

All Web browsers have routines for entering URLs. They can be typed into the slot above the display area (labelled **Address:** in Internet Explorer, **Go to:** in Navigator 4.0 and **Location:** in Navigator 4.5), or into the **Open** (IE) or **Open Page** (Navigator) dialog box that is reached from the File menu.

Finding URLs

Of course, before you can use a URL, you must know what it is. So where do you find them? There are dozens scattered through this book and listed – with more – in Chapter 15; they are given in magazines and newspaper articles, on posters, in TV ads and programmes – the URL for the BBC's news service (used opposite) is given at the end of every newscast.

Basic steps

1 Have the URL to hand – they're easy to mistype!

❑ Internet Explorer

2 From the File menu select Open.

3 Type in the URL.

4 Click OK.

or

5 Type the URL into the Address box and press [Enter].

❑ Navigator

Follow the steps above, using File – Open Page or the Location box.

Take note

All domain names (site addresses) must be registered with InterNIC, the controlling body, to make sure that each is unique. If you want a domain name for your business (or personal) site, talk to your access provider.

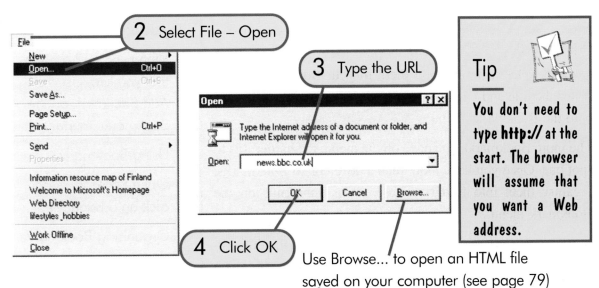

2 Select File – Open

3 Type the URL

4 Click OK

Use Browse... to open an HTML file
saved on your computer (see page 79)

Tip

You don't need to type **http://** at the start. The browser will assume that you want a Web address.

5 Type the URL into the Address box

Netscape Bookmarks

Some good places are easy to find; others you discover over a long and painful search or by sheer chance. If you want to return to these pages in future, add them to your Bookmarks. This stores the title and URL of the page in a file, and puts the title onto the Bookmarks menu.

The more Bookmarks you have on the menu, the harder it is to spot one. Once you have more than a dozen or so Bookmarks, organise them into folders. These act as submenus on the Bookmark menu.

Before you start, work out which ones have something in common, and what to call their folders. Odds and ends can be left on the main menu and grouped later.

❑ Adding Bookmarks

1 When you find a page that you like, just click Add Bookmark on the Bookmarks menu.

❑ Using Bookmarks

2 Open Bookmarks and click on a page title.

❑ Organising Bookmarks

3 Open the Bookmarks menu and select Go to Bookmarks.

4 The new folder will be inserted below the selected item. For this first folder, select the Header – the top line.

5 Use Item – Insert Folder

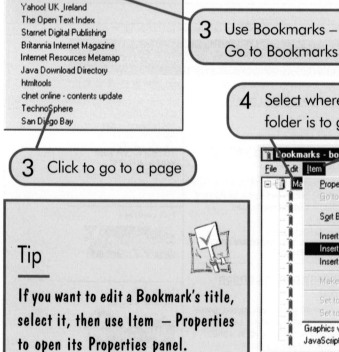

1 Add a Bookmark

3 Use Bookmarks – Go to Bookmarks

3 Click to go to a page

4 Select where the folder is to go

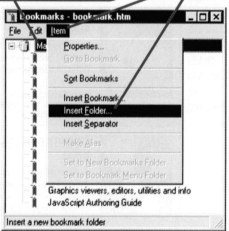

Tip

If you want to edit a Bookmark's title, select it, then use Item – Properties to open its Properties panel.

72

5 Open the Item menu and select Insert Folder.

6 Replace *New Folder* with a name to use on the Bookmarks menu.

7 Select an item and drag it onto the folder.

8 Repeat step 7 for all items for that folder.

9 Repeat steps 4 to 8 to create more folders.

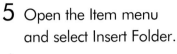
6 Name the new folder

Bookmark Properties

General

Name: Directories

Location (URL):

Description:

There are no aliases to this bookmark   Select Aliases

Last Visited:

Added on: Mon Dec 16 10:26:32 1997

OK   Cancel   Help

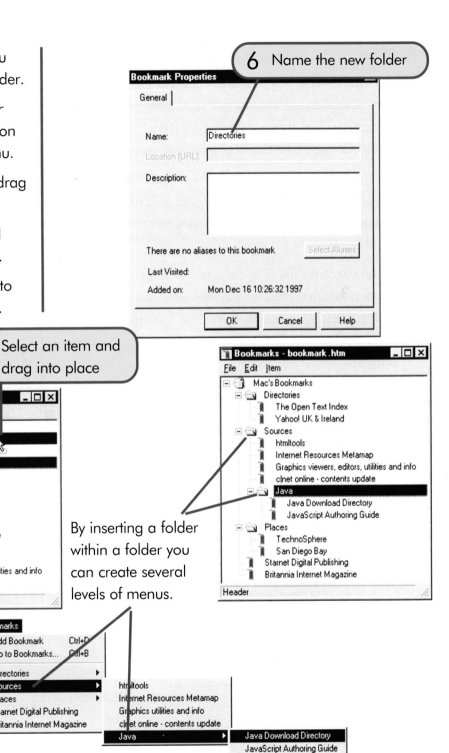

7 Select an item and drag into place

Bookmarks - bookmark.htm

File Edit Item

Mac's Bookmarks
  Directories
    Yahoo! UK & Ireland
    The Open Text Index
  Starnet Digital Publishing
  Britannia Internet Magazine
  Internet Resources Metamap
  Java Download Directory
  htmltools
  c|net online - contents update
  TechnoSphere
  San Diego Bay
  Graphics viewers, editors, utilities and info
  JavaScript Authoring Guide

http://index.opentext.net/

By inserting a folder within a folder you can create several levels of menus.

Bookmarks - bookmark.htm

File Edit Item

Mac's Bookmarks
  Directories
    The Open Text Index
    Yahoo! UK & Ireland
  Sources
    htmltools
    Internet Resources Metamap
    Graphics viewers, editors, utilities and info
    c|net online - contents update
    Java
      Java Download Directory
      JavaScript Authoring Guide
  Places
    TechnoSphere
    San Diego Bay
  Starnet Digital Publishing
  Britannia Internet Magazine

Header

Bookmarks

Add Bookmark   Ctrl+D
Go to Bookmarks...   Ctrl+B

Directories   ▶
Sources   ▶
Places   ▶
Starnet Digital Publishing
Britannia Internet Magazine

htmltools
Internet Resources Metamap
Graphics utilities and info
c|net online - contents update
Java   ▶

Java Download Directory
JavaScript Authoring Guide

Favorites

Favorites are Internet Explorer's equivalent to Bookmarks. They work in the same way, and are created in a similar fashion. The main differences are that you can store a Favorite in a folder as you create it, and that you will be offered the chance to subscribe to the page (if it runs a channel) as you add it to your Favorites.

● You must have the page open to be able to add it to the Favorites – but you can do this offline by opening the page from the History list (page 76).

● If the Favorites list is opened from the menu bar, it just drops down the screen and closes after you have chosen. Using the toolbar button opens the Favorites list in the Explorer bar, where it stays at hand until you choose to close it.

Basic steps

❑ Adding Favorites

1 Find a good page!

2 Open Favorites.

3 Select Add to Favorites.

4 Edit the name if necessary.

5 To add it to the main menu, click OK.

or

6 To store it in a folder, click Create in>>.

7 Select the folder.

8 Click OK.

❑ Using Favorites

9 Open Favorites and select the page title.

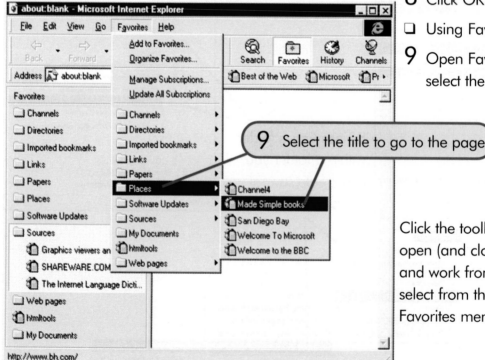

9 Select the title to go to the page

Click the toolbar button to open (and close) the sidebar and work from there, or select from the drop-down Favorites menu.

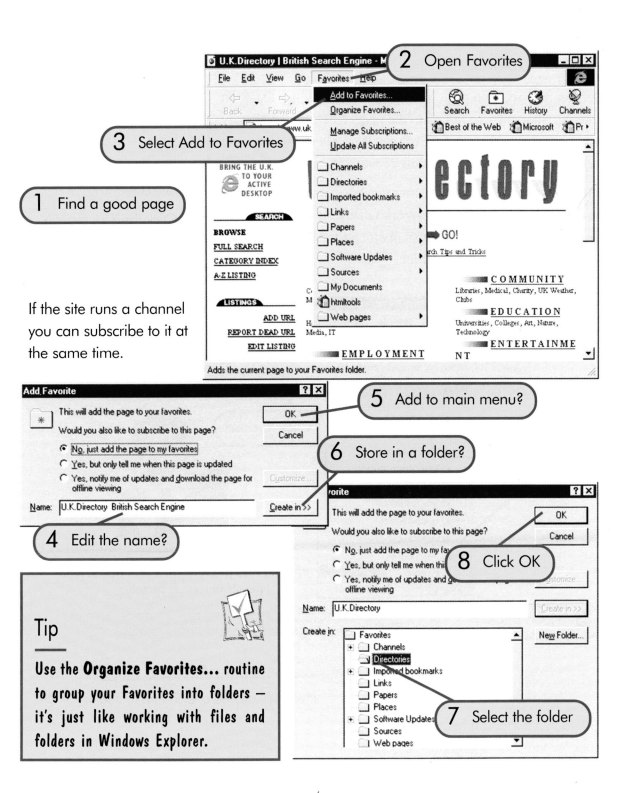

2 Open Favorites

U.K.Directory | British Search Engine - M

File   Edit   View   Go   Favorites   Help

Add to Favorites...

3 Select Add to Favorites

Organize Favorites...

Manage Subscriptions...

Update All Subscriptions

Search   Favorites   History   Channels

Best of the Web   Microsoft   Pr

BRING THE U.K.
TO YOUR
ACTIVE
DESKTOP

Channels

Directories

Imported bookmarks

Links

Papers

Places

Software Updates

Sources

My Documents

htmltools

Web pages

ectory

GO!

1   Find a good page

SEARCH

BROWSE

FULL SEARCH

CATEGORY INDEX

A-Z LISTING

LISTINGS

ADD URL

REPORT DEAD URL

EDIT LISTING

rch Tips and Tricks

COMMUNITY
Libraries, Medical, Charity, UK Weather,
Clubs

EDUCATION
Universities, Colleges, Art, Nature,
Technology

ENTERTAINME
NT

If the site runs a channel
you can subscribe to it at
the same time.

Media, IT

EMPLOYMENT

Adds the current page to your Favorites folder.

Add Favorite

This will add the page to your favorites.

Would you also like to subscribe to this page?

OK

Cancel

5   Add to main menu?

● No, just add the page to my favorites

○ Yes, but only tell me when this page is updated

○ Yes, notify me of updates and download the page for offline viewing

Customize...

6   Store in a folder?

orite

This will add the page to your favorites.

OK

Name: U.K.Directory British Search Engine

Create in >>

Would you also like to subscribe to this page?

Cancel

4   Edit the name?

● No, just add the page to my fa

○ Yes, but only tell me when thi

○ Yes, notify me of updates and g offline viewing

8   Click OK

omize...

Name: U.K.Directory

Create in >>

Tip

Use the **Organize Favorites...** routine
to group your Favorites into folders —
it's just like working with files and
folders in Windows Explorer.

Create in: Favorites

Channels

Directories

Imported bookmarks

Links

Papers

Places

Software Updates

Sources

Web pages

New Folder...

7   Select the folder

The History list

Internet Explorer

As you browse, each page is recorded in the History list as an Internet Shortcut – i.e. a link to the page. Clicking the History button opens the list in the Explorer Bar, where the links are organised into folders, according to site.

If you want to use the History after you have gone offline, open the File menu and turn on the Work Offline. If a page actively draws from its home site – typically to get fresh adverts – you will not be able to open it offline.

Basic steps

1 Click the History button to open the list in the Explorer Bar.

2 Click to open a site's folder.

3 Select the page.

4 Click the X at the top right of the Explorer Bar to close it.

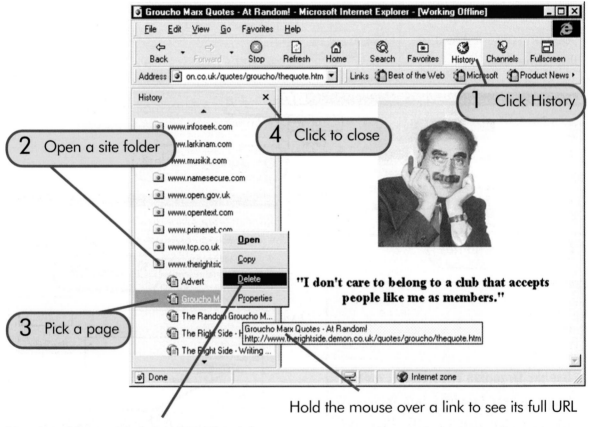

Hold the mouse over a link to see its full URL

Unwanted items can be removed – right click for the short menu and select Delete

Basic steps

Navigator History

1 Open the Communicator menu, point to Tools and select History, or press [Ctrl] and [H].

2 Select the page.

❏ To return to a page

3 Double-click on it or select Go to Page from the File menu.

❏ To bookmark a page

4 Open the File menu and select Add to Bookmarks.

In Navigator, the History list is displayed in its own separate window. This stays open after you have selected a page – though it may not be obvious if you are running Navigator in a maximized window.

● If you want to do a lot of browsing through the History, reduce the Navigator window a little and arrange that and the History window so that they are overlapping. You can then switch easily between them.

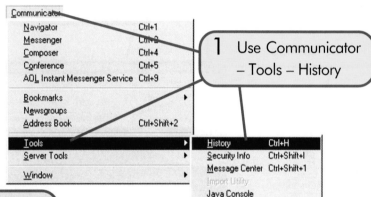

1 Use Communicator – Tools – History

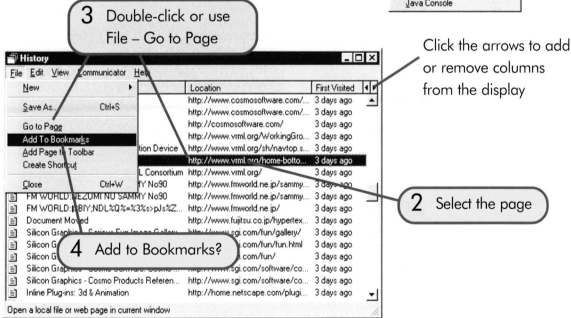

3 Double-click or use File – Go to Page

Click the arrows to add or remove columns from the display

2 Select the page

4 Add to Bookmarks?

Desktop shortcuts

Do you use desktop shortcuts to your most-used applications, or to documents that you want to reopen in a hurry? You can also create desktop shortcuts to Internet sites. One click on the shortcut will then start the browser and make the connection.

The process is the same in Navigator and Internet Explorer – and if you have both browsers installed, the shortcut will always run Internet Explorer.

Basic steps

1 Go to the page.

2 Drag 🏃 (Navigator) or 🮷 (Explorer) onto the desktop.

Or

3 Right-click and select Create Shortcut.

4 Edit the Description as required.

5 Click OK.

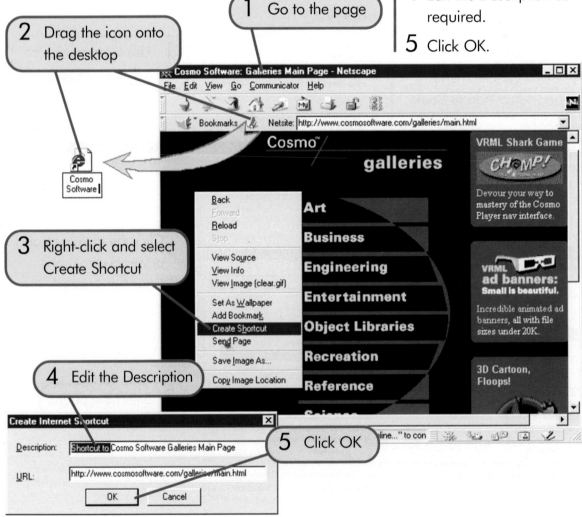

1 Go to the page

2 Drag the icon onto the desktop

3 Right-click and select Create Shortcut

4 Edit the Description

5 Click OK

78

Basic steps

❏ Saving pages

1 From the File menu select Save As ...

2 Set the folder and filename and save as normal.

❏ Opening filed pages

3 Open the File menu and select Open.

4 Click Browse.

5 Find and select the file.

6 Click Open, then back at the Open panel, click OK.

Saving pages

Page files are erased from the History list after a while – how long depends on you (see page 32 for Explorer and page 52 for Navigator). If you want to keep a page for long-term reference, save it as a file on disk. It can then be opened from there at any time later.

● The Save routine is the same in Navigator and Explorer.

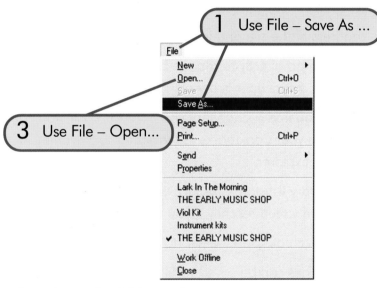

1 Use File – Save As ...

3 Use File – Open...

If you know the folder and filename, you can type it here

4 Click Browse

5 Select the file

6 Click Open, then OK

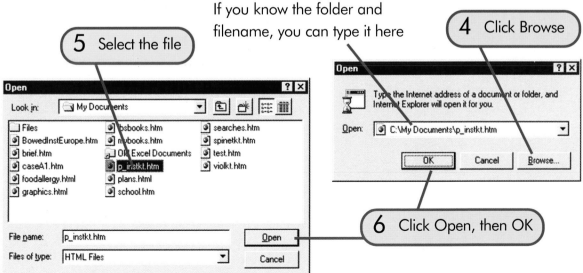

Summary

- ◆ Hypertext links can be built into text or attached to images or image maps.

- ◆ Internet Explorer offers a number of start pages at MSN, with links to search engines, directories and other resources. From Navigator you can reach a similar, but more extensive, service at Netcenter.

- ◆ Every Web page has a unique URL which gives the address of the site and the location of the page file.

- ◆ You can go directly to a page by typing its URL into the Address slot of your browser.

- ◆ When you find a page that you want to revisit, you can add it to your Bookmarks in Navigator or Favorites in Internet Explorer.

- ◆ The History list stores links to, and files from, the places you have visited recently – you can even revisit offline!

- ◆ You can create Desktop shortcuts to Web addresses.

- ◆ Web pages can be saved as files, for later reference.

6 Net directories

Yahoo

The Web hosts a dozen or so large, general-purpose directories, plus many more specialist ones. Have a look at them – they can be excellent places to start browsing.

Yahoo was one of the first, and is still one of the biggest and best Net directories. It has links to over a million selected Web pages and newsgroups, organised into a hierarchy of categories with extensive cross-referencing.

Once you get past the first level, you find a mixture of links to pages and lists of subcategories, with the links increasing as you go down the hierarchy.

Basic steps

1 Go to Yahoo at
   www.yahoo.com
   or www.yahoo.co.uk

2 Click on a category on the main menu.

3 Select a category from the next menu – repeat as necessary.

4 When you reach the links, select one.

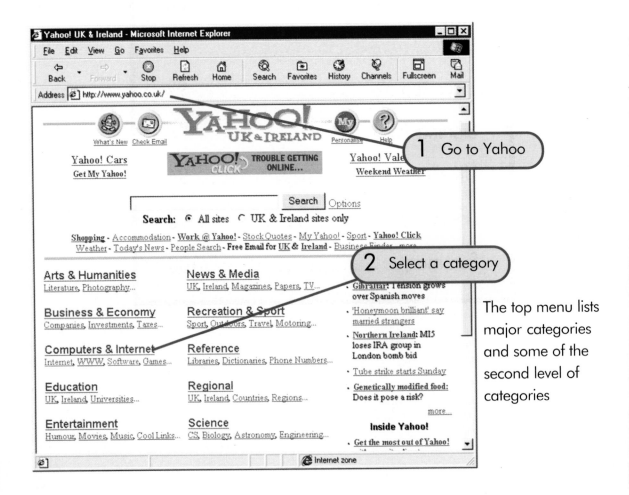

The top menu lists major categories and some of the second level of categories

82

Click Back or use these links to return to a higher level

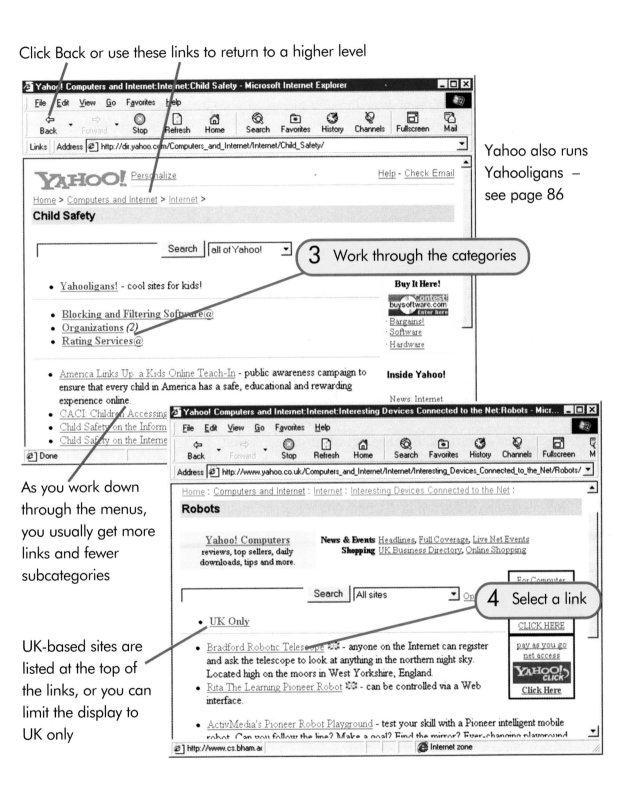

Yahoo also runs
Yahooligans –
see page 86

3 Work through the categories

As you work down
through the menus,
you usually get more
links and fewer
subcategories

UK-based sites are
listed at the top of
the links, or you can
limit the display to
UK only

4 Select a link

Searching Yahoo

If you are looking for information on a specific topic, organisation, artist, piece of software, or whatever, it is often quicker to search for it, than to work your way through menus or the descriptions of linked pages.

A successful search will give you a list of categories, if any, and a list of links that contain the given word(s).

Simple search

A simple search looks for pages that contain matches for all the words you enter (the *keys*), but treats the words as *substrings*. For instance, if you entered 'graphic software' it would look for pages with 'graphic', 'graphics' and 'graphical' and with 'software'.

- If you are in the UK, restrict the search to **UK & Ireland** only if you are looking for suppliers or societies, where being local is important.

- Restrict the search to **This category only** to reduce search times and cut out irrelevant material from other categories – even if your words do not have more than one meaning, they may crop up as a passing reference in an otherwise unrelated page.

1 Enter one or more words to describe what you are looking for – try to be specific.

2 Restrict the search, if appropriate.

3 Click ⬚Search⬚.

4 When the results appear, go to a Category to browse through a menu page of related links.

Or

5 Work through the Sites or Pages and select from there.

6 If you would like to try a more closely defined search, click Options.

Tip

The Yahoo menu structure is very good, but it isn't always obvious where you should start looking for a topic. Rather than hunt up and down the menus, run a search to find the category headings.

Tip

If you are looking for a company on the Web, start in the Business section and just type the main part of its name.

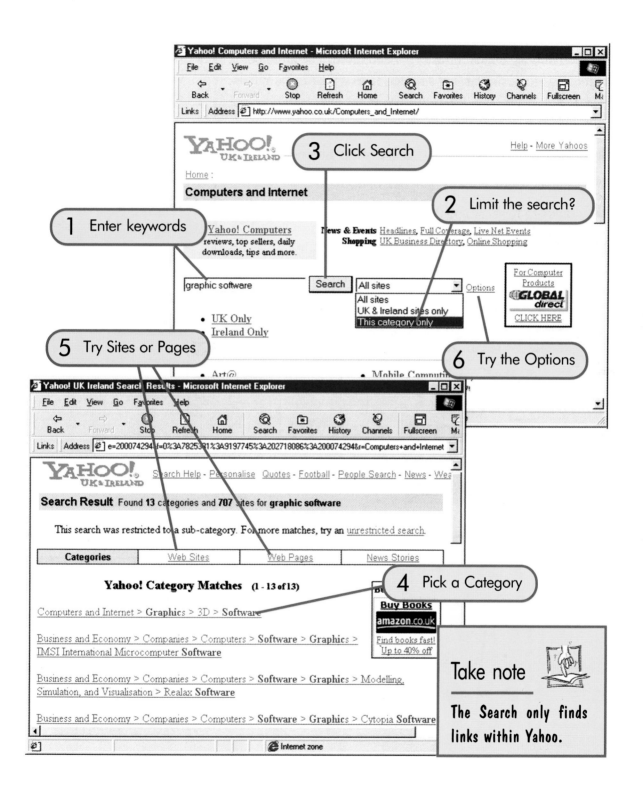

Take note

The Search only finds links within Yahoo.

Yahooligans

Yahooligans is a kids' directory – and more. The directory is organised along similar, but simpler, lines as the main Yahoo, and its links have been carefully chosen for their suitability for children. The site also offers, amongst other things:

- a *Club*, to encourage active use of the Internet,
- guidance for *Parents and Teachers*,
- links to forthcoming *Net Events*,
- and the *Downloader* (see opposite).

Basic steps

1 Go to Yahooligans at www.yahooligans.com

2 Click on a category and work through the menus to the links on a topic.

Or

3 Click on a link to an activity within the site.

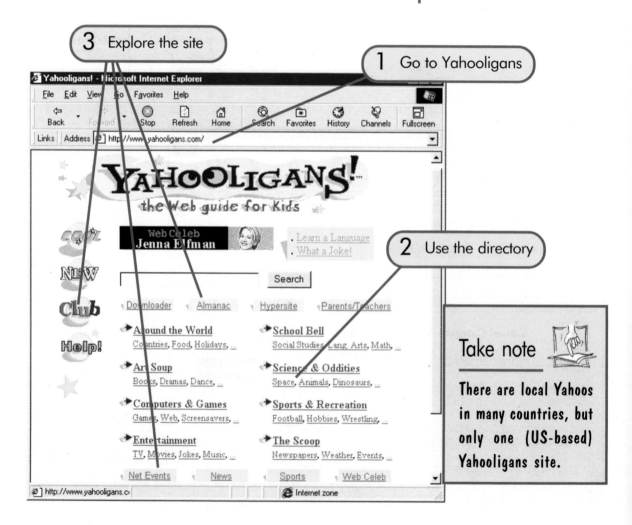

3 Explore the site

1 Go to Yahooligans

2 Use the directory

Take note

There are local Yahoos in many countries, but only one (US-based) Yahooligans site.

86

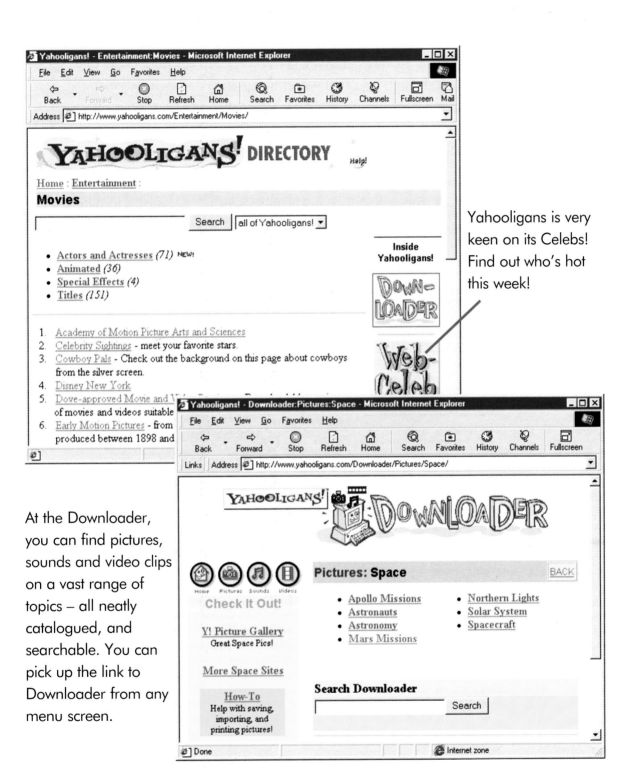

Yahooligans is very keen on its Celebs! Find out who's hot this week!

At the Downloader, you can find pictures, sounds and video clips on a vast range of topics – all neatly catalogued, and searchable. You can pick up the link to Downloader from any menu screen.

Excite

There is an awful lot of junk on the Internet, and you can waste an awful lot of time sifting through it to find useful material. Save yourself some time and start from Excite. Here you will find a comprehensive catalogue of selected sites, with brief but thoughtful reviews, enabling you to find relevant stuff quickly.

Excite also offers many other services, including a powerful search engine (which can also be reached through Magellan, see page 110), Communities (opposite), My Excite (page 90) and Web mail (page 166).

Basic steps

1 Go to Excite at www.excite.co.uk

2 Click on a category heading or subheading.

3 The display at the next level varies, but always has links to different aspects of the category – follow the links!

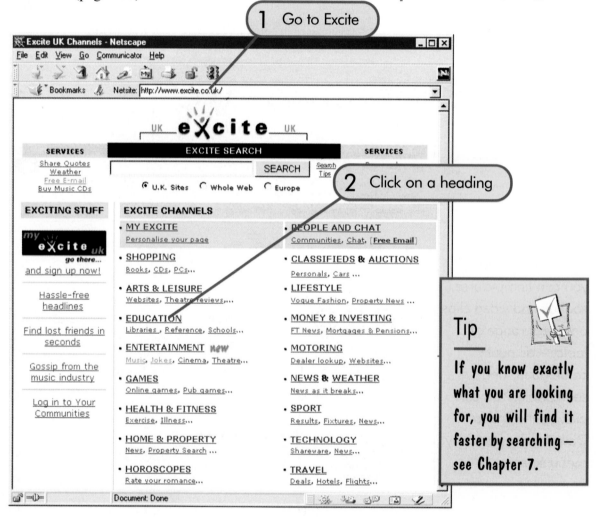

1 Go to Excite

2 Click on a heading

Tip

If you know exactly what you are looking for, you will find it faster by searching — see Chapter 7.

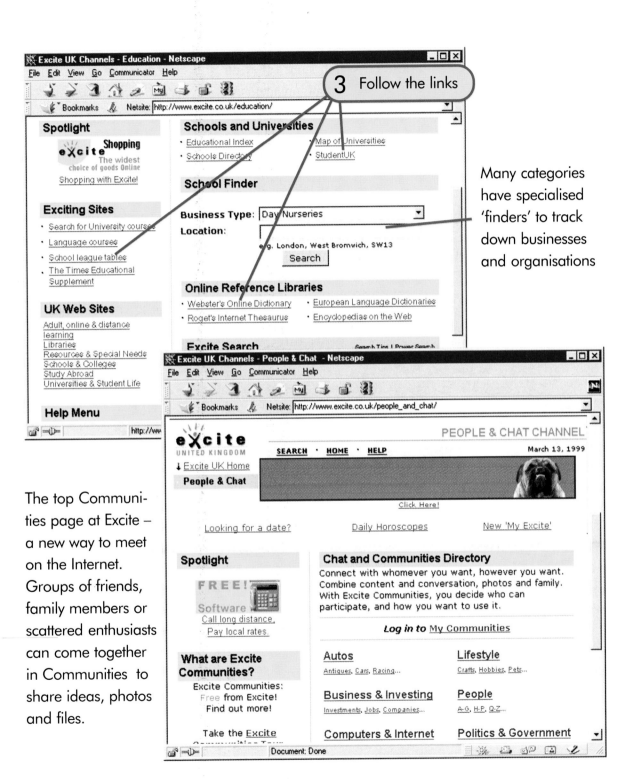

Many categories have specialised 'finders' to track down businesses and organisations

The top Communities page at Excite – a new way to meet on the Internet. Groups of friends, family members or scattered enthusiasts can come together in Communities to share ideas, photos and files.

My Channel

Excite, like most other directories and search sites, relies on advertising for its income – and rates depend upon readership. The personalised My Channel facility is one of the things that they hope will encourage you to keep coming back, and to spend more time there.

You can choose what topics to include on these pages, and set up your own selections of favourite links. The choices are stored on your computer, as a 'cookie' – coded data in Netscape's *cookie.txt* file, or Internet Explorer's *cookie* folder – so that they are in place when you revisit.

Basic steps

1 Go to Excite at www.excite.co.uk

2 Select My Excite.

❏ The first time you try to personalise the page, you will be asked to register. On later visits, just sign in.

3 Click Contents in the Personalisation Manager to choose which sections to include.

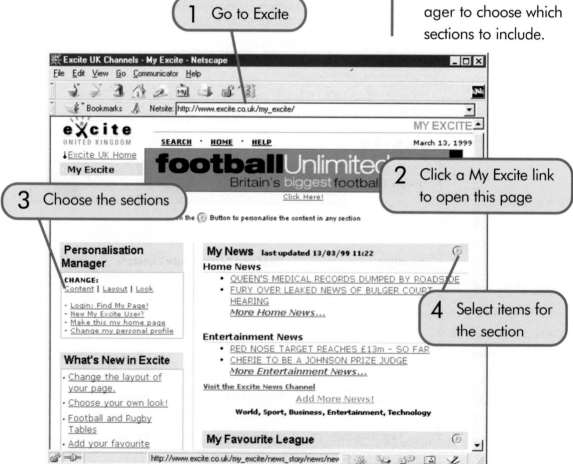

1 Go to Excite

2 Click a My Excite link to open this page

3 Choose the sections

4 Select items for the section

4 Click 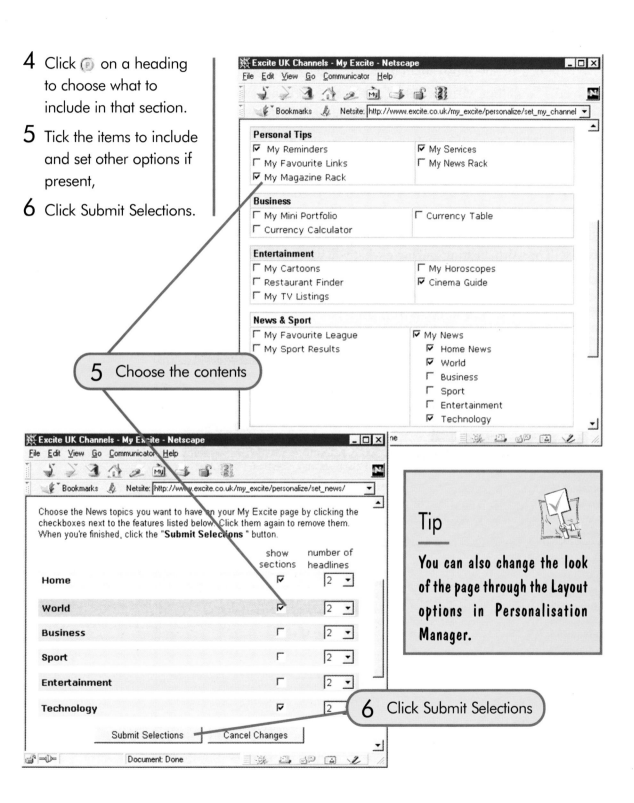 on a heading to choose what to include in that section.

5 Tick the items to include and set other options if present,

6 Click Submit Selections.

5 Choose the contents

Tip

You can also change the look of the page through the Layout options in Personalisation Manager.

6 Click Submit Selections

Lycos Top 5%

Lycos is one of the most popular sites on the Web, with a claimed 13+ million visitors a day! It has an excellent search engine, which has indexed a very large proportion of the Web, a neat *Personal Guide* and good range of other services, but our main interest here is its directory of the Top 5% Sites.

Its Top 5% Sites are rated on content and/or design, and each link is accompanied by a brief review. So, although these cover only a small fraction of the Web, you can be reasonably sure that a site will be worth visiting and have what you want, before you link to it.

1 Go to Lycos Top 5% at http://point-uk.lycos.com

2 Select a Topic.

3 Read through the list to find suitable sites.

Or

4 Click on a heading for a more specialised list.

Or

5 Sort by Content, Date, Design or Alphabet.

1 Go to Lycos Top 5%

2 Click on a Topic

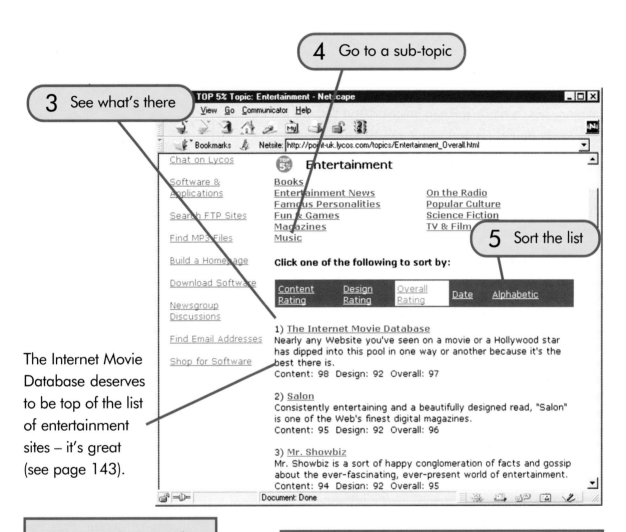

3 See what's there

4 Go to a sub-topic

5 Sort the list

The Internet Movie Database deserves to be top of the list of entertainment sites – it's great (see page 143).

TOP 5% Topic: Entertainment - Netscape

View   Go   Communicator   Help

Bookmarks   Netsite: http://point-uk.lycos.com/topics/Entertainment_Overall.html

Chat on Lycos

Software & Applications

Search FTP Sites

Find MP3 Files

Build a Homepage

Download Software

Newsgroup Discussions

Find Email Addresses

Shop for Software

Entertainment

Books
Entertainment News   On the Radio
Famous Personalities   Popular Culture
Fun & Games   Science Fiction
Magazines   TV & Film
Music

Click one of the following to sort by:

Content Rating	Design Rating	Overall Rating	Date	Alphabetic

1) The Internet Movie Database
Nearly any Website you've seen on a movie or a Hollywood star has dipped into this pool in one way or another because it's the best there is.
Content: 98 Design: 92 Overall: 97

2) Salon
Consistently entertaining and a beautifully designed read, "Salon" is one of the Web's finest digital magazines.
Content: 95 Design: 92 Overall: 96

3) Mr. Showbiz
Mr. Showbiz is a sort of happy conglomeration of facts and gossip about the ever-fascinating, ever-present world of entertainment.
Content: 94 Design: 92 Overall: 95

Document: Done

Take note

If you live in the UK you are automatically redirected to the UK version of the site.

Tip

At the time of writing, Lycos was suffering from its own success. It was often so busy that each page took several minutes to download. They may have improved access by the time you read this.

Starting Point

Starting Point is a well-organised and easy-to-use directory, with a more mature (not 'adult') emphasis than most. Judging by the style and content, Starting Point sees its target audience as professional men and women – even the Women and Family category has as many links to business and finance pages as it does to shopping, fashion and domestic stuff.

In the top pages for each category you will find links to selected sites, accompanied by short reviews; at lower level pages, the links have only one-line descriptions.

Basic steps

1 Go to Starting Point at:
http://www.stpt.com

2 Select a Category from the sidebar.

3 Browse through the top page's selected links.

Or

4 Pick a subcategory.

5 Browse through the links.

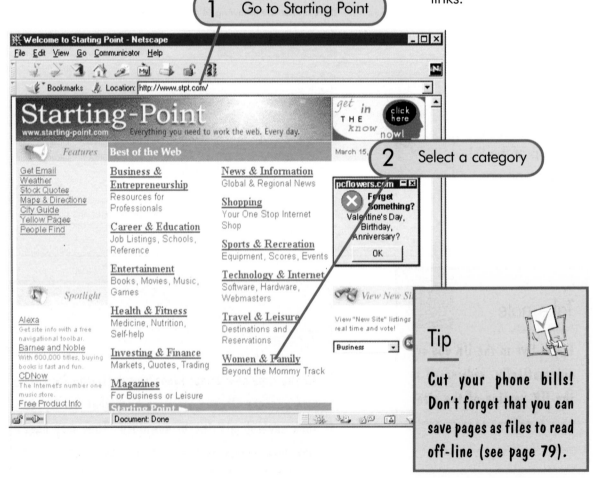

1 Go to Starting Point

2 Select a category

Tip

Cut your phone bills! Don't forget that you can save pages as files to read off-line (see page 79).

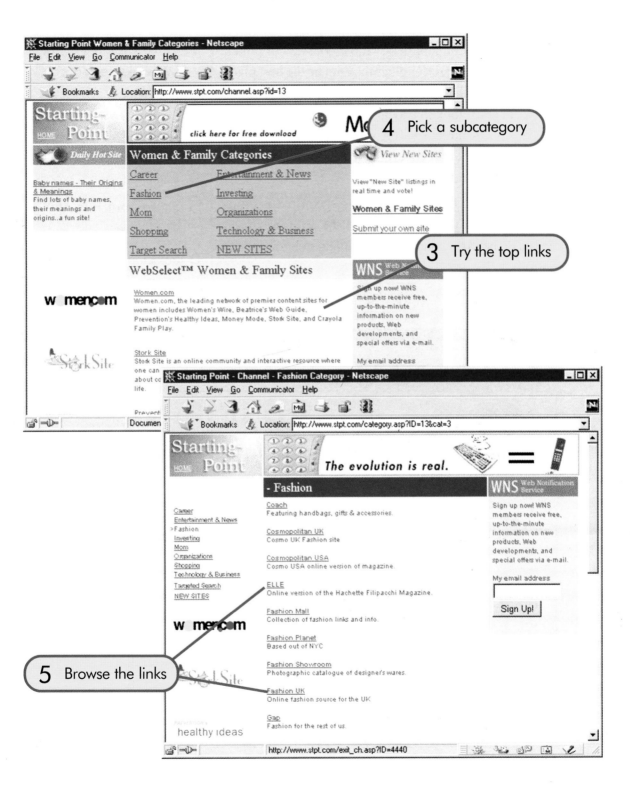

4 Pick a subcategory

3 Try the top links

5 Browse the links

UK directory

If you want to find local suppliers, clubs, courses, the main Internet directories and search engines may not be the best place to look – simply because you will get too many irrelevant links. If you want local stuff, look in a local directory. In the UK, the first place to try is UK directory. It has links to UK businesses, shops, schools, colleges and government organisations, news, travel, entertainment and other services.

Unless you are looking for something very specific it is probably simplest to work your way through the well-organised catalog. If you do need to search, use the Full Search routine for better control.

Basic steps

1 Go to UK directory at: www.ukdirectory.co.uk

2 Browse the catalog.

or

3 Click on Full Search.

4 Enter the search words.

5 Set the match to ANY or ALL words.

6 Select the categories to search.

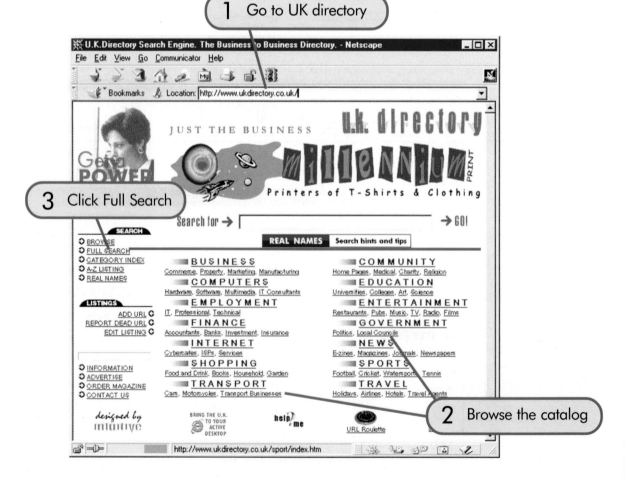

7 Enter any words to Exclude, if appropriate.

8 Click ➡ GO!

9 Follow the links.

Here I was looking for specialists in boat insurance – excluding 'car' has cut out the general insurance firms and given me just what I wanted

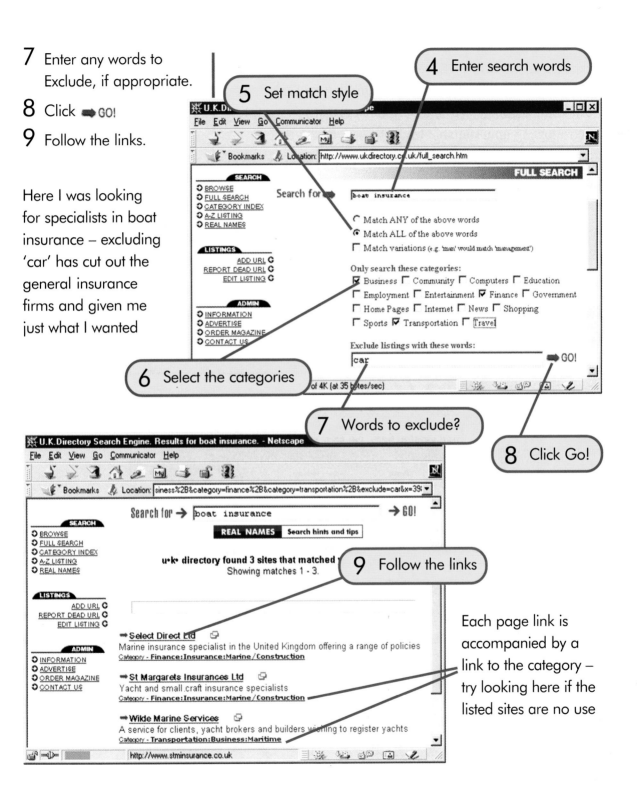

Each page link is accompanied by a link to the category – try looking here if the listed sites are no use

Lifestyle.uk

All the sites listed in this UK-based directory have been selected and are checked regularly to make sure that they still exist. Also, the links are accompanied by descriptions so that you waste less time following up unsuitable leads.

Lifestyle.uk aims to keep things simple, easy to use and fast to download – and they generally succeed. The page design is clear and simple, with minimal use of graphics for faster downloading, though the logo background makes the leftmost text hard to read on some pages.

1 Go to Lifestyle.uk at: www.lifestyle.co.uk

2 Select a Direct Access category.

Or

3 Click on a Channel and select from within it.

4 Read the descriptions.

5 Click on a link!

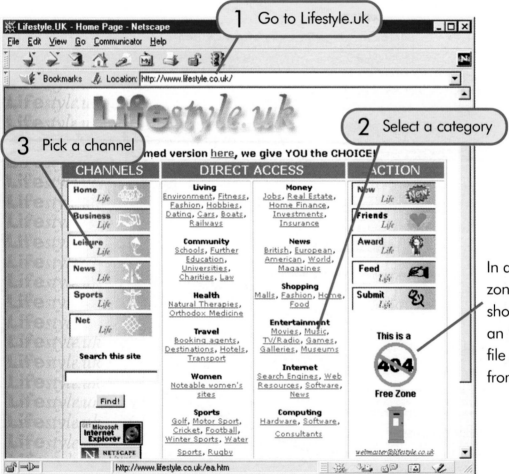

In a 404 free zone you shouldn't get an 'Error 404 file not found' from any links

Routes into Lifestyle.uk

Take note

You can also search for stuff at Lifestyle.uk — see page 114.

Loads of links! Four pages – over 80 links – for Classical Music. I didn't try to count the links for more popular topics.

The **Channels** section has selections of top links, and the top page of each Channel leads to further subdivisions within it.

Direct Access holds the main catalogue, with each heading leading direct to several pages of links. These would be easier to use if they were subdivided or alphabetically arranged – as it is, you just have to browse through them, but at least the pages load in quickly.

The **Action** section has lists of new and award-winning sites, and is for interaction with visitors. If you have a Web site, go to **Submit** and tell them about it!

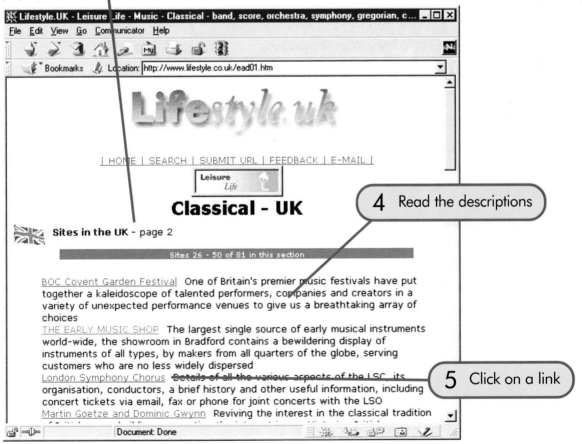

Summary

- Yahoo is probably the best directory on the Web, and is always a good place to start browsing.

- Searches at Yahoo will find any matching links within the site.

- Yahooligans is for children and teenagers, with on-line activities and a catalogue of links to great sites.

- Excite holds many links to reviewed sites, with the best being revisited and checked regularly.

- You can set up a My Channel page at Excite, to give simple access to your favourite links, selected news and other information.

- Lycos has links to the best and busiest sites in its Top 5% selection, as well as a very large database.

- The Starting Point directory is well-organised and pre-sented, making it simple to use – and it has some well-chosen sets of links.

- If you want to find companies, organisations or people in the UK, the UK directory is the best place to start looking.

- At Lifestyle.uk the emphasis is on quality, but there is no lack of quantity either! You will find an excellent range of good links here.

7 Search engines

Search techniques

Search engines vary, but the techniques that you must use to search their databases are broadly similar.

Simple searches

If you enter a single word, then – as you would expect – the engines will search for that word. If you enter two or more words, there are several possible responses:

- Most engines will search for pages that contain any of the words, but display first those those contain all of the words. e.g. a search for 'Beijing Peking' would find pages with references to the capital of China, however it was spelt. A search for 'graphics conversion software' would find all those pages containing the word 'graphics', plus those containing 'conversion' and those containing 'software' – and the total could run to millions. However, pages containing all three words – though not necessarily in that order, or related to each other – would be among the first results displayed.

- Some engines will only return those pages that contain all of the given words.

- If the given words are enclosed in "double quotes", most engines will search only for that phrase. Look for "greenhouse effect" and you should find stuff on global warming, and not get pages on gardening!

Plurals and other endings

Some engines automatically truncate and extend words to cater for different possible endings. With these, a search for '**musicals**' would also find 'music' and 'musicians'.

Take note

Some search engines just search the title and keywords – if the page's author has defined any. Others also search through the top 10 or 20 lines of text. A few do full text searches, so that the whole page is indexed.

Advanced searches

These are much more varied than simple searches. Most support the use of logical operators.

Logical operators

Also known as Boolean operators, these can be used to link keywords. They are normally written in capitals.

> **AND** every word must match to produce a hit.
>
> **OR** any matching word will produce a hit
>
> **NOT** ignore pages containing this word.

If you use a mixture of operators, they will normally be evaluated in the order NOT, AND then OR, e.g.

> boat AND sail OR yacht

will find pages with references to boats where sails are also mentioned, or to yachts.

> boat AND sail OR paddle

will again find references to sailing boats, but will also pick up all 'paddle' pages – whether they relate to boats or not. This can be changed by putting round brackets () around the part you want to evaluate first. So, to find paddle boats or sail boats, you would need:

> boat AND (sail OR paddle)

Include/exclude

Some engines will allow the use of the modifiers + (include) and –(exclude). Keywords marked + must be present for a page to match; pages containing keywords marked with – are to be ignored, e.g.

> +"Tom Jones" Fielding –song

Should find pages about the book by Henry Fielding, but ignore the singer's fan clubs.

Tip

If you enter words only in lower case, most engines will ignore case when matching – so 'windows' also finds 'Windows'.

If you use capital initials, most engines will return only those pages with matching capitals, so that 'Gates' will find the boss of Microsoft, but ignore garden portals.

Words written entirely in capitals will rarely find anything!

AltaVista

This is one of the most popular search engines – fast, simple to use and with a huge database. A search at AltaVista can produce thousands of hits – if this happens, you can refine the search to focus on the things that you want. This doesn't always work that well – in the example shown here, I never got below 28,000 hits!

● No matter how many hits there are, those that best match your query will generally turn up in the first dozen.

In this example, and the next at Infoseek, the search is for steam railways in Wales. At AltaVista, you simply write in the words or phrase which describes what you want. If you like, you could write a proper sentence, e.g. 'Where can I find out about steam railways in Wales?'

1 Go to AltaVista at:
   www.altavista.com/

2 Type what you are looking for.

3 Click Search.

4 If you get a reasonable number of hits, follow the most likely links.

Otherwise...

5 Click Refine your search.

6 Tick Require or Exclude beside each set of words.

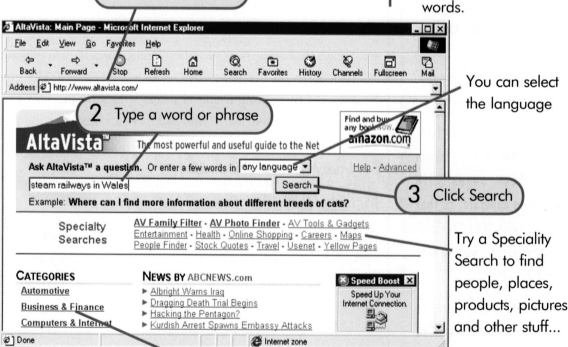

AltaVista also has an organised directory of links

Searches can produce
thousands of hits!

AltaVista will offer similar questions to which it
knows the answers – if one is suitable, click Answer

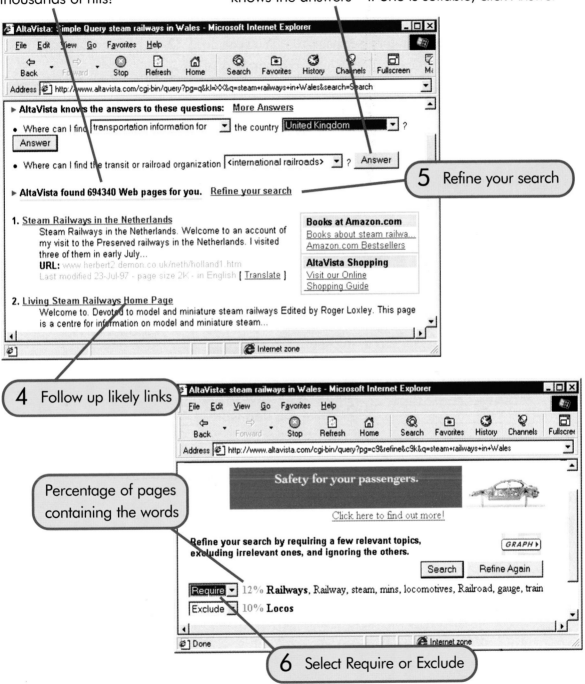

5 Refine your search

4 Follow up likely links

Percentage of pages
containing the words

6 Select Require or Exclude

Infoseek

AltaVista is unusual in accepting questions for its searches. At most search engines you simply enter one or more words, perhaps linked by logical operators (see page 103). You can do this at Infoseek – though it can produce ludicrous numbers of 'matching' pages. A search for 'steam railways Wales' will give you millions of hits – all the pages containing 'steam', plus all those with 'railways' plus all those with 'Wales'.

But don't despair, Infoseek offers a very effective way to find what you want. You can run a series of searches, each based on the results of the last. In the example, we start by entering just one of the key words – 'steam'. This produced 850,000 hits. Searching through these hits for those that also contained 'railway' brought the number down to 6,000. A final filter with 'Wales' reduced this to 183 – and a high proportion of these were relevant.

1 Go to Infoseek at:
http://infoseek.go.com

2 Enter the first word.

3 Select Web Sites – other areas can be searched.

4 Click Search.

5 At the results page, enter the next word, select Search within these results and click Search again.

6 Repeat step 5 to get a reasonably-sized set.

7 Follow the links.

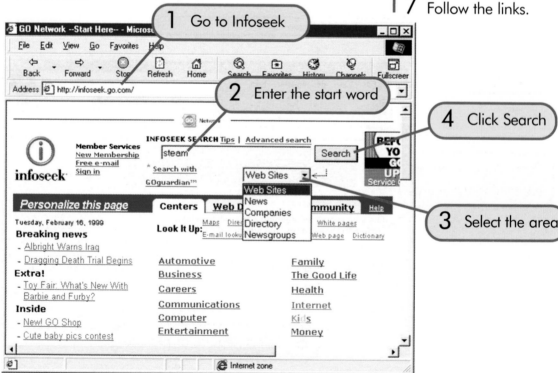

106

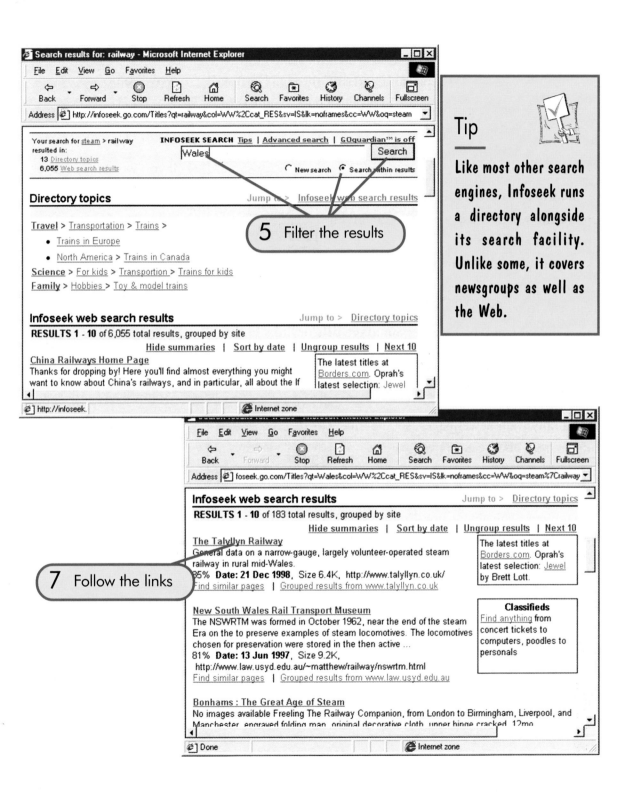

Search results for: railway - Microsoft Internet Explorer

File   Edit   View   Go   Favorites   Help

Back   Forward   Stop   Refresh   Home   Search   Favorites   History   Channels   Fullscreen

Address http://infoseek.go.com/Titles?qt=railway&col=WW%2Ccat_RES&sv=IS&lk=noframes&cc=WW&oq=steam

Your search for steam > railway resulted in:
13 Directory topics
6,055 Web search results

INFOSEEK SEARCH   Tips | Advanced search | GOguardian™ is off

Wales   Search

New search   Search within results

Directory topics   Jump to > Infoseek web search results

Travel > Transportation > Trains >
- Trains in Europe
- North America > Trains in Canada
Science > For kids > Transportation > Trains for kids
Family > Hobbies > Toy & model trains

5   Filter the results

Infoseek web search results   Jump to > Directory topics

RESULTS 1 - 10 of 6,055 total results, grouped by site
Hide summaries | Sort by date | Ungroup results | Next 10

China Railways Home Page
Thanks for dropping by! Here you'll find almost everything you might
want to know about China's railways, and in particular, all about the If

The latest titles at
Borders.com. Oprah's
latest selection: Jewel

http://infoseek.   Internet zone

File   Edit   View   Go   Favorites   Help

Back   Forward   Stop   Refresh   Home   Search   Favorites   History   Channels   Fullscreen

Address foseek.go.com/Titles?qt=Wales&col=WW%2Ccat_RES&sv=IS&lk=noframes&cc=WW&oq=steam%7Crailway

Infoseek web search results   Jump to > Directory topics

RESULTS 1 - 10 of 183 total results, grouped by site
Hide summaries | Sort by date | Ungroup results | Next 10

The Talyllyn Railway
General data on a narrow-gauge, largely volunteer-operated steam
railway in rural mid-Wales.
85% Date: 21 Dec 1998, Size 6.4K, http://www.talyllyn.co.uk/
Find similar pages | Grouped results from www.talyllyn.co.uk

7   Follow the links

New South Wales Rail Transport Museum
The NSWRTM was formed in October 1962, near the end of the steam
Era on the to preserve examples of steam locomotives. The locomotives
chosen for preservation were stored in the then active ...
81% Date: 13 Jun 1997, Size 9.2K,
http://www.law.usyd.edu.au/~matthew/railway/nswrtm.html
Find similar pages | Grouped results from www.law.usyd.edu.au

Bonhams : The Great Age of Steam
No images available Freeling The Railway Companion, from London to Birmingham, Liverpool, and
Manchester, engraved folding map, original decorative cloth, upper hinge cracked, 12mo

The latest titles at
Borders.com. Oprah's
latest selection: Jewel
by Brett Lott.

Classifieds
Find anything from
concert tickets to
computers, poodles to
personals

Done   Internet zone

HotBot

HotBot has a highly efficient 'crawler' which constantly travels the Web indexing sites – if you can't find stuff through HotBot, it probably isn't there! Searches can produce huge numbers of hits, but the menus make it easy to run a tightly defined search.

Type of search

all the words – the same as linking with AND

any of the words – use when you are giving alternative spellings

exact phrase – quotes are not needed

Boolean phrase – select this for complex searches, using the AND, OR and NOT operators

The search can also be for a **person**, **page title** or **links to this URL** – find out how many sites have links to yours!

> exact phrase ▼
> all the words
> any of the words
> exact phrase
> the page title
> the person
> links to this URL
> Boolean phrase

Date

If you only want newer pages, set the time limit – from one week to two years.

> anytime ▼
> anytime
> in the last week
> in the last 2 weeks
> in the last month
> in the last 3 months
> in the last 6 months
> in the last year
> in the last 2 years

Language

Though most valuable to non-English speakers, this is also useful to English speakers to filter out other languages.

> English ▼
> any language
> Dutch
> English
> Finnish
> French
> German
> Italian
> Portuguese
> Spanish
> Swedish

Results display

How many do you want to see at a time?

> 25 ▼
> 10
> 25
> 50
> 100

How much detail do you want? **brief descriptions** will pack more in a page, but **URLs only** is rarely much use.

> full descriptions ▼
> full descriptions
> brief descriptions
> URLs only

Basic steps

1 Go to HotBot at: www.hotbot.com

2 Enter the keywords.

3 Set the type of search.

4 If you want only newer pages, set the time limit.

5 Select the language.

6 Set the number of results per page, and the amount of information to be displayed.

7 Click Search.

8 Click Top 10 Most Visited Sites… if you want to find the most popular sites or to try related searches.

Take note

You can also search for images, sounds, video clips and JavaScript (why?!) – just tick the **Pages must include** boxes.

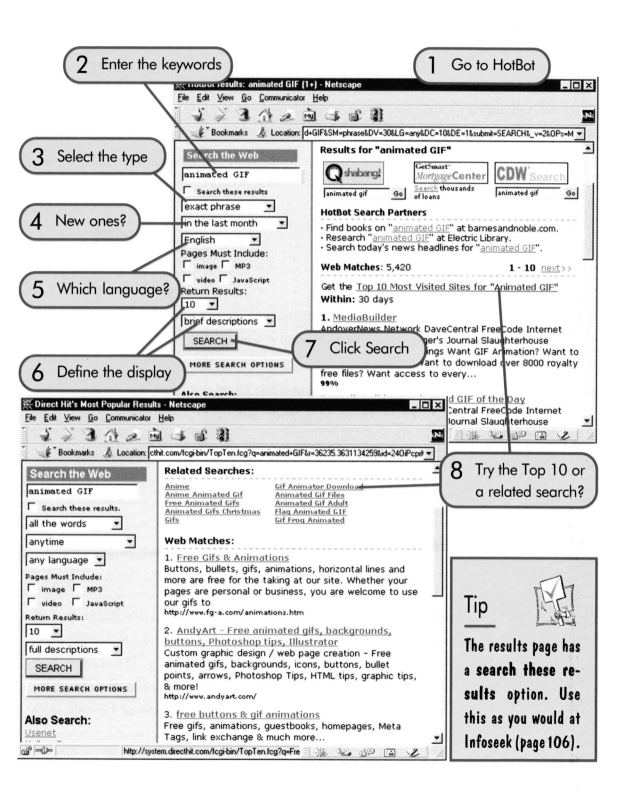

2 Enter the keywords

1 Go to HotBot

3 Select the type

4 New ones?

5 Which language?

6 Define the display

7 Click Search

8 Try the Top 10 or a related search?

Tip

The results page has a **search these results** option. Use this as you would at Infoseek (page 106).

Magellan

Magellan has two unique features. First, it has a database of **Green Light** sites – sites that have been reviewed and found suitable for children. (It also has a database of well over 50 million unreviewed sites.)

The second feature is **concept-based searching**. As the search engine travels the Web building its index, it reads documents and learns which words and ideas are associated with one another. So, if you search for 'movies', it will also look for 'video', 'films', 'cinema' and similar.

Search expressions

With a simple list of words, Magellan will look for pages containing any of them, but put those that contain all – or most – at the top of the results list.

● You can link keywords with AND, OR and AND NOT (e.g. spice AND NOT girls). These must be written in CAPITALS.

● The + and – modifiers can be used to insist that words are present or absent from a page.

Find similar

If your keywords have several meanings, the initial results display may cover a range of topics. To focus on the ones you want, read through to find the most suitable result and click on its **find similar**. This is the concept-based searching in action! In the example, the search for 'amazon' found material on the river, as well as stuff on parrots, the bookshop, sushi (!) and other irrelevancies. (And if it hadn't been restricted to Green Light sites, it would also have found feminist and girlie pages.) The **find similar** link by the Amazon home page turned up a wealth of material on the river basin – the object of the search.

1 Go to Magellan at: magellan.excite.com

2 Enter your search word(s) or expression.

3 Select the area to search – Green Light sites or The Entire Web.

4 Click search .

5 Scroll through and view the results or click find similar to get more pages on the same topic.

Take note

Magellan is now part of Excite. A search here, using The Entire Web option is the same as a search at Excite's main site (www.excite.com).

110

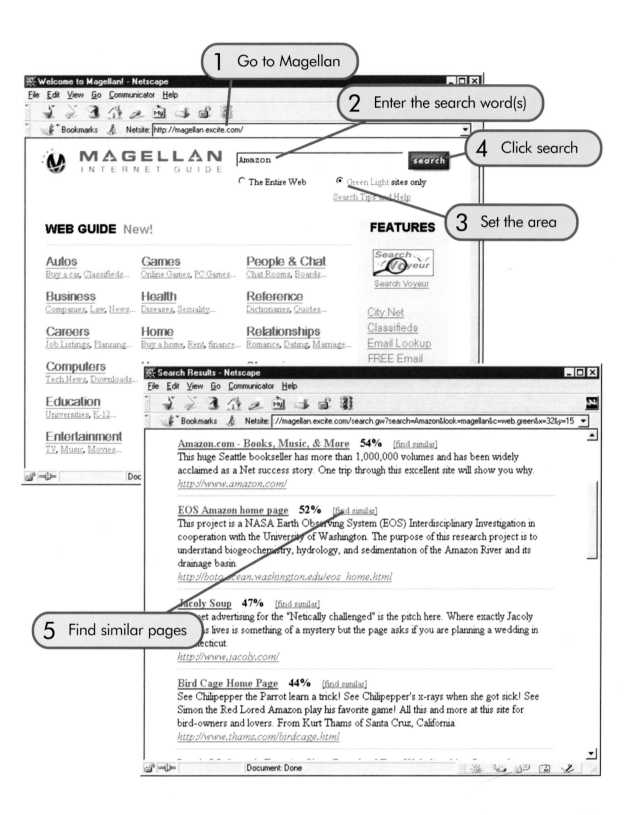

1 Go to Magellan

2 Enter the search word(s)

4 Click search

3 Set the area

5 Find similar pages

Welcome to Magellan! - Netscape

File Edit View Go Communicator Help

Bookmarks Netsite: http://magellan.excite.com/

MAGELLAN
INTERNET GUIDE

Amazon   search

○ The Entire Web   ● Green Light sites only
              Search Tips and Help

WEB GUIDE New!   **FEATURES**

Autos   **Games**   **People & Chat**
Buy a car, Classifieds... Online Games, PC Games... Chat Rooms, Boards...   Search Voyeur

Business   **Health**   **Reference**
Companies, Law, News... Diseases, Sexuality... Dictionaries, Quotes...

Careers   **Home**   **Relationships**   City.Net
Job Listings, Planning... Buy a home, Rent, finance... Romance, Dating, Marriage... Classifieds

Computers   Email Lookup
Tech News, Downloads...   FREE Email

Education
Universities, K-12...

Entertainment
TV, Music, Movies...

Search Results - Netscape

File Edit View Go Communicator Help

Bookmarks Netsite: ://magellan.excite.com/search.gw?search=Amazon&look=magellan&c=web.green&x=32&y=15

Amazon.com - Books, Music, & More **54%** [find similar]
This huge Seattle bookseller has more than 1,000,000 volumes and has been widely
acclaimed as a Net success story. One trip through this excellent site will show you why.
http://www.amazon.com/

EOS Amazon home page **52%** [find similar]
This project is a NASA Earth Observing System (EOS) Interdisciplinary Investigation in
cooperation with the University of Washington. The purpose of this research project is to
understand biogeochemistry, hydrology, and sedimentation of the Amazon River and its
drainage basin.
http://boto.ocean.washington.edu/eos_home.html

Jacoly Soup **47%** [find similar]
et advertising for the "Netically challenged" is the pitch here. Where exactly Jacoly
s lives is something of a mystery but the page asks if you are planning a wedding in
ecticut.
http://www.jacoly.com/

Bird Cage Home Page **44%** [find similar]
See Chilipepper the Parrot learn a trick! See Chilipepper's x-rays when she got sick! See
Simon the Red Lored Amazon play his favorite game! All this and more at this site for
bird-owners and lovers. From Kurt Thams of Santa Cruz, California.
http://www.thams.com/birdcage.html

Document: Done

Ask Jeeves

Ask Jeeves is a mixture of marketing organisation and search site. Ask Jeeves a question here and – if he does not have the answer at his fingertips – he will pass it on to half a dozen or so search engines and show you what they find.

The sorts of questions that Jeeves can answer directly are those which can be looked up in an encyclopedia and those of the 'where can I buy...' type. Companies advertise their wares there – as they do on most content providers' sites – and the Jeeves organisation also markets goods itself.

Whatever the question, ask it in ordinary English – but be prepared to ask the question more than once, and in different ways, as Jeeves may not get your drift the first time.

Basic steps

1 Go to Ask Jeeves at: www.askjeeves.com

2 Type in your question.

3 Click **ASK!**.

4 Select a subject from the drop-down list of a question and click **ASK!**.

Or

5 Select from a list of hits and click **ASK!** to go to the search engine.

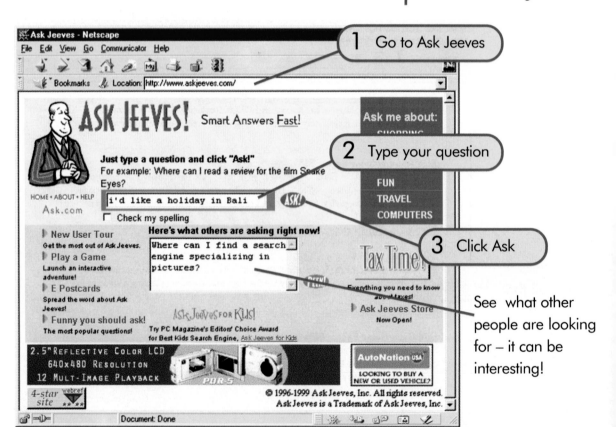

See what other people are looking for – it can be interesting!

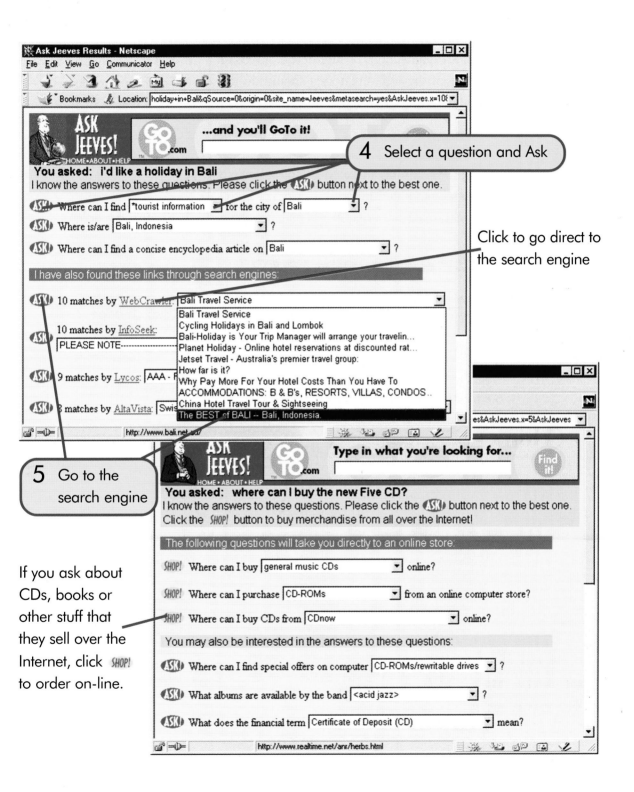

4 Select a question and Ask

Click to go direct to the search engine

5 Go to the search engine

If you ask about CDs, books or other stuff that they sell over the Internet, click *SHOP!* to order on-line.

Searching the UK

If you are looking for UK organisations or suppliers of goods or services, a search at one of the UK directories should do the trick. Here are some you might like to try first.

Lifestyle.uk

As you saw earlier (page 98), this has an excellent and extensive catalogue of selected and annotated links. If you don't know where to start looking in the catalog, a search will pick up all the relevant entries.

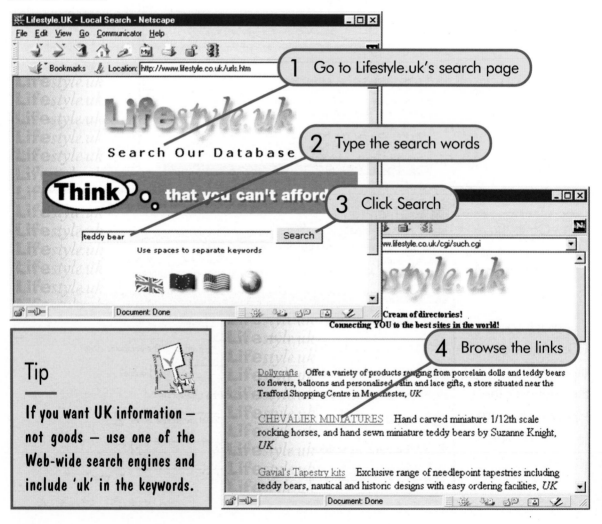

Tip

If you want UK information — not goods — use one of the Web-wide search engines and include 'uk' in the keywords.

Basic steps

1 Go to UK Index at:
   www.ukindex.co.uk

2 Enter up to two separate
   words or one phrase.

3 Select AND, OR or
   PHRASE.

4 Tick the categories to
   search.

5 Click Submit.

6 Browse the results.

UK Index

This is a good source of links to suppliers and other commercial organisations, though not so good for non-commercial.

The searches only hunt through the UK Index, not Web sites or pages in general, but are easy to set up. The organisation of entries by categories makes it very easy to focus a search.

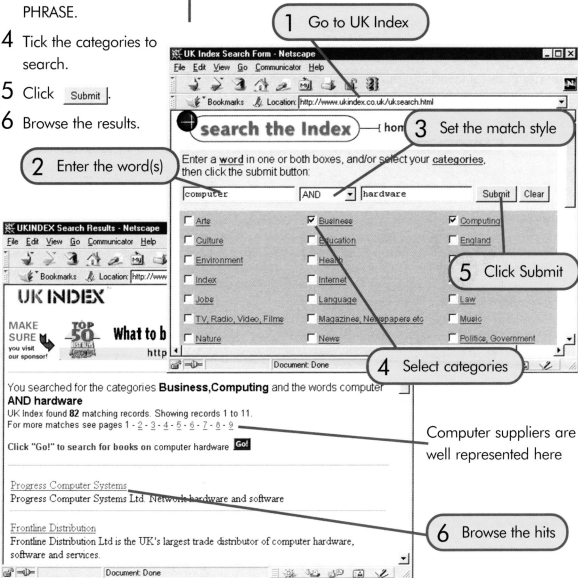

1 Go to UK Index

3 Set the match style

2 Enter the word(s)

5 Click Submit

4 Select categories

Computer suppliers are well represented here

6 Browse the hits

115

Yell

If you want to find a business in the UK, you need Yell, the Electronic Yellow Pages. It has one big advantage over the printed version – it covers the whole UK, not just your area.

If you are searching for a supplier or service – rather than by company name – you must get the **business type** exactly right. There's an index of types at the site, or you can look them up in your printed Yellow Pages before you start.

Also at Yell: UK Web Search (see opposite); an entertainment guide (find out what's on at your local cinema), shopping and travel services.

Basic steps

1 Go to Yell at: www.yell.co.uk

2 Enter the business type or company name.

3 Enter the Location.

4 Click the search icon.

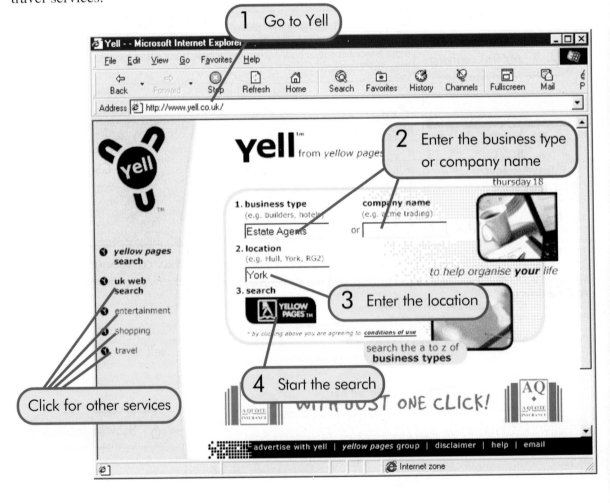

1 Go to Yell

2 Enter the business type or company name

3 Enter the location

4 Start the search

Click for other services

Basic steps

UK Web Search

1 Click uk web search.

2 Enter your key words.

3 Click the search icon.

4 Follow the links.

This is not just for business. There are also lots of links to information pages and non-commercial organisations – and all the linked pages are hand-picked. Browse the catalog, if you can see a likely heading, or run a search.

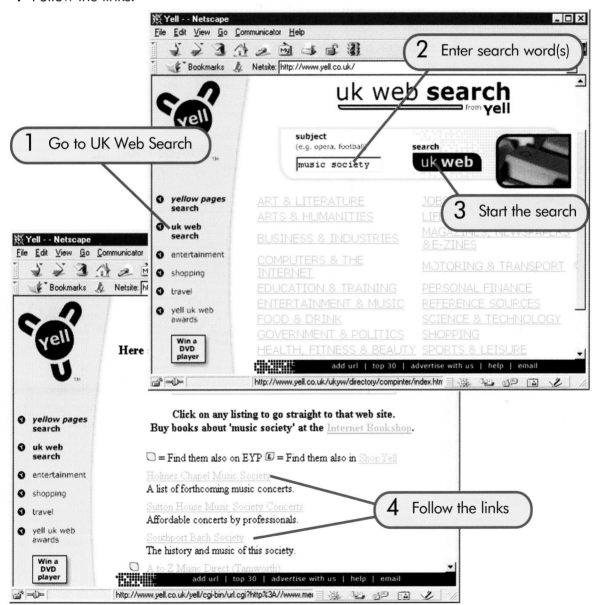

Netscape Search

Netscape users have easy access to six of the best search sites through the Search Internet option on the Edit menu. This links to the search page at Netcenter. You can set up simple searches, or select a catalog heading from here, and are then transferred to the search site for the results.

●   If a search at one site doesn't give you what you want, go back to Netscape Search and try another.

Basic steps

1 Open the Edit menu.

2 Select Search Internet.

3 Choose a search site.

4 Type the search words.

5 Click Seek .

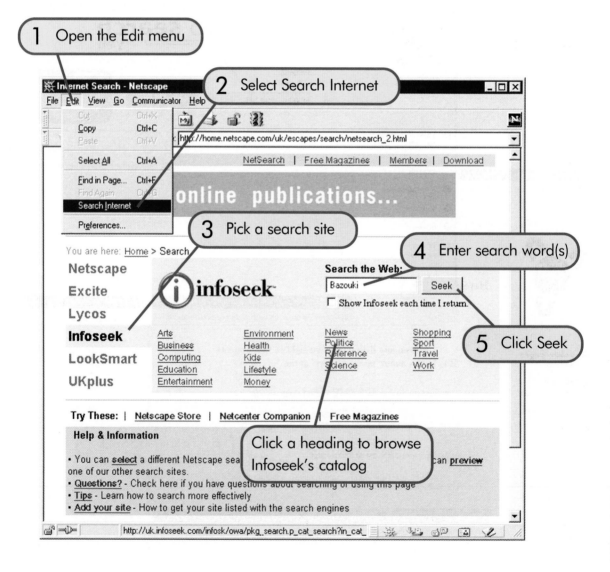

1 Open the Edit menu

2 Select Search Internet

3 Pick a search site

4 Enter search word(s)

5 Click Seek

Click a heading to browse Infoseek's catalog

Basic steps

1 Open the Help menu, point to Microsoft on the Web and select Search the Web.

2 Type a word to describe what you are looking for.

3 Select where to search.

4 Click Find it!

Searches at MSN

On Internet Explorer's Help menu, you will find a **Search the Web** link, which will take you to a page at MSN (MicroSoft Network) where you can search not just for Web pages, but also for flowers (!), books and specialist information.

Tip

You can also run searches from the Explorer bar (see next page).

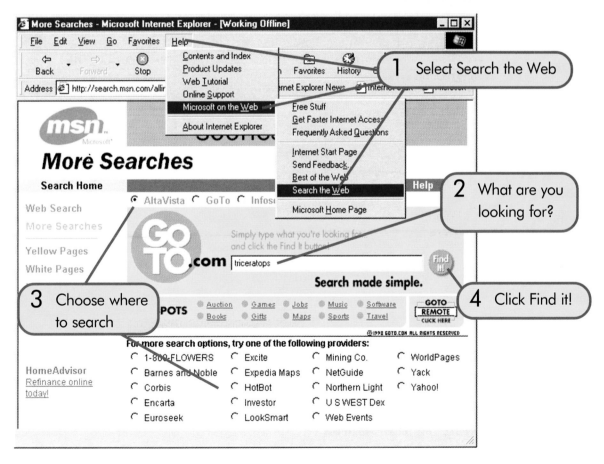

Searching from Explorer

Rather than going to MSN or one of the search engines, you can run a search from the Search button. This gives you simple access to five of the best directories and search engines. But it is only simple access – you cannot do any carefully defined searches here. If you want to search efficiently, use a search engine at its home site.

The one big advantage of searches from the Explorer bar is convenience – you can switch easily between viewing results and running new searches.

1 Click the Search tool to open the Explorer Bar.

2 Enter a word or phrase.

3 Select a search site.

4 Click Search!.

5 If you don't find what you want at one site, start a new search.

Search the Web on the Help menu links to AOL NetFind – where you can search the Web and more

1 Click Search

2 Enter your search word(s)

3 Pick a site

4 Click Search

File Edit View Go Favorites Help

Back Forward Stop Refresh Home Search Favorites History Channels Fullscreen Mail Print

Address http://www.aol.com/netfind/

AOL.COM | AOL NetFind | Web Centers | My News | Shopping | Pro

AOL NetFind | Search the Web

Enter the word or words you are searching for:

triceratops

Search

Select a search engine:

○ ⓘ infoseek sm
◉ LYCOS
○ UKplus
○ Yell®
○ YAHOO!

AOL NetFind Tip: For the best results, type in more than one word and put AND in between them. For example: games AND checkers

You can also search using these other AOL NetFind products:

* AOL Yellow Pages   * Kids Only   * Search Newsgroups
* AOL White Pages   * Maps & Directions   * Search Personal Pages
* E-Mail Finder

New! International Phone Listings on AOL NetFind...Try it!

Search!

Travel
Travel Made Simple

Search thousands of personal home pages.

NATIONAL GEOGRAPHIC **ONLY**
Trip Planner DELUXE $4.99

SAVERS

Top Web Searches
Find an Apartment or Home
Buy a Computer

Get things done. Use the V

• Find Travel Barg
• Find the Perfect
• Research an Illn

Internet zone

Tip

Try Infoseek, Lycos or Yahoo for general stuff; UKplus for UK sites and Yell for UK business.

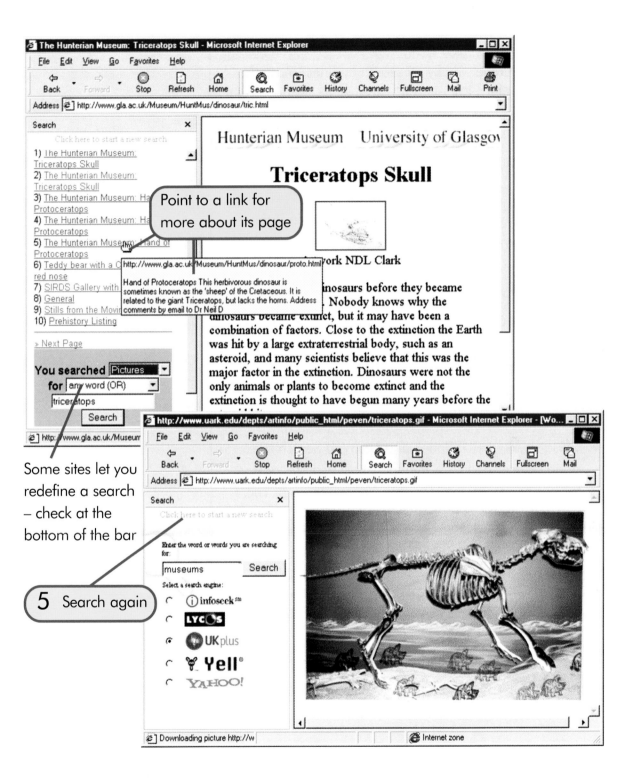

Point to a link for more about its page

Some sites let you redefine a search – check at the bottom of the bar

5 Search again

Summary

- Simple searches – just using keywords – are handled in almost the same way by all search engines. Most also accept the AND, OR and NOT logical operators, and the +/– modifiers.

- At AltaVista you can keep the returns down to a reasonable number by refining the search or by specifying an advanced search.

- At InfoSeek you can narrow a search down in stages, searching within a set of results for a new keyword.

- HotBot has indexed almost all the Web, but its option-based search form makes it easy to focus a search.

- Magellan's Green Light sites make this a prime site for children to use – but it also has reviewed sites across the full range of topics, and links to most of the Web.

- You can Ask Jeeves about almost anything and he will point you in the right direction.

- Lifesdtyle.uk, the UK Index and UK Web Search are good sources of links within the UK. If you are looking for businesses, try the Electronic Yellow Pages at Yell.

- Both Netscape and MSN offer simple access to some of the best search engines from their search pages.

- If you run a search from Internet Explorer's Explorer bar, you can keep the results list at hand while you view the linked pages.

8 Online interaction

On-line services

It would be an impossible task to list all the services that are now available over the Internet – there are just too many, with new ones appearing all the time. There are thousands of firms large and small, government departments, agencies and councils, voluntary organisations and individuals who are providing information, offering services or selling goods over the Internet.

What follows in the next few pages is just a taster of the possibilities. If you want to know more about what's available on-line – with the focus on the UK – head for:

- **the UK directory** at www.ukdirectory.co.uk or

- **UK Plus** at www.ukplus.co.uk.

Take note

Outside the UK, one of the best ways to find local services is through Yahoo. Go to Regional, select Countries, then pick your country from the list.

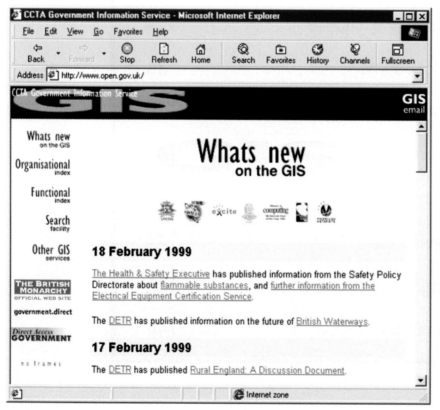

The UK government is putting a lot of information on-line through GIS, the Government Information Service – and it is increasingly a two-way process. Many departments and agencies are actively seeking feedback from visitors to their sites. Start at: www.open.gov.uk

By 'arrivals' they mean 'destinations'!

British Midlands is just one of the airlines offering on-line bookings.

And if you are travelling by road, the RAC's traffic reports will help you miss the jams – go to: www.rac.co.uk

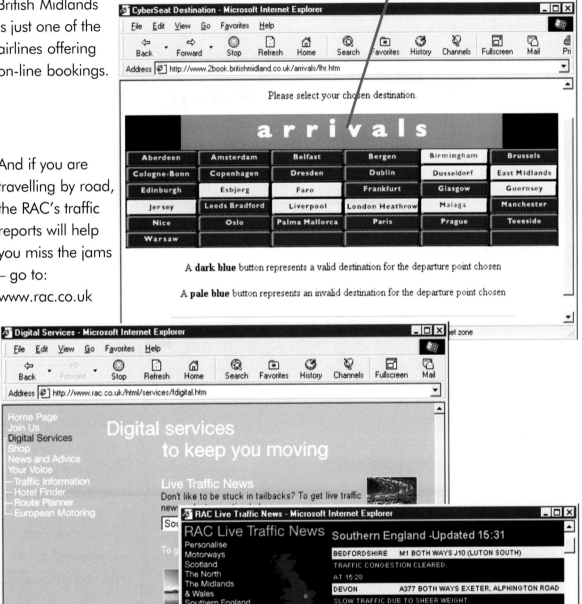

Looking for a new job? Try the Telegraph's Appointments Plus page – this search produced some interesting possibilities for me, though not quite tempting enough to give up writing!

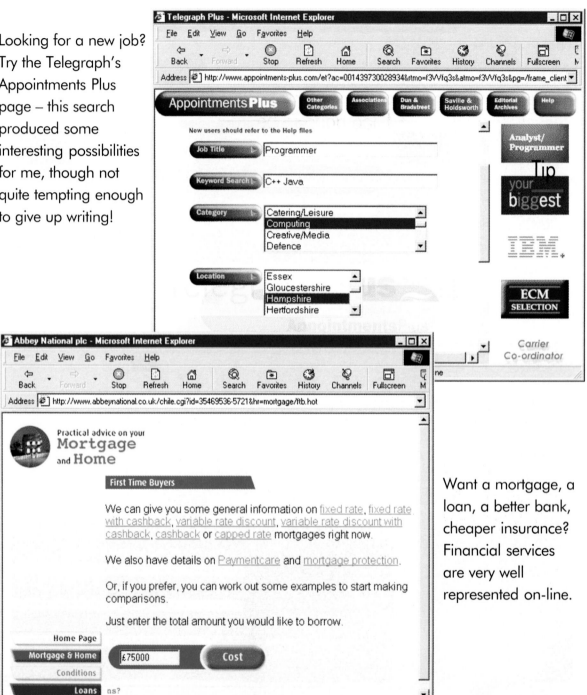

Want a mortgage, a loan, a better bank, cheaper insurance? Financial services are very well represented on-line.

Shop safely

The Internet has its fair share of crooks, but if you observe a few sensible precautions, you should be able to buy goods and services on-line as safely as you can by mail order or in the high street.

Too good to be true?

It is cheaper to trade on the Internet than it is in the high street, or even by by mail order or telephone, so you should expect to get a better deal, a faster service or a lower price. But if an offer sounds too good to be true, it probably is!

Who are these people?

Don't deal with people you don't know or with those that you can only contact over the Internet. If a firm is new to you, check that they really exist by looking up their address at Yell in the Electronic Yellow Pages (page 116) or the Companies lists at Yahoo.

It's not just credit card fraud

In fact credit card fraud makes up less than 20% of Internet fraud. Most victims paid by cheque, cash, money orders or bank debits.

You are as safe paying by credit card over the Internet as you are over the phone – which is not completely safe. Make sure that the *SSL security checking* is enabled on your browser – on the **General Options** in Netscape, and the **Advanced Internet Options** of Explorer. This ensures that the transactions you have with the firm cannot be 'eavesdropped' over the Internet.

Shopping on the Web

So what do they sell on the World Wide Web? You will find the kinds of goods that, five years ago, would have been sold by mail order or over the phone – the Web is a natural extension of these approaches.

The Web is a good place to sell anything which people buy on specification rather than by sitting on or trying on, e.g. computer hardware and software, books and CDs. It is also a logical place to sell those specialist goods that can be difficult to find in your local high street – a good range of organic foods, collectors' items, or almost anything hand-made.

Tip

If you are buying from a US-based firm, remember that there will be VAT to add to the cost, plus the delivery charges. Check the final total before confirming the order.

We've been using the phone to order flower deliveries for years. Now you can do it on the Web and see what you will get for your money! Chocolates, champagne, teddy bears – all sorts of gifts for delivery – can be ordered via the Web. Start at: http://www.giftstore.co.uk

128

CD Now has an enormous range of titles – probably the largest on the Web – including loads of Louis Jordan that I've not seen over here! It is US-based, but delivers worldwide. See for yourself at www.cdnow.com

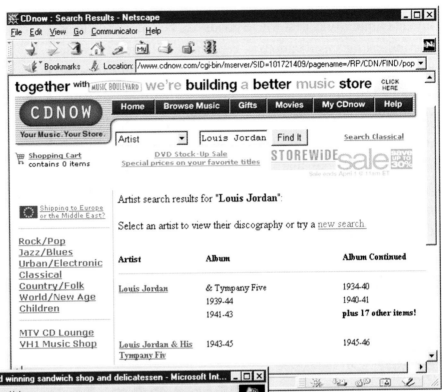

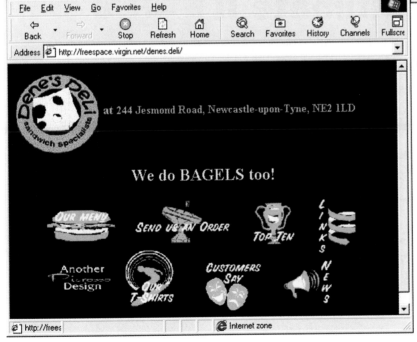

The Web can be a handy marketing medium even if you are only aiming at the local market. You can order your lunch online from Dene's Deli in Newcastle – as long as you are within reach of their delivery service!

Buying online

Buying online works best where goods can be ordered on their descriptions or specifications – especially if there is a wide range or many options. At Dan (below), as at many hardware suppliers, you can order a custom-built PC, checking the cost as you pick the components.

At the Internet Bookshop, they have in stock, or can quickly get, just about every book that's in print in the UK. Finding books is simpler here than on the shelves of a high street shop – though you can't browse them in the same way! The quick search will normally do the job, but there is also a full search where you can hunt by author, title, ISBN, publisher and other features.

Advantages/disadvantages

✔ there is often a wider choice of goods;

✔ you can browse at leisure for the best buy;

✘ you can't try it for size;

✘ returning faulty goods can be expensive in postage.

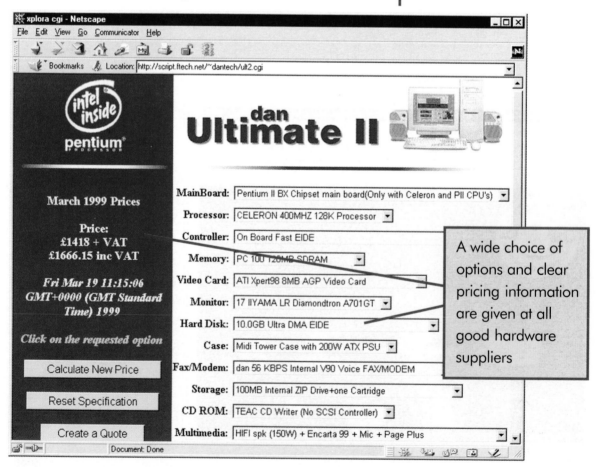

A wide choice of options and clear pricing information are given at all good hardware suppliers

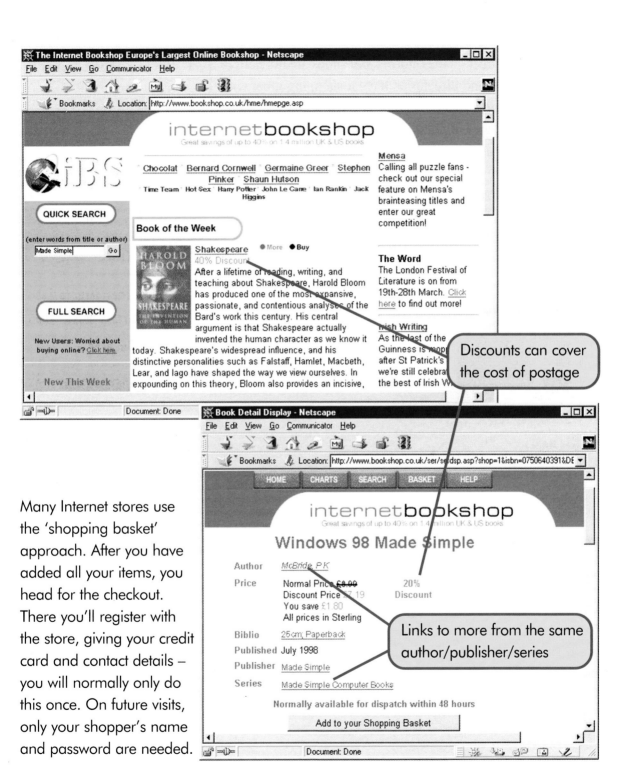

Many Internet stores use the 'shopping basket' approach. After you have added all your items, you head for the checkout. There you'll register with the store, giving your credit card and contact details – you will normally only do this once. On future visits, only your shopper's name and password are needed.

Discounts can cover the cost of postage

Links to more from the same author/publisher/series

Finding the shops

There's no high street on the Internet, but shops are not hard to find. Most portals and directories have a shopping area, with links to online stores. Yahoo's are very good – and try Yahoo UK (if you live in the UK) first, as a local supplier should mean lower delivery costs.

1 Go to Yahoo shopping at:
    shopping.uk.yahoo.com

2 Select the category.

3 Follow the links.

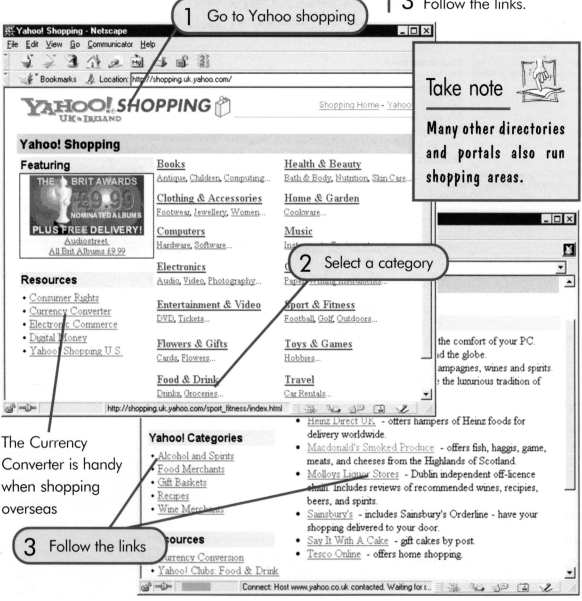

1 Go to Yahoo shopping

Take note

Many other directories and portals also run shopping areas.

2 Select a category

The Currency Converter is handy when shopping overseas

3 Follow the links

Basic steps

1 Go to Buyer's Index at:
   www.buyersindex.com

2 Type the item you want.

3 Click Search .

4 Select an online store
   from the list.

5 When you reach the
   site, you will probably
   need to work through
   their catalog.

You can also browse
for types of goods

Tracking down the unusual

Here's a neat approach to finding specific things. Instead of browsing round the stores to see if they stock an item, you can run a search at the Buyer's Index and get a list of stores, with descriptions (and, of course the links).

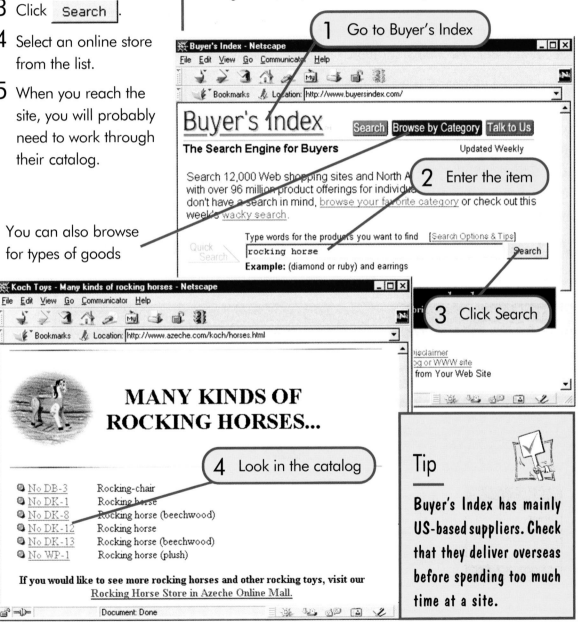

Tip

Buyer's Index has mainly US-based suppliers. Check that they deliver overseas before spending too much time at a site.

Banks and finance

Does your bank offer an online banking facility? For keeping track of your money, paying bills and moving cash between accounts online is as convenient as telephone banking and offers greater control. You can *see* what you are doing while you online, and – if you have suitable software – you can download your account information for further work offline. See *Money 99 Made Simple* for more on online banking.

If you want a mortgage, pension, ISA or insurance, check out the Web. Most companies now run sites where you can, at the very least, read about their services. At the more interactive sites, you can get instant quotations or calculations based on your figures. While you don't want to rush into long-term financial commitments, it's good to be able to get high-quality information online.

Take note

Security should not be a problem with established high street and telephone banks, which use secure systems and have good reputations to protect. But online, offshore banks should be approached with great care.

Virgin One (below) uses applets to calculate personal examples. Virgin Direct (right) sticks to basic information, referring you to a phone number if you want to take things further.

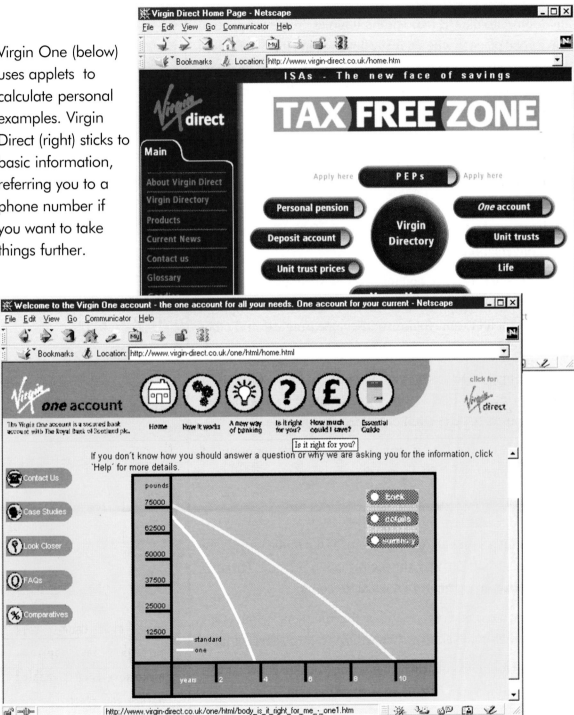

Chat rooms

Chat rooms are the CB radio of the Internet. Some people find them a good place to wile away the hours – but I have to confess I am not one of them. It is very difficult to find a chat room where you can get an interesting conversation going. There are some practical problems:

- Most chat rooms will accommodate anything up to 20 or 30 people at a time. It is difficult to get this number of strangers chatting together, even where you are meeting face to face. If you are lucky and find a room with only a few guests, there's a better chance of starting a sensible conversation.

- The 'chat' is typed and takes a few seconds to reach the screen. In between you reading something that you want to respond to and your response appearing, several other messages could have hit the screen.

- Too many chat users seem to be there for getting off or showing off. This is true even for those rooms that are supposed to be centred on a specific topic.

But don't let me put you off trying. You may get more out of chat rooms that I do.

Places to go

The major directories all run chat rooms. Two of the busiest are at Yahoo (**http://chat.yahoo.com**) and Excite (**http://www.excite.com** or **http://www.excite.co.uk**).

Some individuals and organisations also run them – Spurs fans should try their room at **http://www.link-it.com/soccer/spurs**.

If you want to set up your own chat room, you can get what you need from Ultranet at **http://www.ultranet.org**.

Tip

A chat rooms can be a good place to meet up with friends and family from around the world. You can set up private rooms at most chat sites. Agree a time and a site (by e-mail or during a meeting once you are organised) and get together online.

Take note

Most chat rooms work through a Java applet — make sure Java is enabled before you start.

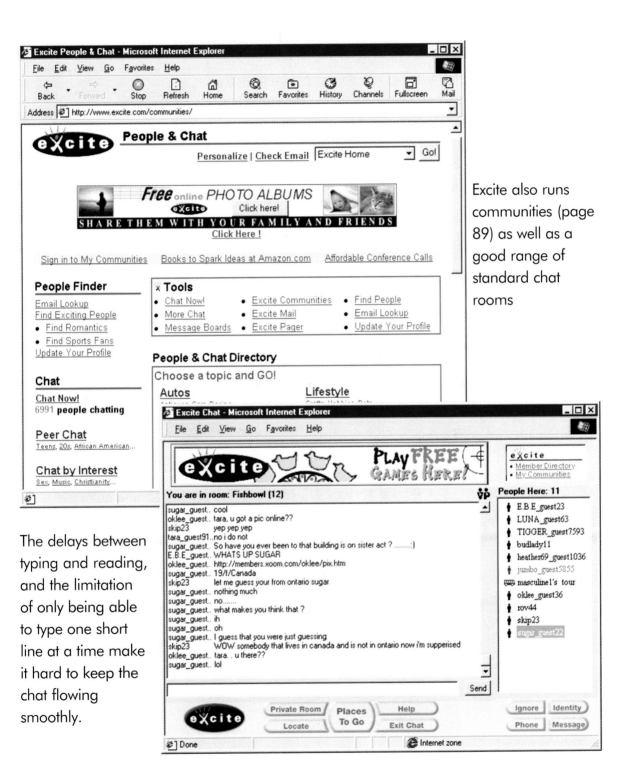

Excite also runs communities (page 89) as well as a good range of standard chat rooms

The delays between typing and reading, and the limitation of only being able to type one short line at a time make it hard to keep the chat flowing smoothly.

Communities

The Communities we noticed at Excite are by no means the only ones on the Web. FortuneCity and its sister organisation, Acme City, specialise in creating communities. They offer not just free Web space and free e-mail, but also a chance to meet and mix with others who share your interests and to be actively involved in the development of your neghbourhood. Volunteer 'ministers' help to organise events, develop the sites and guide newcomers.

Acme City (below) is run in association with Warner Brothers and is mainly for fans of ER, Friends and 'Looney Toons'. Fortune City (opposite) has areas for all kinds of people – I moved in to Tin Pan Alley. The neighbours are noisy, but interesting!

Acme City is mainly built by the residents, with some input from the professionals

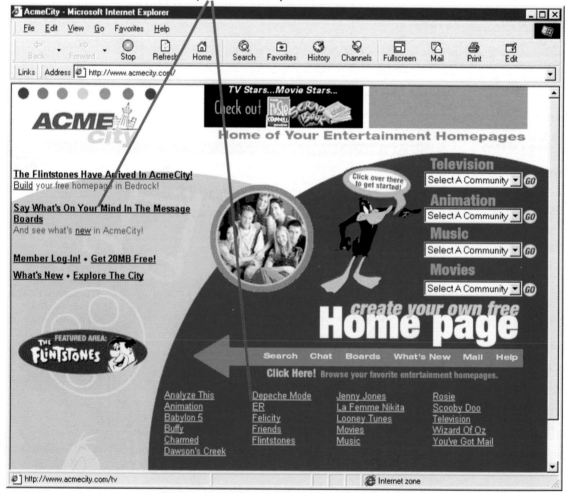

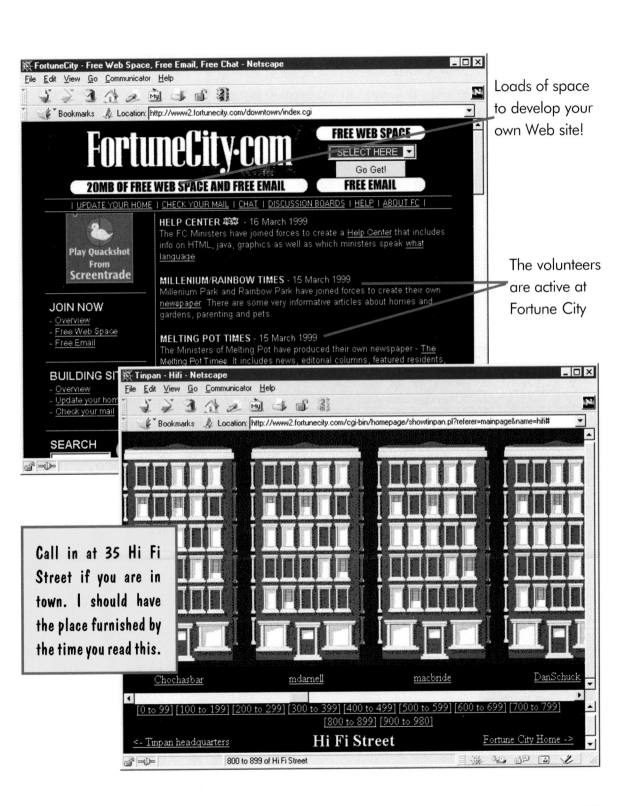

Loads of space to develop your own Web site!

The volunteers are active at Fortune City

Call in at 35 Hi Fi Street if you are in town. I should have the place furnished by the time you read this.

Games

Head for Yahoo's Games section and you will find links to something like 20,000 sites covering all manner of games. Many of these sites act as newsletters and discussion forums for games played offline – use these to track down your nearest bridge club, discuss chess strategies or get the cheats that will help you survive in a game on your PlayStation.

Some sites hold stores of games for playing on- or offline – there are loads of solitaires, word games, 'arcade action' and computerised board games. Where the play is online, games are usually Java applets, Shockwave or ActiveX programs and these can only deliver slick action if they are very well written.

Games Domain has a huge stock of online games (star-rated to point you towards the best) as well as carrying news, reviews, demos and cheats for computer and video games. Visit it at:

www.gamesdomain.co.uk

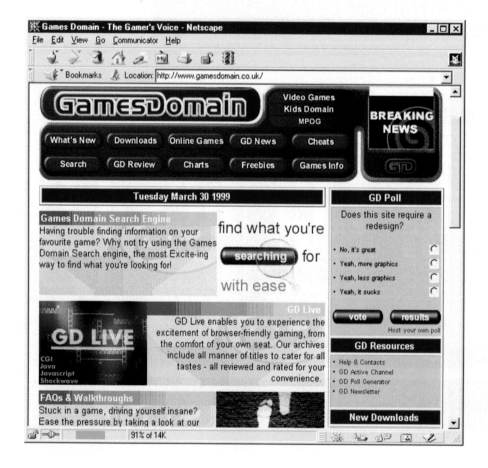

140

Interactive online games

There are hundreds of these, ranging from multi-user adventure and action games through to card games in chat rooms. Most multi-user games need special software, which can sometimes be downloaded free from the game site, but more often must be bought and installed before you go online. All action and some adventure games are played in real-time, some adventure and tactical games are played by turns, with the moves assessed by an online referree – these are normally charged for.

The more casual chat/games rooms can be a nice way to get to know people. The software can usually be downloaded quickly at the start – and will be in your cache if you revisit regularly. Head for the the social lounges, if you are more interested in chatting than playing!

People used to play cribbage in the ale houses of Shake-speare's time, now they play it online – and it is still one of the great card games. Try it in Yahoo's Games rooms.

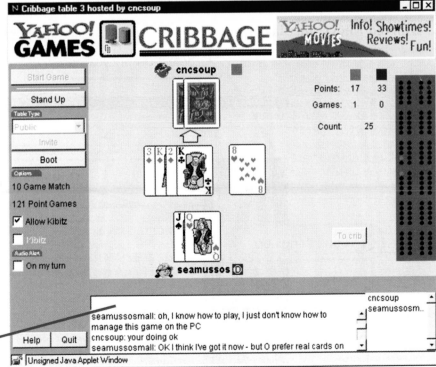

Type here to chat to the other player(s)

Fact-finding

The Internet is a wonderful source of information, but it's not well organised and the quality varies. If you want succinct and accurate information, your best source may be an encyclopedia – and there are plenty on the Web! You'll find links to many of them at EDIS, the Encyclopedia of Delay-Insensitive Systems.

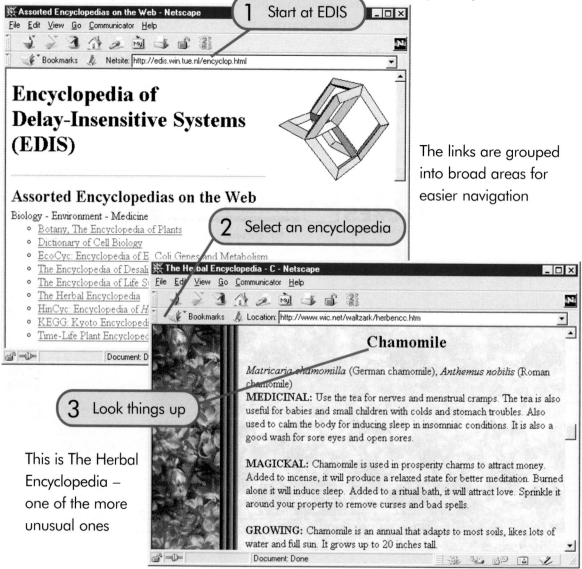

Basic steps

1 Go to Edis at: edis.win.tue.nl/encyclop.html

2 Browse the list and select an encyclopedia.

3 Look up the information you require.

The links are grouped into broad areas for easier navigation

This is The Herbal Encyclopedia – one of the more unusual ones

Basic steps

The Internet Movie Database

1 Go to the IMDb at:
   www.imdb.com
   or us.imdb.com

2 Enter all or part of the title or name.

3 Select Title or Name.

4 Click GO.

5 Click on a link to read more about the film or one of the cast or crew.

This is the prime site for film buffs. I have yet to find a film where it did not have the full (credited) cast and crew, usually with reviews, awards, plot summary, trivia and goofs. Enter any actor's or actress's name and it will tell you all their films and major TV appearances, along with biographical information. Directors, producers, gaff operators, animal trainers – they are all in there. The whole lot is interlinked, so that you can start from one film then dig into the credits of just about everyone associated with it. It's great for tracking down people – that long-haired assassin in *The Replacement Killers*, where have I seen him before? Two minutes later, I know it was Danny Trejo, who played Johnny Baca in *Con Air* – one of his 52 films!

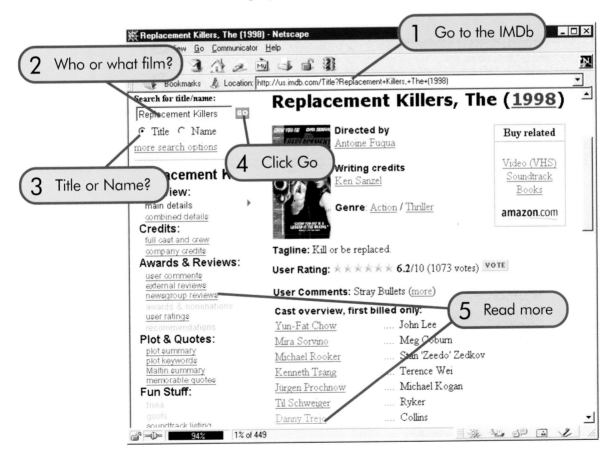

Newspapers

Most of the directories and portals carry some news stories and sports results, but if you really want to read the news, then turn to the papers. Many of the national papers and some of the local ones now have Web sites, and these normally carry the same stories and range of features as the printed editions.

The Telegraph (**www.telegraph.co.uk**) was the first of the UK nationals to go on-line with its *Electronic Telegraph*. It has now been joined by *The Times* and its associated papers (**www.thetimes.co.uk**), *The Guardian* (**www.guardian.co.uk**), the *Financial Times* (**www.ft.com**) and the *Daily* and *Sunday Mirror* (**www.mirror.co.uk**). The *Daily Mail* publishes its IT section on-line (**www.dailymail.co.uk**).

Take note

The broadsheet papers will ask you to register before you can access their site, but registration is free — they need to be able to tell their advertisers how many readers they attract.

Immediate access to major stories, and simple ways to reach the different sections of the paper are key features of the Guardian's site.

Tip

If you want a foreign newspaper and can't get it locally, see if it is published online.

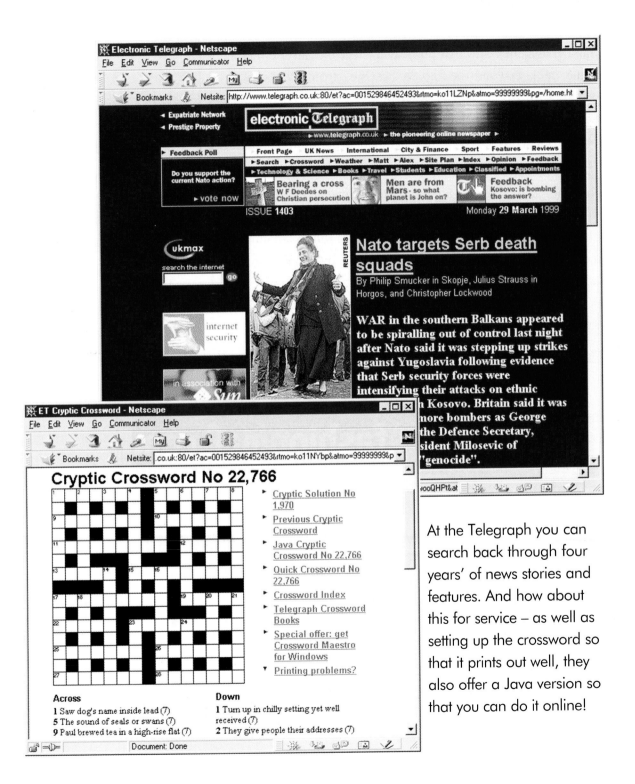

At the Telegraph you can search back through four years' of news stories and features. And how about this for service – as well as setting up the crossword so that it prints out well, they also offer a Java version so that you can do it online!

Magazines and e-zines

Many magazines are also published electronically, either in whole or part – and the choice stretches from *Private Eye*, through *Cosmopolitan* to *Scientific American*, with most computer mags in between. Some are subscription-only, but most are free and none are as convenient as their paper equivalents for reading on the train or in the bath!

There are also an increasing number of 'magazines' which are only published electronically. These include the excellent *Vzine*, which focuses on Web design and Web-based programming and is one of many devoted to computers and the Internet. But there are many others on a wide range of special interests, plus a whole bunch of 'alternative' magazines covering music, politics, film, sex, free speech, the occult and the weird.

Tip

Yahoo has a comprehensive listing of magazines. Go to 'News and Media' then 'Magazines' and pick a subject — any subject!

Vzine, the magazine for Web developers, is at www.vzine.com

Basic steps

1 Go to In-Box Direct at home.netscape.com/ibd

2 Select a topic from the Browse by Subject list.

3 Read the descriptions, clicking View Sample if you want to see more.

4 Click Select to add to your list.

5 Click Subscribe to confirm your choices.

In-Box Direct

At Netcenter, you can arrange to have electronic magazines mailed to you. Like channels, In-Box Direct is an example of 'push technology' – i.e. information is sent out to you by providers, rather than you having to pull it off the Web – but it is much more efficient. As they are sent by e-mail, you pick them up along with your other messages when it suits you, and it is far quicker to get stuff from your mail server than to have it sent across the Web from a channel provider.

The publishers will normally only send the top page, with tasters of the lead stories and a contents list – all linked so that you can follow up any that interest you.

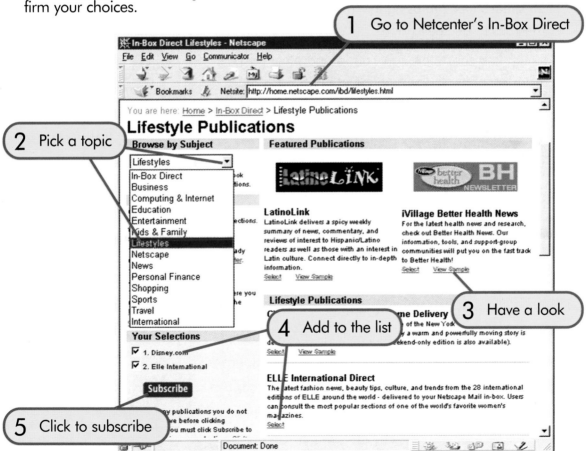

1 Go to Netcenter's In-Box Direct

2 Pick a topic

3 Have a look

4 Add to the list

5 Click to subscribe

147

Summary

- Governments, commercial and voluntary organisations publish a great deal of information online.

- There are risks in purchasing goods and services over the Internet, but take sensible precautions and it should be no riskier than buying by mail or in the high street.

- Cheaper running costs should enable Internet-based traders to offer god deals – but amazing bargains are often a sign of a con man at work.

- A wide range of goods can now be bought over the Internet and delivered to the door.

- High street shops are using the Web to advertise, and sometimes to sell their goods.

- You can find shops through Yahoo and other large directories, or track down goods at the Buyer's Index.

- Many banks now offer online banking – try it, it's a more convenient alternative to telephone banking.

- Chat rooms are where people can get together in real-time to exchange ideas and gossip.

- Communities can be sociable places to set up your Web site.

- All manner of games are supported on the Web in one form or another. Whatever you like to play, there will be a site devoted to it somewhere!

- The Internet is a great reference library, with stores of organised information in encyclopedias and databases.

- Most quality newspapers and many magazines also publish online editions. E-zines publish only online.

Take note

With a microphone, sound card and speakers, you can turn your PC into an 'Internet telephone' – at least, that's the theory. At present, it does not work very well in practice – the connections are simply not fast enough for a proper conversation, but it is improving. Watch out for developments, especially if you have friends and family overseas and would like to cut down your phone bill!

9 E-mail

Electronic mail

These are messages sent to other individuals on the Internet. Think of them more like memos than postal mail. A message can be easily copied to other users; and when you receive an incoming message, you can attach your reply to it, or forward it on to a third party. You can also attach documents and graphics files to messages (see *Files by mail*, page 158).

The mail will sometimes get through almost instantaneously, but at worst it will be there within a few hours. The delay is because not all of the computers that handle mail are constantly in touch with each other. Instead, they will **log on** at regular intervals to deal with the mail and other services.

Key points about e-mail:

- E-mail is **fast**, **cheap** and (generally) very **reliable**.

- Every service provider offers **e-mail** access.

- The cheapest and most convenient way of dealing with your mail is to read and compose it **offline**.

- As with snail mail, to send someone e-mail you need their address (see *Finding people*, page 168).

Netscape Composer and Microsoft's Outlook Express can be run offline – this is the most efficient way to handle your mail. Just go online to collect your mail and to send any messages that you have written already, then hang up the phone and read your mail and write your replies or new messages at your leisure, without clocking up phone charges.

Jargon

Log on – connect to a multi-user computer, either directly or over a phone line.

E-mail – electronic mail.

Snail mail – the good old postal service.

Take note

There are many organised **MAIL LISTS** on the Internet, each dealing with its own special topic of interest. Subscribers can post messages to a central point, from which they are sent out to all other subscribers. As a means of sharing ideas, they are similar to Newsgroups (see the next chapter) with the one key difference that you must join mail lists to get the messages.

E-mail addresses

Tip

There are utilities on the Internet that will help you to find people's e-mail addresses (page 168), but the simplest way to do it is to phone them and ask them to e-mail to you. Every message carries its sender's address.

The standard pattern for a person's e-mail address is:

> name@provider

However, there are quite a few variations to the basic pattern. Here, for example, are some of the names that I have had over the last few years. At TCP (Total Connectivity Providers), they follow the standard pattern:

> macbride@tcp.co.uk

When I joined CompuServe it gave its users numbers. Now you can have a name as well, if you like.

> 100407.2521@compuserve.co.uk

> macbride@compuserve.co.uk

At **WinNet**, they allocates domain names (**macdesign**) to their users, as well as personal names (**macbride**). This is because they use the same format for companies and for home users.

> macbride@macdesign.win-uk.net

You will see the same pattern in commercial and other organisations. For example, if you wanted to e-mail my publisher – perhaps to ask about some other Made Simple books – his address is:

> mike.cash@repp.co.uk

Take note

It is easy to mistype an e-mail address, but you should only have to type it once for each person. Every mail system has an Address Book file where you can store addresses (see page 162).

Outlook Express

Outlook Express is the mail and news application that comes with Internet Explorer. If you do not have an existing mail connection, the first time you use Outlook, a Wizard will run to collect the details needed to set it up. Get this information from your access provider and have it to hand:

● your user name and password;

● your e-mail name, e.g. JoSmith@mynet.co.uk;

● the names of your service provider's Incoming and Outgoing Mail Servers – these may well be the same.

To read your mail, select the Inbox and click on a header in the Header pane to display its message in the Preview pane.

Take note

The only fixed part of the window is the Header pane – all the rest are optional. As the Folder and Outlook bars do the same job, turn one off. If the Preview Pane is turned off, a new window will open to display a message when you click on it.

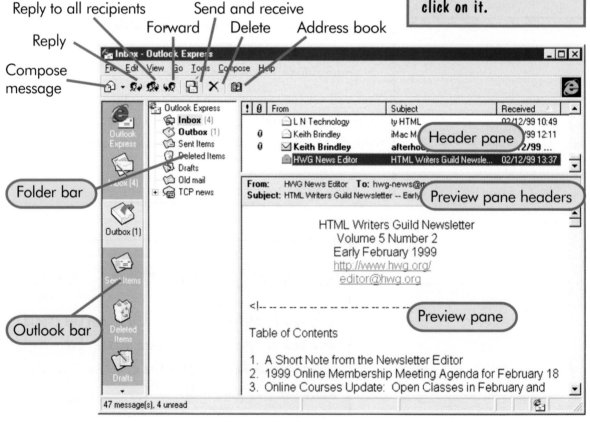

Basic steps

1 Open the View menu, select Layout...

2 Set the screen layout.

3 Open the View menu, and select Columns.

4 Select from the Available list and click
Add >> to include.

5 Select from the Displayed list and click
<< Remove to remove.

6 Adjust the positions with the Move buttons.

Display options

You can set the layout and what to include in the headers.

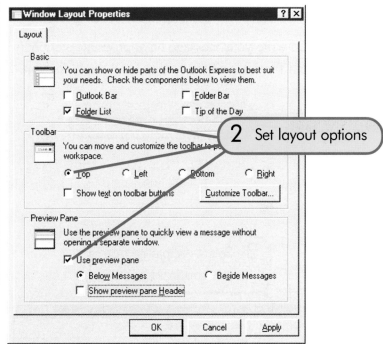

2 Set layout options

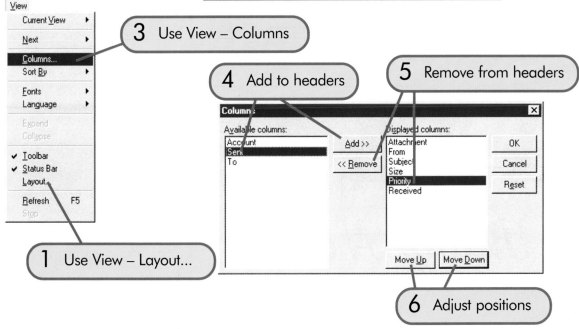

3 Use View – Columns

4 Add to headers

5 Remove from headers

1 Use View – Layout...

6 Adjust positions

153

Sending messages

To send e-mail, all you need is the address – and something to say! Messages can be composed and sent immediately if you are online, or composed offline and stored for sending later.

To add impact, write your message on appropriate stationery! These have text formats and backgrounds all ready for you.

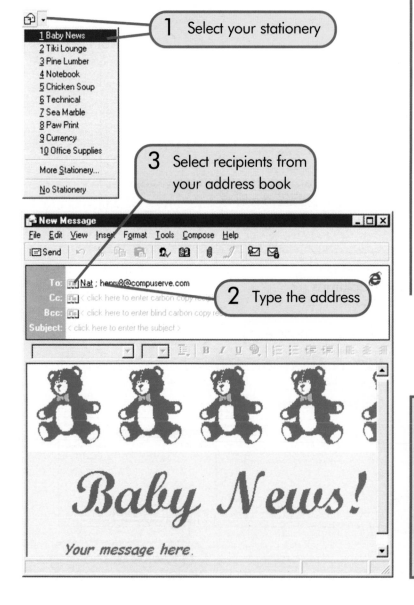

1 Select your stationery

3 Select recipients from your address book

2 Type the address

1 Click the arrow beside Compose ⏥▾ and select your stationery.

❑ Use No stationery – or simply click ⏥ for plain paper.

2 Type the address in the To: slot.

or

3 Click ▦ beside To: to open the Select Recipients panel.

4 Select a name and click the To: button, then OK to copy the address.

❑ To send copies, repeat from step 2 for the Cc: text box.

Take note

Subject lines are important as they help your recipients to organise their messages. Make them brief, but clear.

154

5 Type a Subject.

6 Type your message.

7 Click 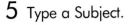 .

or

8 Open the File menu
   and select Send Mes-
   sage, for immediate
   delivery, or Send Later.

9 Your spelling will be
   checked before the
   message is sent.

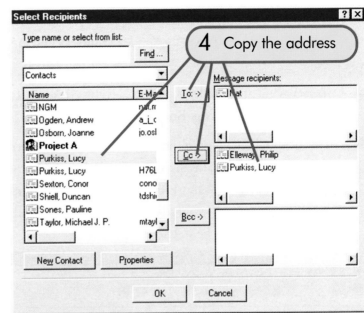

4 Copy the address

7 Send it

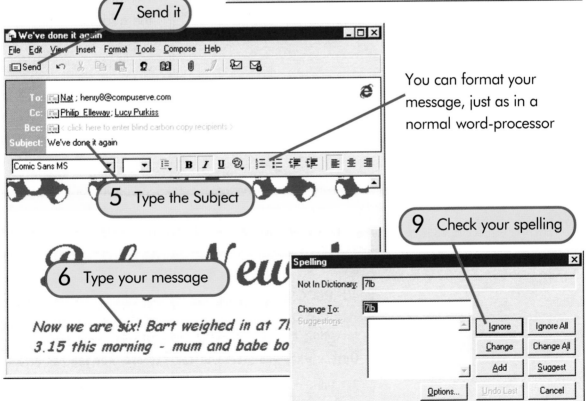

You can format your
message, just as in a
normal word-processor

5 Type the Subject

6 Type your message

9 Check your spelling

Replying

When you reply to an incoming message, the system will open the Compose window and copy the sender's address into the To: text box.

- If you want the sender's address, right-click on it and select **Add to Address Book** from the short menu.

- The original message is normally also copied into the main text area with > at the start of each line. This can be very handy if you want to respond to the mail point-by-point. You can insert your text between the lines, and any unwanted lines can be deleted.

Tip

Copying messages into a Reply is an option. If you don't want it, go to the Options panel (from the Tools menu), switch to the Send tab and turn it off.

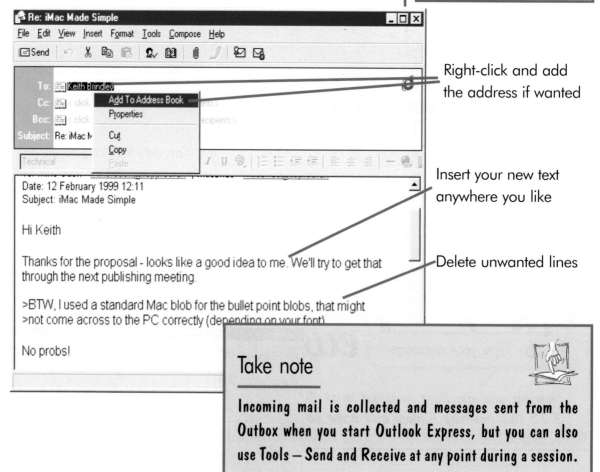

Right-click and add the address if wanted

Insert your new text anywhere you like

Delete unwanted lines

Take note

Incoming mail is collected and messages sent from the Outbox when you start Outlook Express, but you can also use Tools – Send and Receive at any point during a session.

Basic steps

❑ Forwarding mail

1 Select the message in the header pane.

2 Click the Forwad button.

3 Type or select the address(es) of the recipient(s).

4 Delete any unwanted headers or other text and add your own comments.

5 Click ▣Send .

Forward

You can send a message on to another person – perhaps after adding your own comments to it.

Reply to all

If you get a message that has been sent to several people, you can reply to all those listed in the **To:** and **Cc:** boxes. Click 🐾, instead of 🐾, and continue as for a normal reply. Your message will be copied to all the recipients of the original message.

> 3 Type or select the recipients

> 5 Click Send

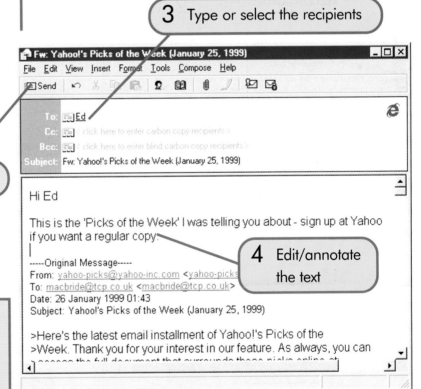

> 4 Edit/annotate the text

Take note

The **Bcc:** box is for 'Blind carbon copies'. Any Bcc: recipients are not listed on the copies sent to other people.

Files by mail

Files of any type – graphics, word-processor and spreadsheet documents, audio and video clips – and URL links, can be attached to messages and sent by e-mail. Compared to sending files printed or on disk in the post, e-mail is almost always quicker, often more reliable and cheaper.

● If you use the Rich Text format, rather than plain text, you can also insert pictures directly into a message.

Basic steps

1 Compose the message.

2 From the Insert menu select File Attachment.

❑ To attach a file

3 Browse for the file and click Attach.

❑ To insert a picture

4 Open the Format menu and select Rich Text.

5 Browse for the picture source and click OK.

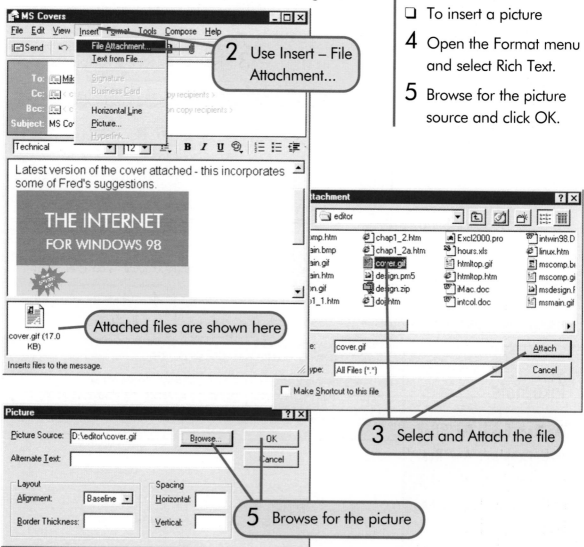

2 Use Insert – File Attachment...

Latest version of the cover attached - this incorporates some of Fred's suggestions.

THE INTERNET FOR WINDOWS 98

cover.gif (17.0 KB)

Attached files are shown here

Inserts files to the message.

3 Select and Attach the file

Picture

Picture Source: D:\editor\cover.gif   Browse...   OK
Alternate Text: Cancel

Layout
Alignment: Baseline
Border Thickness:

Spacing
Horizontal:
Vertical:

5 Browse for the picture

Basic steps

1 Click on the ✐ , then select the filename.

Or

2 Double-click on the message to open it in its own window.

3 Click on the name.

❑ Either the file will be opened in a suitable application or you will be offered the choice of opening or saving it.

Detaching binary files

Detaching binary files from messages used to be hard work – they had to be cut out from the text of the message and processed through special decoding software. With Outlook Express, it's a piece of cake. If the preview pane header bar is open, an attached file is shown by a paperclip icon. If it is not, you must open the message in its own window – the file icon will be in the bottom pane. In either case, Outlook Express handles all the detaching and decoding.

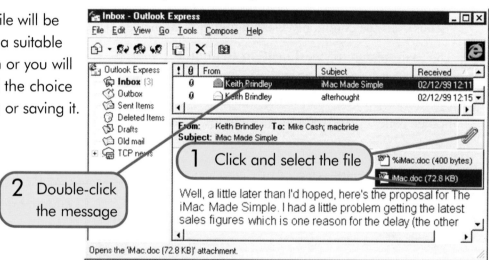

1 Click and select the file

2 Double-click the message

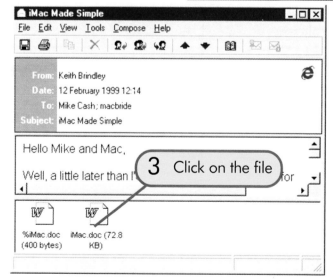

3 Click on the file

Take note

If a message has an embedded picture, Outlook will display it. To save it, right-click on the image and select **Save As..** from the short menu.

159

Messenger

Messenger is the mail and news application in Netscape's Communicator suite. Its facilities and commands are almost identical to those of Outlook Express.

The Messenger Window

- The **Header pane** and the **Menu bar** are the only fixed components – everything else is optional.

- The **Message toolbar** is much quicker to use than the menus – all the commonly-used commands are here.

- The main feature of the **Location toolbar** is the drop-down list of folders. If you have a small screen, or like to run Messenger in a small window, use this instead of the Folder pane – it leaves the full window width for the messages.

- If the **Message pane** is turned off, messages are displayed in a new window. This can make sense with a small screen, but it is usually more convenient to display everything in one window.

- The **Folder pane** offers the simplest way to switch between your various mail and news folders.

Composition

Messenger does not offer the ready-made 'stationery' that you find in Outlook Express, but messages can be formatted if required. The formatting options includes the full range of HTML tags – colours, font sizes, background images, etc.

Tip

The screen layout can be adjusted in the **Window Settings** panel of the **Edit – Preferences** dialog box, so that either the Message pane runs the full width or the Folder pane runs the full depth of the window. Explore these, and other preferences, after you have used Messenger for a while.

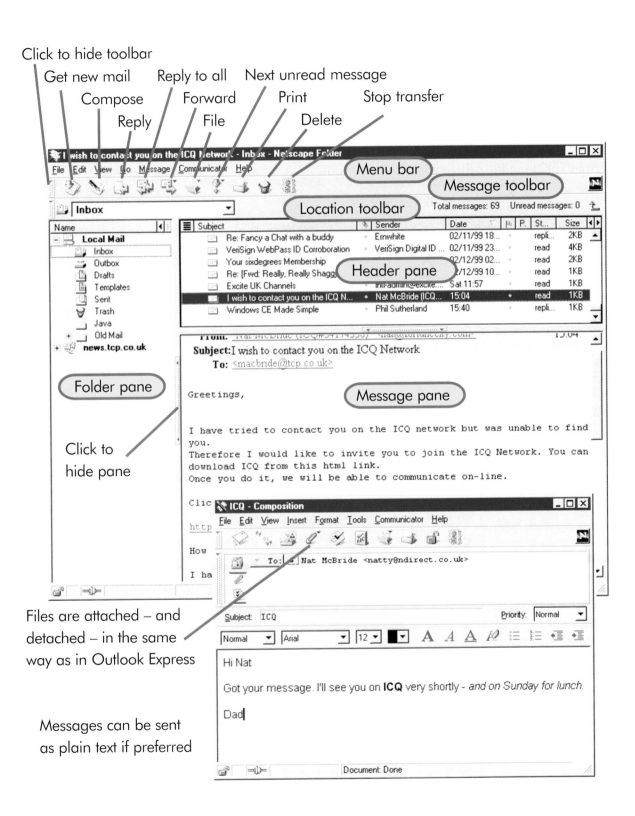

Click to hide toolbar

Get new mail

Compose

Reply to all

Next unread message

Reply

Forward

File

Print

Delete

Stop transfer

Menu bar

Message toolbar

Location toolbar

Header pane

Folder pane

Message pane

Click to hide pane

Files are attached – and detached – in the same way as in Outlook Express

Messages can be sent as plain text if preferred

Address Book

Typing e-mail addresses is a pain – one slip and the mail comes bouncing back the next day with a 'recipient unknown' label. The simple solution is to use the Address Book. Type the address in once correctly – or add it when replying to a message (page 156) – and it's there whenever you want it.

(page 156)

1 Click the Address Book button 📖 .

2 Click 🗔 New Contact .

3 Enter the First, Middle and Last names – contacts are normally listed alphabetically.

4 Type the address and click [Add].

5 If the person has several addresses, add them and set one as the Default.

6 Click OK.

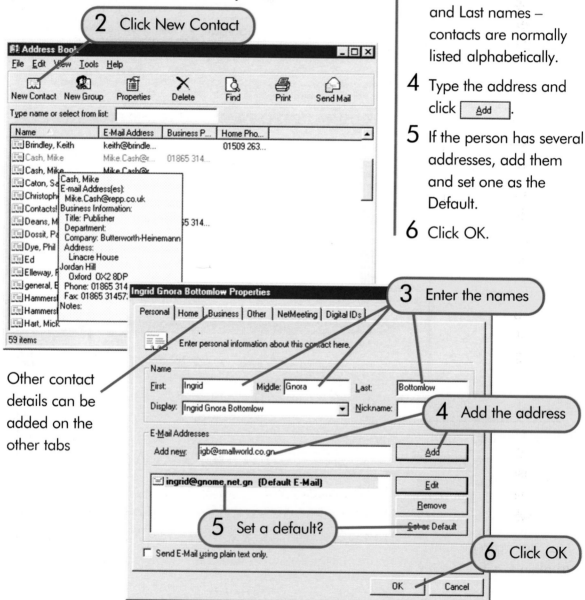

2 Click New Contact

Other contact details can be added on the other tabs

3 Enter the names

4 Add the address

5 Set a default?

6 Click OK

162

E-mail etiquette

- Small is beautiful. Short messages are quick and cheap to download.

- Test first. When sending anything other than plain text, try a short test file first to make sure that the other person can receive it properly.

- Zip it up! If you are sending files, compress them with WinZip.

- Subject matters! Always type a Subject line so that the other person can identify the message.

- Short signatures. If you create a signature file (see page 165), keep it short.

- Don't SHOUT. Using capitals is known as shouting. It's OK to emphasise the odd word this way, but don't shout whole messages.

When you send someone a paper letter, you know that what they receive will be the same as you send, and if you enclose lots of material, you will pay the extra postage.

E-mail is different. Your recipients actively download your messages, which takes time and can cost money. Further, if they are using different Mail software to yours, it can affect the appearance – and sometimes the *delivery* – of your messages.

Formatted text

Most modern e-mail software can display formatted text, but few people bother with formatting. The essence of e-mail is that it is quick and informal – plain text is very much the norm. Save your fancy stationery for special announcements and greetings.

Size

Some e-mail systems set a limit to the size of messages, typically 1000 lines (roughly 70Kb). You are hardly likely to write this much, but an attached file (see page 158) can easily push the message size over the limit.

Even where there is no limit, file size is still a factor. The larger the file, the longer it takes to download, and the higher your recipients' phone bills – especially if they are paying long-distance charges to their providers.With a good modem and a standard phone line, e-mail usually comes in at around 3Kb per second, or 1Mb in 5 minutes.

Use the standard WinZip software to compress data files before attaching them. Graphics and documents files can be reduced to 10% or less of their original size this way. Even executable files – the most difficult to compress – show some reduction.

Subject lines

A clear Subject line identifies a message. Your recipients need this when the mail arrives, to see which to deal with first – and which to ignore completely! They also need it when organising old mail, so that they know which to delete and which to place in what folder.

Emphasis

If your recipient's Mail system can handle formatted text, then you can use <u>underline</u> or **bold** for emphasis. If you are sending plain text, and want to make a word stand out, enclose it in *asterisks* or _underscores_, or write it in CAPITALS.

Smileys

E-mail messages tend to be brief, and as your receipients cannot see your expression or hear the tone of your voice, there is a possibility of being misunderstood – especially when joking. Smileys, also known as *emoticons,* are little pictures, composed of ASCII characters, that can help to convey your meaning.

The basic smiley of **:-)** is the one you will see most often, though there are many other weird and wonderful smileys around. Here are a few of the more common ones.

:-)	It's a joke
'-)	Wink
:-(	I'm feeling sad
:-o	Wow!
:-C	I don't believe it!
(-:	I'm left handed
%-)	I've been staring at a screen for hours!
8-)	I'm wearing sunglasses

<aside>
Take note

If you want to add your 'signature' to messages, create the file in NotePad or other editor, saving it as plain text. Go to the **Identity** panel in **Mail and News** Preferences and link it in there.
</aside>

Abbreviations

BTW	By The Way
BWQ	Buzz Word Quotient
FYI	For Your Information
IMHO	In My Humble Opinion (ironic)
MOTSS	Member Of The Same Sex
POV	Point Of View
TIA	Thanks In Advance
TTFN	Ta Ta For Now
WRT	With Reference To
<g>	Grin

If you are an indifferent typist, or like to keep your messages short, or are likely to be getting mail from old 'netties', then it's worth learning a few of the standard abbreviations. You will also find these used in real-time conferences and chat lines, and in newsgroup articles.

If you want to track down more abbreviations or the acronyms used elsewhere in the computing world, an excellent list called Babel is maintained by Irving Kind at Temple University in the States. Get a copy at this URL:

http://www.access.digex.net/~ikind/babel.html

Signatures

A signature file can be added to the end of every message. This is a plain text file, usually saved as *personal.sig* or something similar, containing your name, e-mail address and any other contact details you want to give. People's signatures often also contain a favourite quote, advert, or a picture or name created from ASCII characters. e.g.

Example 1

```
-------------
P.K. McBride      |macbride@tcp.co.uk
Computing's Made Simple at http://www.madesimple.co.uk
-------------
```

Example 2

```
                      _\  |  /_
                       @ @    =
_____ooO_(_)_Ooo_____
Declan Quinn,
```

Web mail

Go to almost any of the major directories and portals and you will be offered free Web mail. What is it and how does it work?

The crucial difference between Web mail and ordinary e-mail is that your mail folders, where you store your messages, are online. With ordinary e-mail, you only need to be online while you are sending and receiving messages – they can be read and written, moved and deleted offline. With Web mail, you must (normally) be online the whole time that you are dealing with your mail. (It is possible to download messages for reading and storage, and to transfer up to the site, messages that you have written in a word-processor.) As a result, dealing with the mail is slower – and more costly if you are paying for the online and telephone time.

The big advantage of Web mail – apart from the fact that it is free – is that you can access your mailbox from anywhere as long as you can get into the Internet somehow. This may be through a terminal in a public library, from a friend's or colleague's desktop anywhere in the world, or through your own (temporary) account at your place of work or study.

A Web mail address is worth having if:

- you are a student and want to be able to keep in touch when you are at home or at college;

- your job takes you to places where you cannot easily access your normal Internet account;

- you are likely to be changing your job/college/Internet Access Provider and don't want the disruption of a change of address.

Web mail providers

❑ There are lots including:

MailCity

   www.mailcity.com

Excite

   mail.excite.co.uk

   mail.excite.com

Yahoo

   mail.yahoo.co.uk

   mail.yahoo.com

Netcenter

   home.netcenter.com

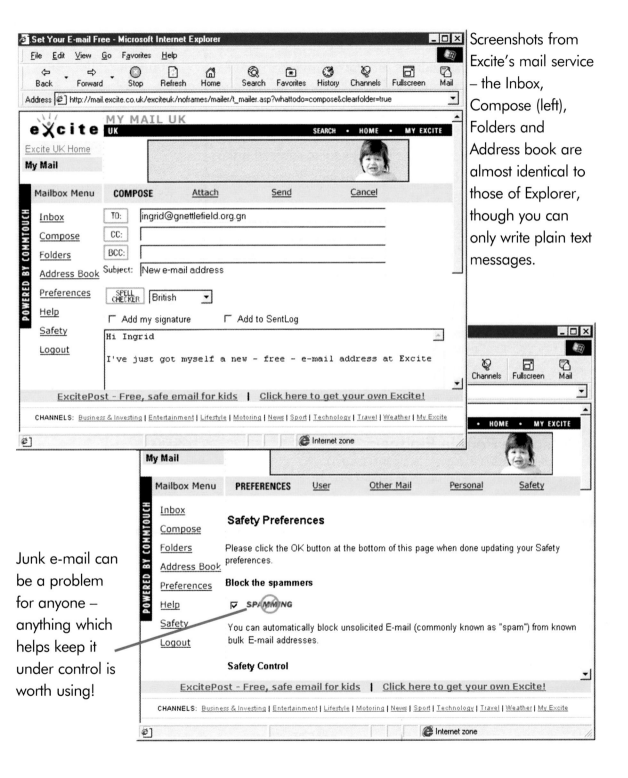

Screenshots from
Excite's mail service
– the Inbox,
Compose (left),
Folders and
Address book are
almost identical to
those of Explorer,
though you can
only write plain text
messages.

Junk e-mail can
be a problem
for anyone –
anything which
helps keep it
under control is
worth using!

Finding people

Finding people on the Internet can be very difficult. Users get online directly through hundreds of access providers or indirectly through thousands of businesses – and there is no single controlling organisation. However, there are sites that are compiling directories of e-mail addresses – but don't expect too much from any of these. You are more likely to succeed if the person is in the States, but the coverage of the UK and the rest of the world can be very patchy.

Netscape People Finder at Netcenter is one of the better ones for finding the e-mail addresses of folk outside of the US (and phone numbers in the US and some other countries).

Basic steps

1 Go to Netcenter at home.netcenter.com

2 Select People Finder.

3 In the e-mail address section, type the Last Name and First Name (or initial).

4 Click Search! .

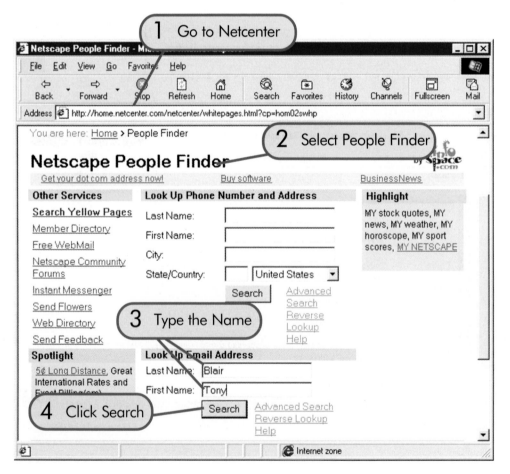

Basic steps

InfoSpace

1 Go to InfoSpace at: www.infospace.com

2 Select White Pages then Email Search.

3 Type the Last Name and First Name.

4 Enter the City and State (for US addresses) or the Country.

5 Click Find Email.

Netcenter's People Finder uses the directory at InfoSpace, and can give you dozens – or hundreds – of matches. At InfoSpace itself, you can restrict the search to a geographical area.

You can also search for phone numbers in the UK and other countries, at InfoSpace.

> ## Tip
>
> If you want other people to be able to find you more easily, add your e-mail address to the InfoSpace directory.

The URL will change as you are moved around within the site

Add your own e-mail address while you are at InfoSpace

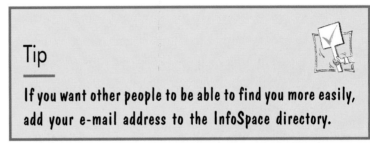

169

Summary

- Electronic mail is faster, cheaper and probably more reliable than the post.

- E-mail addresses normally follow a pattern, but there's no way you can guess someone's address.

- You can customise the Composer and Outlook Express displays to suit yourself – only the header panes are essential.

- When sending messages, start by selecting who they will go to. You should always write the nature of the message in the Subject line.

- When replying, the mail system can copy in the original message for you to add your comments to.

- As well as replying directly to the sender, you can reply to all recipients and forward the message on.

- Use your Address Book and you will only ever have to type a person's e-mail address once – if at all.

- E-mail etiquette is mainly aimed at not wasting other people's time (and phone bills). Mail should be kept short, and should have a clear Subject line.

- Signatures can add something extra to your mail – and long ones can add far too much!

- Files can be attached to e-mail messages and de-tached at the other end. Outlook Express makes this a simple process.

- If you want an e-mail address to use when you are on the move, sign up with a Web mail service.

- You can (sometimes) find people's e-mail addresses at a People Finder site. InfoSpace is one of the best.

10 News

Newsgroups

Newsgroups have developed from e-mail, and consist of groups of users linked so that an **article** sent to the group is **posted** to all its members. There are thousands of groups, each dedicated to a different interest – professions and obsessions, computer programming and TV programs, software, hobbies, politics.

Key points about newsgroups

● **Subscribing** to a group is easy, free of charge and free of entry restrictions.

● The quality and quantity of the communications vary enormously. Some newsgroups circulate large volumes of interesting and relevant information; others carry few articles – or few of any interest.

● Some newsgroups are moderated, i.e. someone checks all incoming articles before broadcasting them to the group. This reduces the quantity of irrelevant and/or boring post.

● The seedier and steamier side of the Internet is mainly in the newsgroups. If you do not want anyone to access this from your system, there are programs that will filter it out for you.

● Some groups are mainly for discussions, others are more like open help-lines, where people can ask for – and get – solutions to technical problems.

● Newsgroups bring together people who share an interest, and so can be good places to make new friends.

● If you decide that a newsgroup is not for you, you can leave at any time.

Jargon

Article – message in a newsgroup.

Post – submit an article.

Subscribing – doesn't involve going onto a membership list. It just places the newsgroup name in a folder for easy access.

Netiquette – like e-mail etiquette (page 163), with the added rules: do read the group's FAQ; don't flame and don't spam.

FAQ– list of Frequently Asked Questions (and answers). Check the FAQ before you post a question to a group.

Flame – overreaction to a breach of netiquette. Can lead to flame wars if the victims believe they are right.

Spam – send article to inappropriate groups.

Lurk – read articles, without posting. It's OK to lurk.

Some major groups

alt – alternative set: a vast and varied collection, largely unmoderated

comp – computing: a great source of help and a good place to meet fellow enthusiasts

rec – recreation: for sports, arts, hobbies and pastimes

sci – science: for academic and amateur scientists

uk – groups mainly for UK residents. There are similar sets for most countries and many smaller regions

Newsgroup names

Newsgroups are organised into a branching structure, with major sections subdivided by topic. Their names reflect this structure. For example, **comp.lang.basic.visual.database** is in the **comp**uter section, which amongst other things covers programming **lang**uages, including **basic**, and this has a **visual** subsection containing several groups, one of which is concerned with **database** programming.

You can see the full list of the newsgroups available on your server, by clicking the Newsgroups button to open this dialog box. (The first time you do this, you will have to go online and download the list of newsgroups from your news server.) You can find groups on particular topics, when you want to select one to subscribe or sample (page 173), but when you have a spare hour or two, work through the full list to see what's there.

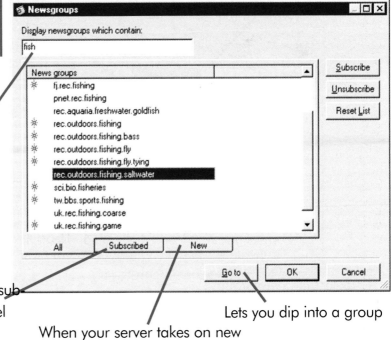

Used for finding the newsgroups on a topic – see page 171

The groups to which you are subscribed are listed on this panel

When your server takes on new groups, they will be listed here

Lets you dip into a group

Reading the news

When you turn to the newsgroups in Outlook Express you will see some minor changes in the toolbar, which reflect the differences between news and e-mail.

- Only the newsgroup headers are downloaded at first – articles come in one at a time as you select them. You can use ⊗ to stop downloading at any point.

- The ✎ **Connect** and ☎ **Hang up** buttons let you go on- and offline easily, so that you can read long articles without running up your phone bill.

- The ▦ **News groups** button lets you find groups.

Right-click on the Toolbar to customise it. You can...

1 Open the news folder and select a group. Wait for the headers to be downloaded into the top right pane.

2 Select an article and wait for it to download into the lower pane.

3 Read it.

... add other buttons

... turn off Text Labels   ... locate the toolbar

2 Select the article

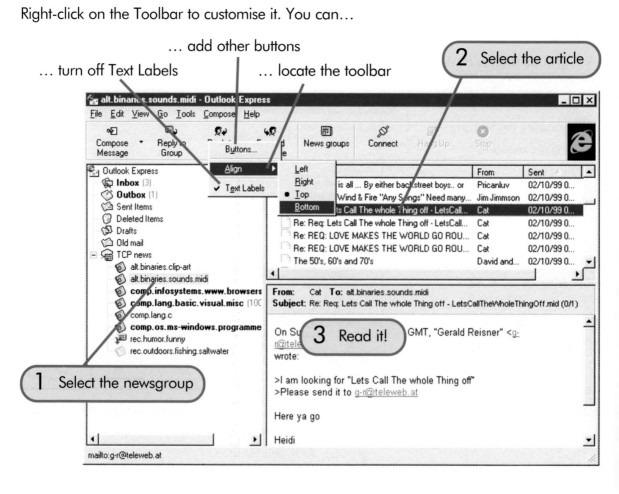

1 Select the newsgroup

3 Read it!

Basic steps

1 From the Tools menu, select Newsgroups... or click the 🔳 button.

2 Open the All groups panel.

3 Type a word to filter the list – if there are still too many, type a second word.

4 Select a group.

5 See what's there by clicking Go to.

or

6 Join the group by clicking Subscribe.

Take note

There may be no groups listed when you first use your news software. To get the list of groups, you must go online and download it – it's a long list and will take some time to download!

Sampling and subscribing

Subscribing to a newsgroup costs nothing and commits you to nothing. It simply means that the group is included in the folder list for easy access.

If you want to read the occasional article in different newsgroups, without cluttering up the folder list, you can use the **Go to** option to pick up the current articles.

Whether you are subscribing or sampling, newsgroups are selected from the **Newsgroups** panel. Rather than struggle with the full list, filter it with one or more words that are likely to be in the name.

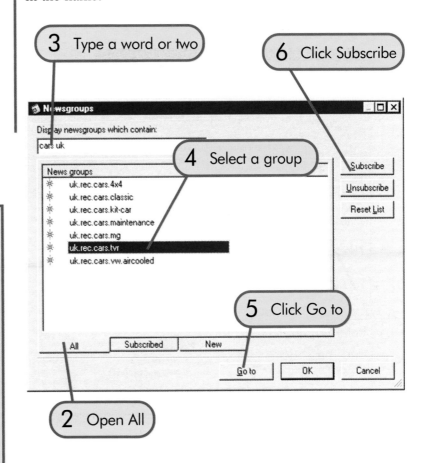

3 Type a word or two

6 Click Subscribe

4 Select a group

5 Click Go to

2 Open All

Posting and replying

Posting articles to a newsgroup is very similar to sending mail, but with a couple of significant differences:

- when posting to a newsgroup, your message goes to thousands of people – observing the netiquette (page 172) is very important.

- when responding to an article, you can reply to the author only (i.e. send a personal e-mail), or post to the whole group, or reply to both at once.

If your message is *truly* relevant to several groups, you can write other group names in the Cc: slot

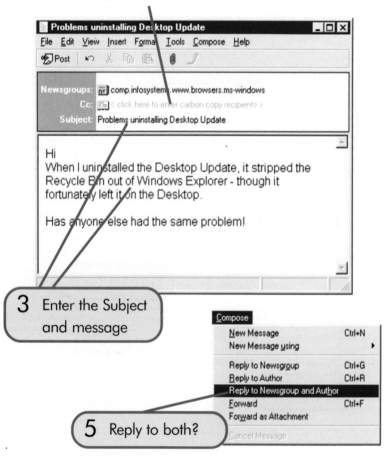

3 Enter the Subject and message

5 Reply to both?

❑ Posting articles

1 From the news folder, select the one in which you want to post.

2 Click the ▪ button or use Compose – New Message.

3 The group's name will be in the Newsgroups: slot. Enter the Subject, and type the message.

❑ Responding to articles

4 Select the article.

5 Use the Compose menu to Reply to Newsgroup and Author.

or

6 Use the buttons to reply to the Author only ▪ or to the Group ▪.

7 Edit unwanted lines from the quoted article.

8 Type your reply.

9 Click the Post button.

176

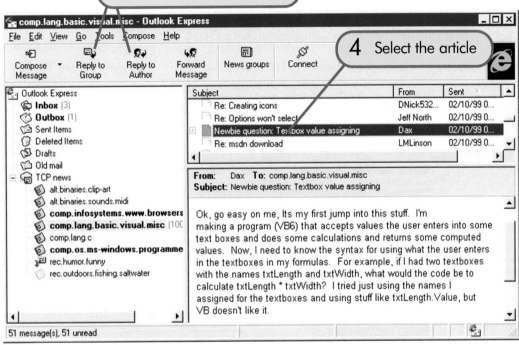

6 Reply to group or author

4 Select the article

9 Post

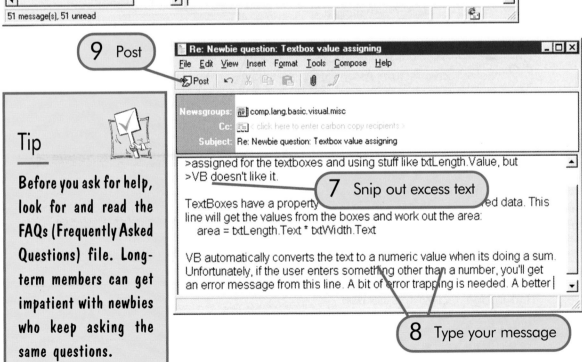

7 Snip out excess text

8 Type your message

Files in the News

Some newsgroups circulate graphics, sounds and other binary (i.e. not plain text) files. Outlook will display (or play) these if it can, and if not, will show their presence with a paperclip icon.

The filename is usually in the Subject line

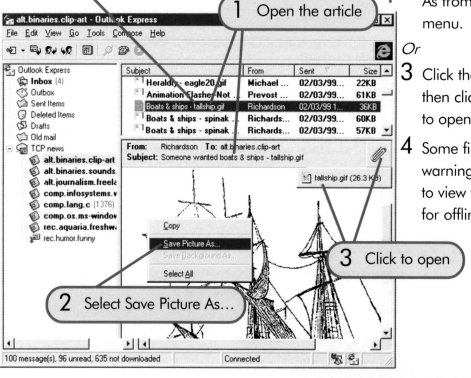

1 Select the article.

2 To save a displayed image, right-click on it and select Save Picture As from the shortcut menu.

Or

3 Click the Paperclip icon then click the filename to open the file.

4 Some files generate a warning. Choose Open to view the file or Save for offline viewing.

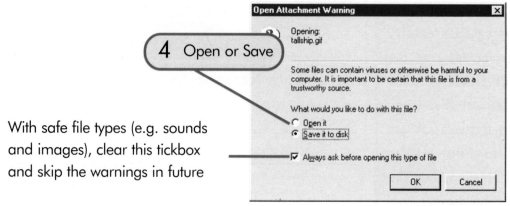

With safe file types (e.g. sounds and images), clear this tickbox and skip the warnings in future

Basic steps

1 Select the articles that contain parts of the file.

2 Open the Tools menu and select Combine and Decode....

3 If a part is in the wrong order, drag it or select it and use Move Up or Move Down to nudge it into place.

4 Click OK.

❑ The file will appear as an attachment to the message – view or save it as normal.

Multi-part files

The news (and e-mail) systems were designed for text messages and binary files must be specially encoding for transfer. You will rarely be aware of this as Outlook Express usually decodes them automatically. However, large binary files are sometimes split into chunks for transfer, and if you try to view a single chunk you will see only gobbledegook. Multi-part files can normally be recovered by the **Combine and Decode** tool, which detaches the parts from their messages, joins them together and produces one decoded file.

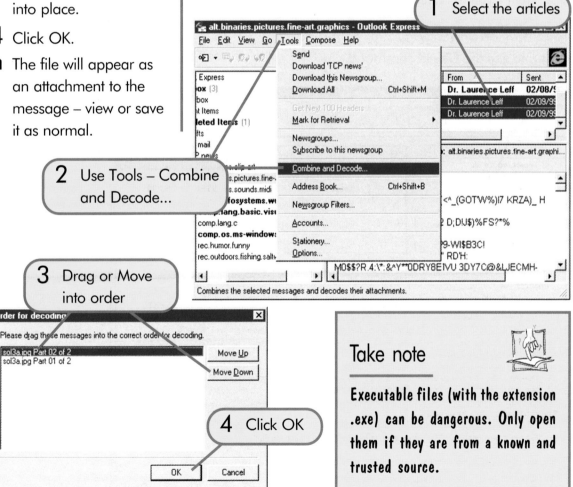

1 Select the articles

2 Use Tools – Combine and Decode...

3 Drag or Move into order

4 Click OK

Take note

Executable files (with the extension .exe) can be dangerous. Only open them if they are from a known and trusted source.

News from Messenger

As Messenger is almost identical to Outlook Express in dealing with e-mail, it should be no surprise that it is also almost identical when dealing with the news. The menus are structured slightly differently, but the commands are pretty much the same – though Messenger gives you a little more control over downloading, allowing you to choose at the time whether you want to download all the new headers or a set number.

There are a couple of features lacking from Messenger which may or may not be significant to you – it depends on which newsgroups you use and how you use them.

To remove an unwanted group, right-click on it and use the Delete command

Reading the news in Messenger – subscribed groups are added to the news server's folder.

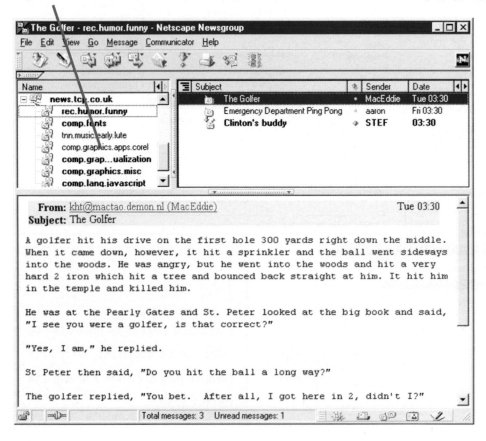

Sampling and subscribing

In Messenger, you cannot dip into a newsgroup without subscribing to it. This is no big deal, as it is simple enough to unsubscribe to a group after sampling in, but when you are first looking around it's a bit of bother you could do without.

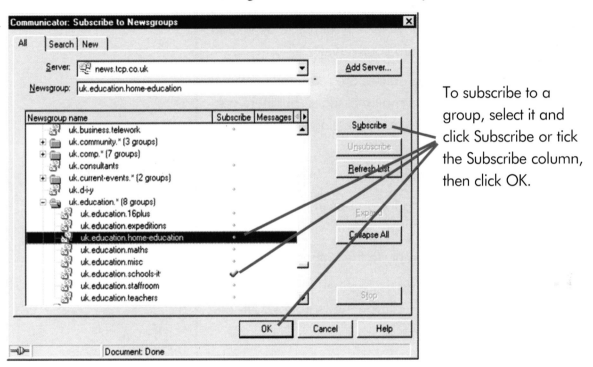

To subscribe to a group, select it and click Subscribe or tick the Subscribe column, then click OK.

Binary files

One-part binary files are displayed or can be saved just as easily as in Outlook Express, but there is no Combine and Decode routine to handle multi-part files for you. In fact, there is no simple way to recombine multi-part files in Messenger – it will automatically decode the first part, but leave the rest in its encoded form and they cannot be joined. If you subscribe to a newsgroup where multi-part files are common, e.g. those that circulate sounds, videos or high-resolution images, switch to Outlook Express, with its Combine and Decode facility.

Summary

◆ There is a newsgroup for almost every conceivable interest, hobby, profession or obsession.

◆ Newsgroups are organised into a hierarchy, branching down from broad areas to highly specialised topics.

◆ The first stage in using any News system is to download the list of newsgroups from your server.

◆ In Outlook Express news articles are read and written in much the same way as e-mail messages, but there are some extra tools available for accessing the newsgroups.

◆ Newsgroups can be sampled easily.

◆ Subscribing saves hunting for groups in the full list.

◆ When responding to an article, you can post a follow-up article to the group, reply to the author, or both.

◆ You can post articles to any subscribed group. Articles should only be posted to relevant newsgroups. Off-topic postings cause offence.

◆ Most binary files can be viewed and saved easily. Multi-part binary files must be joined together and then decoded – Outlook Express's Combine and Decode will do this for you.

Tip

If you are new to the Internet, there is a group specially for you. It's *news.announce.newusers.* (For subscribing see page 175.) And look out for Emily Postnews' *Etiquette for USENET News Postings.* It's posted fairly often to this group.

11 Files from the Net

File transfer

There are gigabytes of files out there, just waiting to be **downloaded**. They include the latest software updates, movie, video and music clips, pictures from high art to low pornography and all sorts of texts. There are also tools for working on the Internet, along with guides on how to use them. You will find files at:

FTP sites

FTP stands for **F**ile **T**ransfer **P**rotocol and is the standard method by which files are copied between different types of computers over the Internet. There are special FTP programs, such as WS_FTP (get a copy from **www.ipswitch.com**), but browsers can also handle the FTP routines to download files.

Many of the FTP sites (also called *archives*) have been up and running from the early days of the Internet. Almost all were active before the World Wide Web got going, though they have all now been brought into its scope. You can reach these sites and download their files through your browser, but if you want to **upload** files, you will need dedicated FTP software.

Shareware sites

Shareware is software that you can download and use – on a trial basis – free, but for which you should pay (typically £5 to £25) if you continue to use it after the trial period. The quality varies. At one extreme, there are excellent, highly professional programs like **Paint Shop Pro** and **WinZip**; at the other end are simple games and utilities written by enthusiastic amateurs.

Some sites exist mainly to distribute shareware. Most of these do not merely store the files (or provide links to the sites where they are stored), they also test and review them. You can be reasonably sure that any file from a good shareware site, will be free of viruses and that it will do what it claims.

Jargon

Downloading – transferring a file from a distant computer onto your machine.

Uploading – sending files from your computer to the online host, for others to download.

Paint Shop Pro – shareware program for creating and editing images, and for converting between graphic formats.

WinZip – the standard Windows software for compressing and for unpacking files. It can reduce file sizes by up to 95%. Files are often Zipped for faster downloading.

Shareware sites can be reached and their files downloaded through your browser. Some will have an area into which you can upload your own efforts – but again you need dedicated FTP software for this.

Software houses

Most computer companies run Web sites – for marketing and technical support, but also to distribute upgrades, bug-fixes and beta-test versions. If you hit problems with any software, or want the latest driver for your printer, head for the manufacturer's site. The files that you need may be there, for you to download.

The URL for a company's home page usually takes the form:

> http://www.companyname.com   (USA/international)
> http://www.companyname.co.uk   (UK)

If this doesn't work, go to Yahoo and look it up in their **Companies** menu.

Enthusiasts' pages and news articles

Individual enthusiasts' pages often include links to files that relate to their particular interests – look out for them as you browse. And don't forget newsgroups – they can also be a good source of files on specialist interests and topics.

Downloading linked files

Downloadable files are usually easy to identify. For a start – like all links – they will be underlined and in a different colour! The names may be shown in filename form, such as *gwaw95.exe*, or as the program title, e.g. *Graphics Workshop*.

If you point to filename, and look in the status line, you will see the URL. This will show you the nature of the link. This may be:

● directly to the file, shown by **ftp://** at the start and a filename at the end, e.g.

ftp://mrcnext.cso.uiuc.edu/pub/win3/desktop/ psp30.zip

If the filename has the **.zip** extension, it is Zip-compressed, and will need WinZip to extract it. Those ending **.exe** are often also Zip-compressed, but are self-extracting.

● to an FTP site, shown by **ftp://** at the start and **/** at the end, e.g.

ftp://gated.cornell.edu/pub/video/

Before you follow this link, make a careful note of the filename as you will have to hunt for the file when you reach the ftp site.

● to a page which contains it, shown by **http://** at the start and **.html** or **.htm** at the end, e.g.

http://pc.inrird.com/cgirend.html

Once there, you should find download instructions.

1 Point to the link and read the URL in the status bar.

❏ File URLs

2 Click on the link.

3 When the Save dialog opens, select the folder but leave the original filename.

❏ FTP site URLs

4 Make a note of the filename.

5 Click on the link, then follow the steps for saving from shareware sites on page 188.

Tip

If the lines to the site are busy, the download speed may be far too slow (under 1 Kb/sec). At times like this, it is often better cancel the download, to write down the URL, and try again later.

Take note

There's loads of Windows 95 software around, but very little
labelled 'Windows 98'. Don't worry about it! Windows 95 and
98 are the same as far as software is concerned.

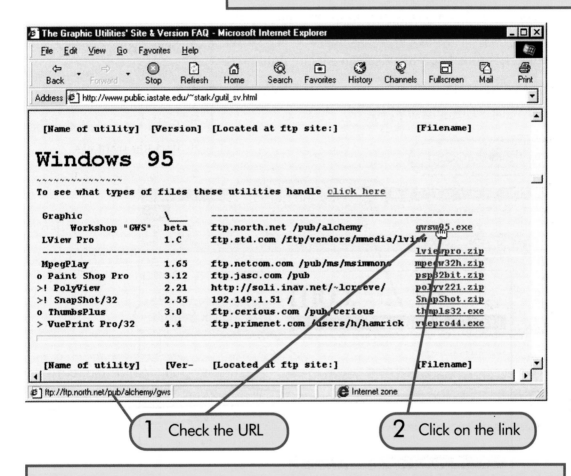

[Name of utility]	[Version]	[Located at ftp site:]	[Filename]

Windows 95

~~~~~~~~~~~~~~

To see what types of files these utilities handle click here

Graphic	___	--	
Workshop "GWS"	beta	ftp.north.net /pub/alchemy	gwsw95.exe
LView Pro	1.C	ftp.std.com /ftp/vendors/mmedia/lview	
-------------------------			lviewpro.zip
MpegPlay	1.65	ftp.netcom.com /pub/ms/msimmons	mpegw32h.zip
o Paint Shop Pro	3.12	ftp.jasc.com /pub	psp32bit.zip
>! PolyView	2.21	http://soli.inav.net/~lcreeve/	polyv221.zip
>! SnapShot/32	2.55	192.149.1.51 /	SnapShot.zip
o ThumbsPlus	3.0	ftp.cerious.com /pub/cerious	thmpls32.exe
> VuePrint Pro/32	4.4	ftp.primenet.com /users/h/hamrick	vuepro44.exe

[Name of utility]	[Ver-	[Located at ftp site:]	[Filename]

ftp://ftp.north.net/pub/alchemy/gws   Internet zone

1 Check the URL

2 Click on the link

Take note

Shareware can be tried without charge, but you should pay the small registration fee if
you are going to use it. Some programs — including some excellent utilities,
programming tools and the hugely successful Linux operating system — are freeware!

Shareware at c|net

One of the best places for shareware (and freeware) programs is **shareware.com**. This is run by c|net which also provides a range of other services to Internet users.

- If you are looking for particular software – and know its name or words that might appear in its brief description – use the Search facility. In the example, A search for 'capture' has found dozens of screen capture utilities.

- If you are just starting to build your shareware collection, try the What's Hot selection.

1 Go to: http://www.shareware.com

2 In the Search slot, type the program name or a descriptive word.

3 Select your operating system.

4 Click Search and wait.

5 Read the descriptions to find the right file.

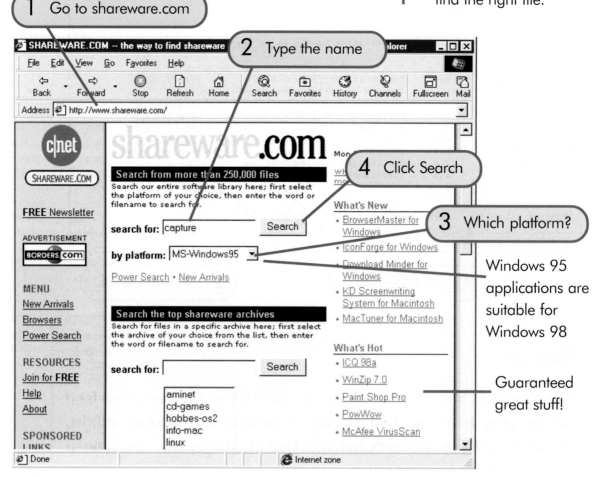

1 Go to shareware.com

2 Type the name

4 Click Search

3 Which platform?

Windows 95 applications are suitable for Windows 98

Guaranteed great stuff!

188

6 Click on the filename to start the download.

7 Select the folder, edit the name if you want to, and click Save to save the file.

Tip

clnet has loads more software for downloading at gamecenter.com and download.com

Check the size – is it worth the download time?

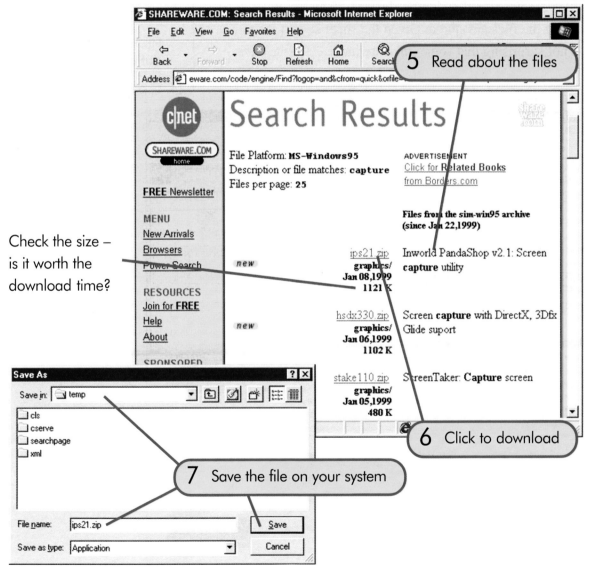

SHAREWARE.COM: Search Results - Microsoft Internet Explorer

File   Edit   View   Go   Favorites   Help

Back   Forward   Stop   Refresh   Home   Searc

Address   eware.com/code/engine/Find?logop=and&cfrom=quick&orfile=

5 Read about the files

Search Results

File Platform: **MS-Windows95**
Description or file matches: **capture**
Files per page: **25**

MENU
New Arrivals
Browsers
Power Search

RESOURCES
Join for **FREE**
Help
About

SPONSORED

ADVERTISEMENT
Click for Related Books
from Borders.com

Files from the sim-win95 archive (since Jan 22,1999)

ips21.zip   Inworld PandaShop v2.1: Screen
new   **graphics/**   **capture** utility
    Jan 08,1999
    1121 K

hsdx330.zip   Screen **capture** with DirectX, 3Dfx
new   **graphics/**   Glide suport
    Jan 06,1999
    1102 K

stake110.zip   ScreenTaker: **Capture** screen
    graphics/
    Jan 05,1999
    480 K

6 Click to download

Save As

Save in: temp

cls
cserve
searchpage
xml

7 Save the file on your system

File name: ips21.zip   Save

Save as type: Application   Cancel

Shareware at Jumbo

At the time of writing, Spring 1999, Jumbo has over 300,000 files at the tip of its trunk – and increasing by nearly 10,000 a month. Despite this rate of growth, the files are well organised, with brief descriptions in the main listings. Fuller descriptions, sometimes accompanied by ratings, are given at the download page for each file.

Files are not stored at Jumbo. Instead, there are links to sites where the files are stored. Given the sheer size of the place, it is not surprising that some links are incorrect or inactive.

1 Go to Jumbo at:
http://www.jumbo.com

2 Select a channel.

3 Work through the sub-divisions to reach the right type of file.

4 Read the descriptions – click on a name to find out more about it.

5 Click 🖫 to download.

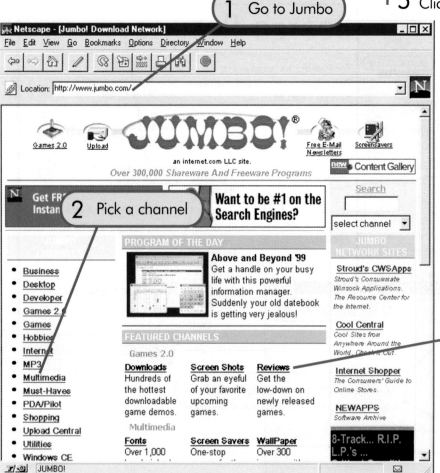

Check out the features if you are just browsing to see what's around

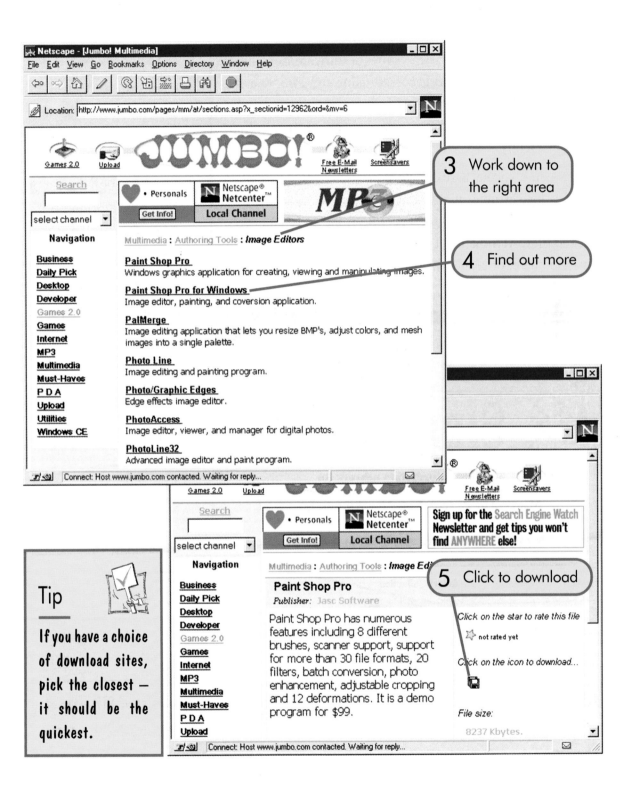

3 Work down to the right area

4 Find out more

5 Click to download

Tip

If you have a choice of download sites, pick the closest — it should be the quickest.

191

FTP sites

There are thousands of FTP sites – stores of software, documents and other files that can be accessed using the File Transfer Protocol. Most universities, most Internet access and service providers, and many government and commercial organisations offer this facility.

At some sites, you get bare directory listings. As these are plain text, they load in quite quickly, but finding stuff can be difficult. Some of the better sites have HTML front ends and well-indexed files. At Simtel.Net you can browse the collections, as illustrated here, or search for particular files. Simtel.Net is at:

http://www.simtel.net/simtel.net/

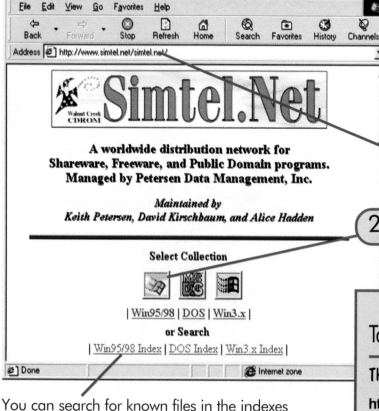

You can search for known files in the indexes

Basic steps

1 Go to Simtel.Net.

2 Click on a collection – and some of the older DOS and Win3.x stuff is worth looking at.

3 Scroll through the list or click a letter to jump down the list.

4 Click on a topic name.

5 Scroll through the files, reading the descriptions.

6 Click on a filename to start downloading and save as usual in the Save As dialog box.

1 Go to the site

2 Pick a collection

Take note

There's a full list of FTP sites at:

http://hoohoo.ncsa.uiuc.edu/ftp

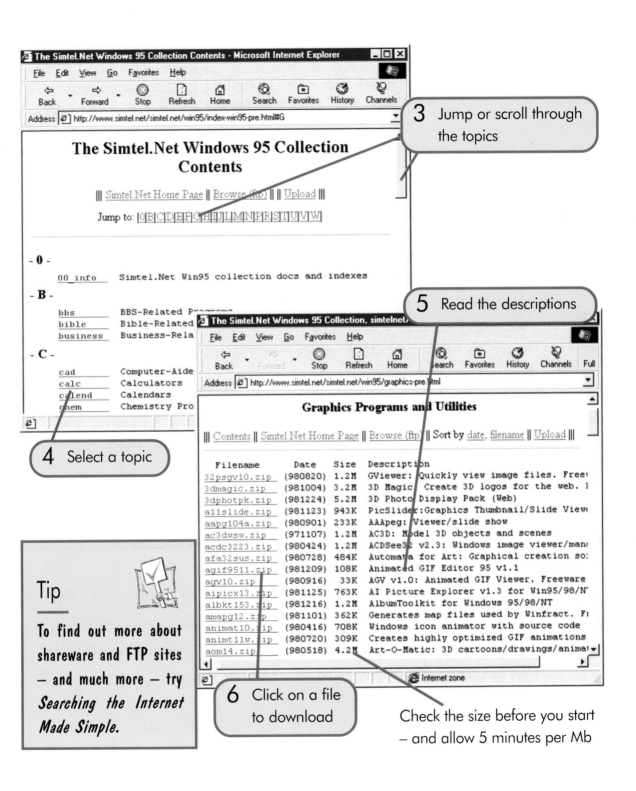

3 Jump or scroll through the topics

5 Read the descriptions

4 Select a topic

Tip

To find out more about shareware and FTP sites – and much more – try *Searching the Internet Made Simple.*

6 Click on a file to download

Check the size before you start – and allow 5 minutes per Mb

WS_FTP

If you use the FTP sites a lot, or you want to upload files, you should get some dedicated FTP software. WS_FTP is probably the best of these – and it's free. There are several versions of WS_FTP. The one illustrated here is for Windows 95/98. Get a copy from the author's (John Junod) home site at:

http://www.ipswitch.com

Anonymous login

When connecting to an FTP site, you normally give 'anonymous' as the user name and your e-mail address as the password. This is known as **anonymous login**. The main exception is when you use FTP to upload your home page files to your access provider's site. Then, you will give the same User ID and password that you use when logging in at the start of a normal session.

With WS_FTP, you give your e-mail address during the installation process, so it is in place when needed in setting up a new connection.

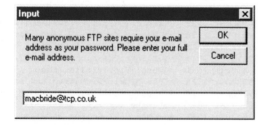

Making the connection

WS_FTP is simple enough to use – just tell it where you want to go, and what directory to start at, then send it off to make the connection. The connection information for a site is stored in its profile, so only has to be entered once. See the steps opposite.

Tip

You can run WS_FTP alongside your browser, or by itself. The only essential is that you are logged onto the Internet.

Take note

You must know the exact host name. If you also know the path to the directory, it speeds things up. If you do not give it, you will start at the top of the directory structure and have to work your way down.

Basic steps

1 Go online then run
   WS_FTP.

2 Pick a site from the
   Profile list – there are a
   dozen already set up.

or

3 Create a profile for a
   new site. Click New
   and enter a profile
   name and the exact
   Host name.

4 If this uses the (normal)
   anonymous login, tick
   Anonymous.

5 Switch to the Startup tab
   and enter the Remote
   Host Directory, if
   known.

6 Click Apply if you
   have set up a new
   profile, or made
   changes that you want
   to keep.

7 Click OK to start
   the connection.

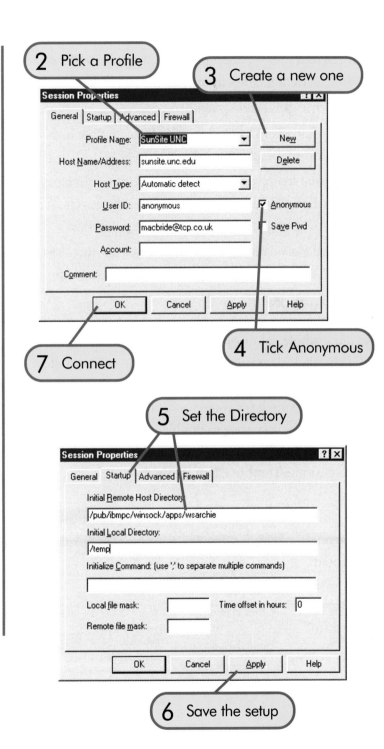

2 Pick a Profile

3 Create a new one

7 Connect

4 Tick Anonymous

5 Set the Directory

6 Save the setup

195

Working at an FTP site

FTP gives you a two-way, interactive connection to the remote host. You can treat its directories and files as if they were in a drive in your own machine – almost.

● Downloading is like copying a file from another disk – but much slower. Be patient.

● If you want to upload a file, only do so into a directory that welcomes contributions – if you can't see one called UPLOADS, they probably don't want your files.

● Don't delete or edit files or directories on the Host – it shouldn't let you, but it might have let its guard slip.

WS_FTP options

There are a whole set of options that you can set to fine-tune WS_FTP – click the **Options** button on the main window to reach them. Most options can be safely left at their defaults until you have been using it for some time, but there is one that you should check. It's very easy to double-click by mistake. What do you want to happen when you do this? Go to the **Advanced** tab, and select the **Double Click Action.**

What should happen when you double-click on a file?

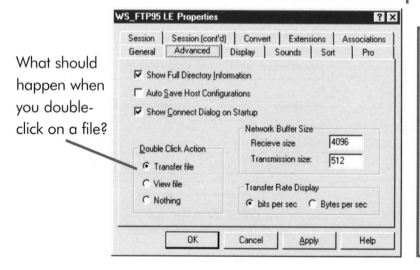

Basic steps

❑ Downloading

1 Change directory if need be – use the same techniques as in any File Manager.

2 Highlight a file that interests you.

3 Set the directory on your local system to receive a file.

4 Opt for ASCII to transfer text files, Binary for any others.

5 Click to download.

6 Use Close to return to the first panel and set up a new session.

7 Click Exit to end.

Take note

There are lots of types of files out there on the Internet – but there are also the applications that you need to view them (see pages 202 to 209).

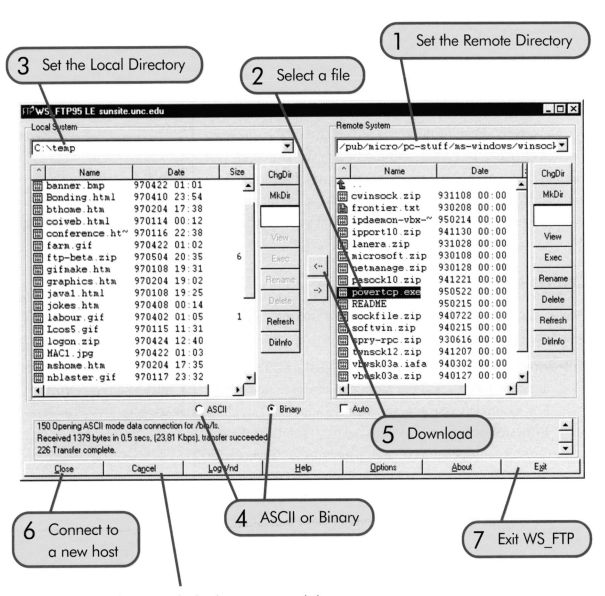

3 Set the Local Directory

2 Select a file

1 Set the Remote Directory

5 Download

4 ASCII or Binary

6 Connect to a new host

7 Exit WS_FTP

This cancels the last command, but leaves you still connected to the host

FTP WS_FTP95 LE sunsite.unc.edu

Local System

C:\temp

Name	Date	Size
banner.bmp	970422 01:01	
Bonding.html	970410 23:54	
bthome.htm	970204 17:38	
coiweb.html	970114 00:12	
conference.ht~	970116 22:38	
farm.gif	970422 01:02	
ftp-beta.zip	970504 20:35	6
gifmake.htm	970108 19:31	
graphics.htm	970204 19:02	
java1.html	970108 19:25	
jokes.htm	970408 00:14	
labour.gif	970402 01:05	1
Lcos5.gif	970115 11:31	
logon.zip	970424 12:40	
MAC1.jpg	970422 01:03	
mshome.htm	970204 17:35	
nblaster.gif	970117 23:32	

ChgDir
MkDir
View
Exec
Rename
Delete
Refresh
DirInfo

Remote System

/pub/micro/pc-stuff/ms-windows/winsock

Name	Date	
..		
cwinsock.zip	931108 00:00	
frontier.txt	930208 00:00	
ipdaemon-vbx-~	950214 00:00	
ipport10.zip	941130 00:00	
lanera.zip	931028 00:00	
microsoft.zip	930108 00:00	
netmanage.zip	930128 00:00	
pasock10.zip	941221 00:00	
powertcp.exe	950522 00:00	
README	950215 00:00	
sockfile.zip	940722 00:00	
softwin.zip	940215 00:00	
spry-rpc.zip	930616 00:00	
twnsck12.zip	941207 00:00	
vbwsk03a.iafa	940302 00:00	
vbwsk03a.zip	940127 00:00	

ChgDir
MkDir
View
Exec
Rename
Delete
Refresh
DirInfo

○ ASCII ● Binary □ Auto

150 Opening ASCII mode data connection for /bin/ls.
Received 1379 bytes in 0.5 secs, (23.81 Kbps), transfer succeeded
226 Transfer complete.

Close | Cancel | LogWnd | Help | Options | About | Exit

197

Archie

Browsing FTP sites is not an efficient way to find a file. You will find it far quicker if you know where to look, and for this you need Archie.

Scattered over the Internet are a number of hosts that act as Archie servers. Each of these has a database of the directory listings of major FTP sites, and a program for searching that database. The Archie servers know the names, locations, sizes and dates of last update of the files of those sites, though they do not know what is in the files, what type they are or what they do.

Search types

Archie can use one of four different matching methods as it searches its database.

Substring: Looks for the given string within the names of files and directories – and the more you can give, the better. For example, a search for Paint Shop Pro (graphics software) with '**psp**' produces nearly 100 hits, including 'crystalswa**psp**eedup.txt' and '**psp**lan.ps.Z'. Trying with '**pspro**' gets around 20 hits, including 'XD**PSpro**to.h', 's**pspro**g.txt' and '**pspro**41.zip' or '**pspro**501ev.zip' – two of the more recent versions of the Paint Shop Pro package.

Substring (case-sensitive): As substring, but matching lower/upper case characters exactly as given. '**pspro**' would not find 'XD**PSpro**to.h' (good), but equally, '**PSPRO**' would not find '**pspro**41.zip' (bad).

Exact: Looks for an exact match. This gets results fastest, but you must know precisely what you want. If you are looking for shareware or beta-test software, this approach

Take note

You can get dedicated Archie software – WsArchie is excellent – but unless you want to find an awful lot of files, it is much simpler to use an Archie gateway on the Web (see page 200).

may miss the latest versions. For example, the latest beta of Netscape at the time of writing was '**n32e45.exe**', but searching for this now will give you an out-of-date copy. A substring search for '**n32e**' will be more productive.

Regex: Use *regular expressions* when matching. These are similar to DOS wildcards. But not that similar – the differences are significant.

Regular expressions

The wildcard '.' (dot) stands for any single character. This was a rotten choice, as dot is an essential part of most filenames. If you want to use dot for its proper meaning – not as a wildcard – put a backslash in front of it '\.'

> 'winzip\.exe' will find the file 'winzip.exe'
>
> 'winzip.exe' will look for 'winzip**A**exe', 'winzip**B**exe', etc. and probably find nothing!

'*' is a repeater, standing for any number of whatever character was written before it. 'A*' means any number of A's. Use '.*' to stand for any set of any characters.

> 'babel.*txt' will look for files that start with 'babel', end with 'txt' and have something (or nothing) in between.

You can specify a set of alternative single characters by enclosing them in square brackets – '[...]'

> 'babel99[**ab**]\.txt' finds 'babel99**a**.txt' and 'babel99**b**.txt'

- Ranges can be defined with '-', e.g. [**A-F**] is the same as [**ABCDEF**];

- '^' at the start of a range means match characters that are *not* in the list, e.g. [**^A-Z**] means ignore all capitals.

Archie through the Web

To run an Archie search from your browser, go to Yahoo and select *Computers and Internet – Internet – FTP Sites – Searching:Archie.* There you will find a number of links labelled Archie Request Form or Archie Gateway.

1 Go to an Archie Request Form.

2 Enter the search string.

3 Set the Database to Anonymous FTP.

4 Select the Search Type.

5 Set the Case.

6 Start the search.

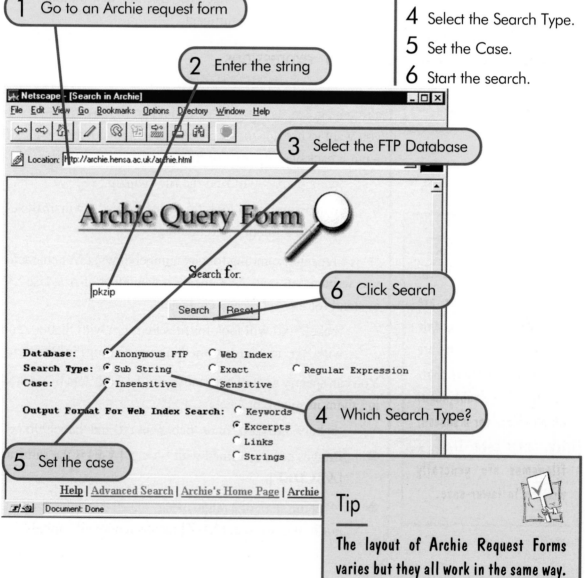

1 Go to an Archie request form

2 Enter the string

3 Select the FTP Database

Netscape - [Search in Archie]

File Edit View Go Bookmarks Options Directory Window Help

Location: http://archie.hensa.ac.uk/archie.html

Archie Query Form

Search for:

pkzip

Search   Reset

6 Click Search

Database: ⦿ Anonymous FTP   ○ Web Index
Search Type: ⦿ Sub String   ○ Exact   ○ Regular Expression
Case: ⦿ Insensitive   ○ Sensitive

Output Format For Web Index Search: ○ Keywords
                                      ⦿ Excerpts
                                      ○ Links
                                      ○ Strings

4 Which Search Type?

5 Set the case

Help | Advanced Search | Archie's Home Page | Archie

Document: Done

Tip

The layout of Archie Request Forms varies but they all work in the same way.

200

Files from an Archie Gateway

7 Scroll through the results to find the file.

8 Click on a filename to download the file.

❑ If the site or directory is linked, you can go to it to browse for files.

If your Archie search is productive, you will get a page or more listing the results. Here you will see the FTP sites, directories and name of the matching files. Sometimes all of these will be hyperlinked; sometimes there will only be a link to the file itself.

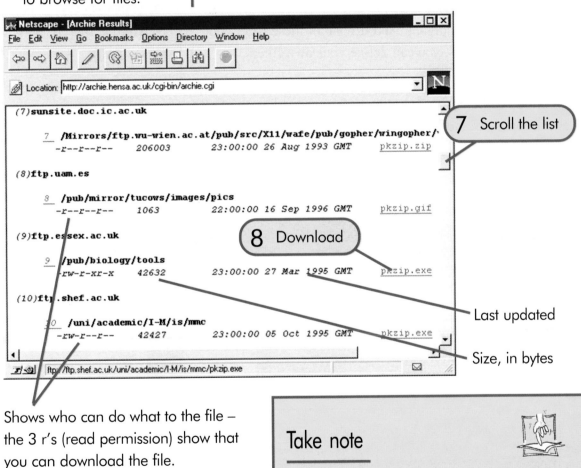

Shows who can do what to the file – the 3 r's (read permission) show that you can download the file.

Some Archie gateways give simpler displays.

Graphics viewers

If you have found images files that you cannot view, you need something like Paint Shop Pro. This great shareware graphics package can cope with just about every graphic format from Word Perfect graphics to Kodak PhotoCD. It also has an excellent set for tools for creating images, and has superb editing facilities for working on existing pictures. Its approach to filters is a good example of its simplicity of use and its power. The Filter Browser gives you a wide range of effects, which you can preview before applying. And if none of these meet your exacting requirements, you can define your own filters.

Paint Shop Pro being used to edit a Monet – gilding the lily?
Monet courtesy of the Web Museum, at http://sunsite.doc.ic.ac.uk/wm/

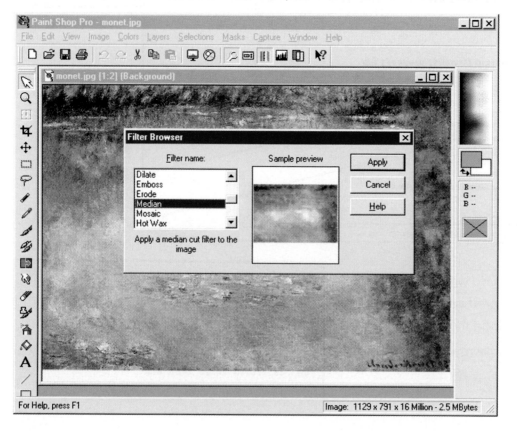

Basic steps

1 Open the File menu and select Batch Conversion...

2 Set the Look in: folder.

3 Set the Files of type for input.

4 Select the files.

Or

5 Click Select All.

6 Set the Output Type.

7 Set the Output folder.

8 Click Start.

Batch conversion

If you have a set of files in one format that you want to convert to another, they can be processed all at once through Paint Shop Pro's efficient batch conversion facility.

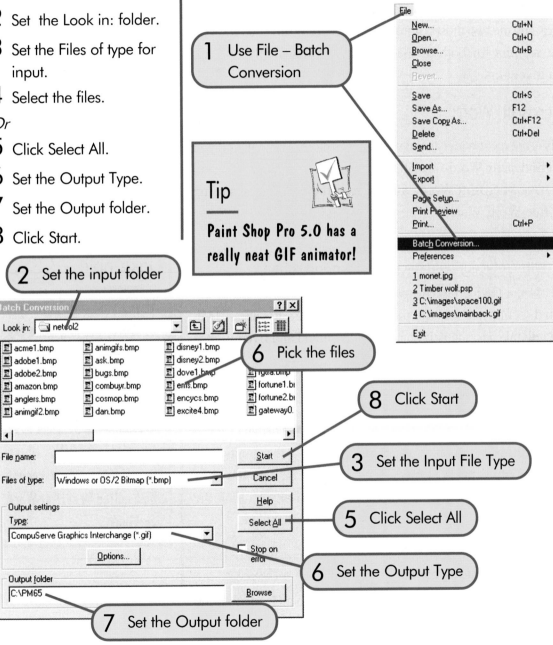

1 Use File – Batch Conversion

Tip

Paint Shop Pro 5.0 has a really neat GIF animator!

File

New...	Ctrl+N
Open...	Ctrl+O
Browse...	Ctrl+B
Close	
Revert...	
Save	Ctrl+S
Save As...	F12
Save Copy As...	Ctrl+F12
Delete	Ctrl+Del
Send...	
Import	▶
Export	▶
Page Setup...	
Print Preview	
Print...	Ctrl+P
Batch Conversion...	
Preferences	▶
1 monet.jpg	
2 Timber wolf.psp	
3 C:\images\space100.gif	
4 C:\images\mainback.gif	
Exit	

2 Set the input folder

Batch Conversion

Look in: netool2

acme1.bmp	animgifs.bmp	disney1.bmp
adobe1.bmp	ask.bmp	disney2.bmp
adobe2.bmp	bugs.bmp	dove1.bmp
amazon.bmp	combuyr.bmp	enfs.bmp
anglers.bmp	cosmop.bmp	encycs.bmp
animgif2.bmp	dan.bmp	excite4.bmp

rgwa.bmp	
fortune1.bi	
fortune2.bi	
gateway0.	

6 Pick the files

8 Click Start

File name:

Files of type: Windows or OS/2 Bitmap (*.bmp)

3 Set the Input File Type

Start

Cancel

Help

Select All

5 Click Select All

Output settings
Type:
CompuServe Graphics Interchange (*.gif)
Options...

☐ Stop on error

6 Set the Output Type

Output folder
C:\PM65

Browse

7 Set the Output folder

203

Text viewers

Much of the text that is on the Web is in HTML format – ideal for browsers; much of the text elsewhere on the Internet is plain ASCII text, that can be read with any editor or word-processor. However, there are also quite a few formatted text files out there, and the two most common formats are Word and Acrobat. The viewers for both of these are distributed freely by their manufacturers.

Microsoft Word

This is the most widely used word-processor at present, and you will find many Word-formatted documents on the Net. If you do not have Microsoft Word, you can read these documents using the free Word Viewer.

Get it through the Web at:

http://officeupdate.microsoft.com/index.htm

This is the Office Update page at Microsoft's site. Go to the **Word** section and look for the Word 97 viewer. It's about 4Mb and will take around half an hour to download and five minutes to install.

Acrobat Reader

This is a viewer for PDF (Portable Document Format) files, a cross-platform format devised by Adobe – the Fonts and PageMaker people. A PDF file can be viewed on a Windows or DOS PC, a Mac or a Unix machine, and will always look the same – as long as suitable reader software is installed.

Get your copy from the Web at:

http://www.adobe.com

and look in the Products section for the Acrobat Reader. At the time of writing version 4.0 was about to be released.

Take note

If you have an old version of Word, you may need the Word Viewer to be able to read some files. Windows 95/98 users are moving over to Word 97 (and soon to Word 2000), which have features that cannot be handled by earlier Word versions.

Tip

It is typically 3 to 4 times faster to download by FTP than off a Web page.

You can also get Acrobat Reader 3.0 by FTP from:

ftp://ftp.adobe.com/pub/adobe/acrobatreader/win/3.x/

where you will find a whole bunch of alternatives – 'ar32e30.exe' is the English language version. Run this to extract the files and install them into an Acrobat directory in one operation.

The control buttons let you zoom in and out, change pages, print and search for items.

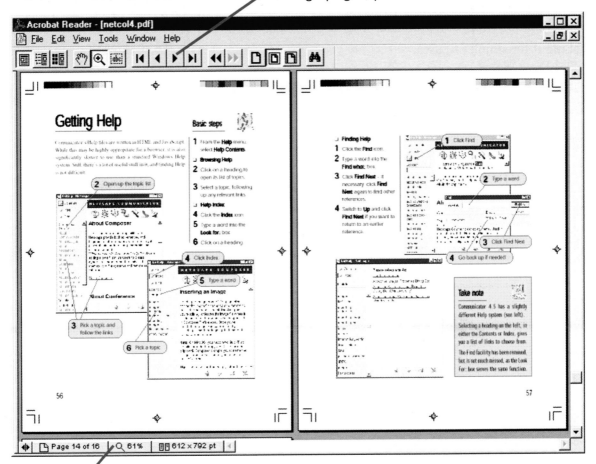

Use this panel to move through the pages, or turn it off for a larger viewing area.

PDF files are quite compact. A double page spread from this heavily-illustrated book is only around 40Kb.

Ghostview & Ghostscript

PostScript is another common document format. If you have a suitable printer, PostScript files present no problems. Simply download them, then pass them directly to the printer. You may not be able to view them on screen, but at least you can get paper copies.

If you do not have a PostScript printer, the answer lies in GhostScript. This can read PostScript files and convert them for screen display – and for output to other printers. Ghostview, its companion program, is a graphical interface to Ghostscript – making it far simpler to use.

Take note

PostScript files are often used for technical diagrams, music scores and other documents with a mixture of formatted text and drawings.

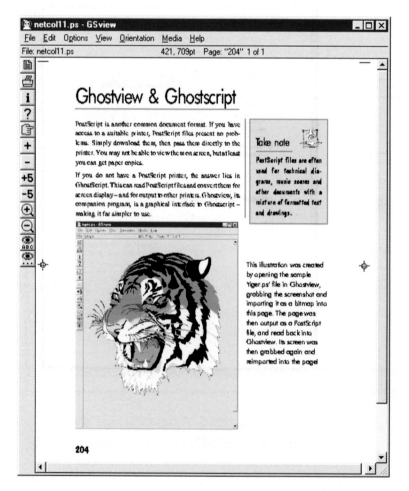

This illustration was created by opening the sample 'tiger.ps' file in Ghostview, grabbing the screenshot and importing the image into this page. The page was then output as a PostScript file, and read back into Ghostview. Its screen was then grabbed again and reimported into the page!

Getting and setting up

At the time of writing, the latest versions were Ghostview 2.7, and Ghostscript 5.50. Updates are posted onto the Internet regularly, so check the numbering and the dates before you download. The simplest way to get them is to go to the Ghostscript page at the University of Wisconsin:

http://www.cs.wisc.edu/~ghost/index.html

From here you can download the self-extracting EXE file, gsv27550.exe, which install both programs and all their files.

If you are working within an organisation that does not let you download EXE files, you can get the software as a set of four Zip files, which you will have to extract and install for yourself.

gs550ini.zip   core files, and samples

gs550w32.zip   GhostScript for Windows

gs550fn1.zip   PostScript fonts

gsv27w32.zip   Ghostview

UnZip *gs550ini.zip* first. This includes *Readme.htm* and *install.htm* which give details of the system and instructions on installation. When unpacked the files will take up just under 6Mb of disk space.

PDFs

The latest version of Ghostscript can also read PDF files, so if you have got this, you don't really need Acrobat Reader – though the Reader is a little slicker and easier to use.

Take note

You can run Ghostscript without Ghostview, but not the other way round. Ghostscript uses complex command lines to load and interpret files; Ghostview gives you simple menu and icon controls and converts these into commands which it then passes to Ghostscript.

Multimedia

As you browse around the Internet you will meet many different kinds of audio and video files. There are dozens of formats, falling into two broad categories – those where the file must be fully downloaded before it can be viewed or played, and those that can be seen or heard in real time.

The main problem with any audio or video files is that they take a lot of bandwidth, and there isn't that much available. Unless you get on-line from within an organisation that links to the Internet through a high-speed, dedicated line, you cannot access it at faster than 56,600 baud (5.5Kb per second). And this is at a quiet time on a good day! More typically, data will come in at 1 to 2 Kb per second – and rarely as a constant, steady flow.

Download first

Files in some of these formats, such as WAV, AVI and MPEG, can be handled by Windows' or the browsers' own routines. For others, including QuickTime, a very popular video format, you need special players or plug-ins. QuickTime is often found on computer magazines' cover CD, or can be downloaded from Apple (www.apple.com). The same package produces the stand-alone and the plug-in software.

Video clips have a very poor download to play time ratio. A 1Mb file – up to 10 minutes to download – will run for 15 to 20 seconds. And it'll be a small, grainy picture. Better compression techniques are improving the ratio and the picture quality, but there's a long way to go before the Internet replaces TV broadcasts!

Take note

Quicktime installs itself as **PLAY32.EXE** (audio/video) and **VIEW32.EXE** (JPGs) in the **WINDOWS** directory, plus other files in **WINDOWS/SYSTEM.**

Real-time multimedia

Macromedia are the leading developers of multimedia players. Shockwave and Flash are much used to create animated and interactive illustrations; and Shockrave can be used to create games.

With 'streaming' audio and video, the files begin to play within seconds of starting to download. It's not quite real time, in the way that TV and radio is, but it's close. The quality is not too bad for voice 'broadcasts', but I wouldn't want to listen to much streamed music or watch streamed videos for long.

Netscape can handle some streaming audio and video through its own Live Audio and Media Player plug-ins, but for the increasingly popular Real formats, you'll need RealPlayer – available through Netcenter or direct from **www.real.com**.

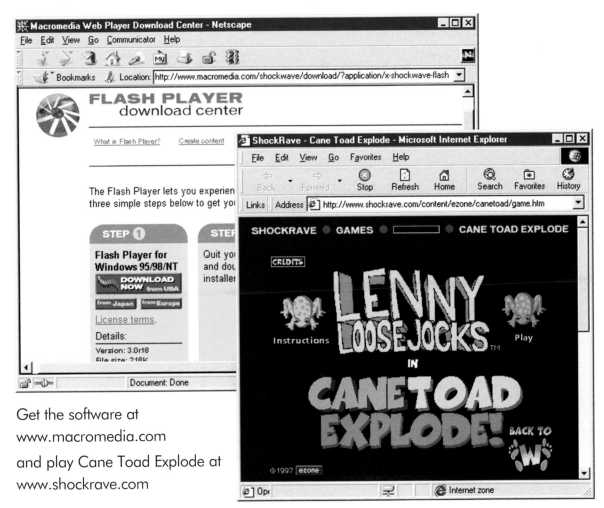

Get the software at
www.macromedia.com
and play Cane Toad Explode at
www.shockrave.com

Summary

◆ You can find files at FTP sites, shareware sites, and in the home pages of companies and individual users.

◆ If you want to download a file that is linked from a Web page, just click on the link.

◆ shareware.com has a large collection of shareware – and an excellent search facility for finding programs.

◆ Jumbo has one of the biggest collections of shareware.

◆ FTP sites hold vast quantities of files, but can be hard to use. Some have catalogs, with descriptions of the files, making the archives much more accessible.

◆ You can reach the FTP sites, browse their directories and download files through your Web browser.

◆ If you want to download files regularly, it is worth getting and learning to use WS_FTP.

◆ Archie is a program for searching for files in the Internet's FTP archives. It lives, alongside its database, on Archie servers.

◆ Archie searches can be for Exact or Substring matches, or can use regular expressions.

◆ You can reach Archie servers through the Web, and run your searches there.

◆ Browsers can cope with the majority of files used on Web pages, but you may need to get extra software to be able to view some types of graphics, formatted text and multimedia files.

12 Creating Web pages

HTML

Most access providers now offer to their customers the facilities to set up their own home pages. People use them to advertise their work, their products, their clubs, their hobbies – themselves!

HTML – HyperText Markup Language – is the system used to produce Web pages. Essentially, it is a set of tags (codes) that specify text styles, draw lines, display images, handle URL links and the other features that create Web pages. It is not difficult to use. There are only a limited number of tags and they follow fairly strict rules. All tags are enclosed in <angle brackets> to mark them off from the text, and they are normally used in pairs – one at the start and one at the end of the text that they affect. For example:

    <H1> This is a main heading </H1>

Notice that the closing tag is the same as the opener, except that it has a forward slash at the start.

All pages have the same outline structure:

```
<HTML>
<HEAD>
    <TITLE>My Gnome Page</TITLE>
</HEAD>
<BODY>
    This page is under construction
</BODY>
</HTML>
```

The whole text is enclosed by **<HTML>** and **</HTML>** tags.

The **<HEAD>** area holds information about the page, and is not displayed – though the Title does appear in the browser's Title bar when loaded. This can be left blank.

The **<BODY>** area is where the main code goes.

Basic steps

1 Type your HTML text into NotePad.

2 Save the document with an '.HTM' extension, e.g. 'MYPAGE.HTM'.

3 Start your browser – don't go online – and use Open File to load in the document.

4 Check the display and return to NotePad to enhance and improve!

Take note

HTML is easy to learn, and 'hand-coding' gives you better control over the appearance of your pages, but it is simpler and quicker to create Web pages with HTML editors such as Composer or FrontPage Express (see Chapters 13 and 14).

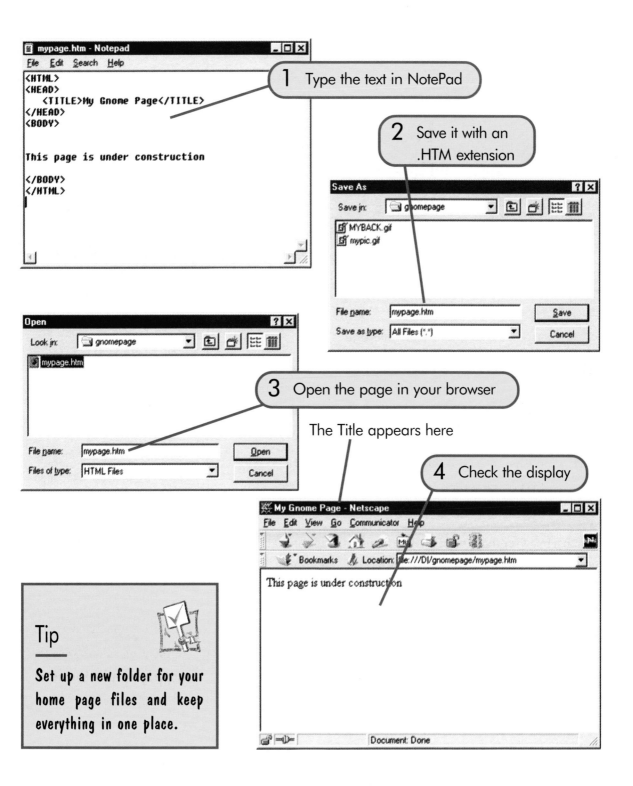

1 Type the text in NotePad

2 Save it with an .HTM extension

3 Open the page in your browser

The Title appears here

4 Check the display

Tip

Set up a new folder for your home page files and keep everything in one place.

213

Text tags

The simplest tags are the ones that format text. These will produce six levels of headings, a small, italicised style (mainly used for e-mail addresses), and bold and italic for emphasis.

<H1>	</H1>	# Heading 1
<H2>	</H2>	## Heading 2
<H3>	</H3>	### Heading 3
<H4>	</H4>	**Heading 4**
<H5>	</H5>	**Heading 5**
<H6>	</H6>	**Heading 6**
<B>	</B>	**Bold**
<I>	</I>	*Italic*
<Address>	</Address>	*Small italic style*

The Heading and Address tags break the text up into separate lines, but untagged text appears as a continuous stream – no matter how you lay it out in NotePad. Create separate paragraphs with these tags:

<P>	Start a new paragaph with a space before and after
</P>	End of paragraph (optional)
 	Start a new line without a space before it

When a browser reads an HTML document, it ignores all spaces (apart from a single space between words), tabs and new lines. What this means is that it doesn't matter how you lay out your HTML text. You can indent it, and add line breaks to make it easier for you to read, but it won't affect what your readers see – only the tags affect the layout of the page in the browser.

Tip

If you come across a great Web page and want to know how it was created, use the View Document Source command to see the HTML code.

If you want to use someone else's page as a model for your own, use File Save As to save it on your hard disk. You can then open it in NotePad or WordPad and study it at leisure.

You should not reuse anyone's text or images without their permission – the page author owns its copyright, whether it is claimed or not.

```
<HTML>
<HEAD>
 <TITLE>My Gnome Page</TITLE>
</HEAD>
<BODY>
 <H1>My Gnome Page</H1>
 <H3>Hello and welcome</H3>
 <H2>Gnomic sayings</H2>
 <P>Every gnome should have one.
 <P>There's gno place like Gnome. (Old Alaskan proverb)
 <P>Gnome is where the heart is.
 <H2>Gnome computing</H2>
 Lots of links to go here!
 <BR>
 <H4>This page is under construction</H4>
 <ADDRESS>Ingrid Bottomlow </ADDRESS>
 <ADDRESS>Last Update: Mudday of this week</ADDRESS>
</BODY>
</HTML>
```

Compare the HTML code with the screen display and note the effect of the <H..> <ADDRESS> <P> and <BR> tags.

Why do these lines have tags at both ends? What would happen if both were enclosed in one set of <ADDRESS> </ADDRESS> tags?

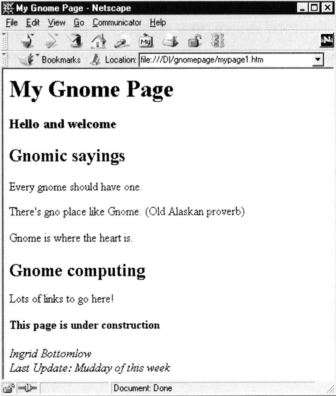
My Gnome Page - Netscape

File Edit View Go Communicator Help

Bookmarks Location: file:///D|/gnomepage/mypage1.htm

My Gnome Page

Hello and welcome

Gnomic sayings

Every gnome should have one.

There's gno place like Gnome. (Old Alaskan proverb)

Gnome is where the heart is.

Gnome computing

Lots of links to go here!

This page is under construction

Ingrid Bottomlow
Last Update: Mudday of this week

Document: Done

Colours

Text-only pages are fast to load, but can be a bit boring. Colour adds impact to your screens, without adding to the loading time.

Colours are defined by the values of their Red, Green and Blue components – given in that order and in hexadecimal digits. These values can be anything from 00 to FF, but are best set at 00 (off), 80 (half/dark) or FF (full power/bright), e.g.:

FFFF00

gives Red and Green at full, with no Blue, resulting in Yellow. Combinations of 00, 80 and FF values should come out true on all screens – other values may not.

BODY colours

The colours of the background and text of the page can be set by the **BGCOLOR** and **TEXT** options in the **BODY** tag.

<BODY BGCOLOR = "#FFFFFF" TEXT = "#008000">

This sets the background to White and the text to Dark Green.

Values are normally enclosed in "quotes" with a # at the start to show that they are hexadecimal. These can be omitted **TEXT = 008000** works just as well.

FONT COLOR

At any point on the page, you can change the colour of the text with the tag:

<FONT COLOR = "#Value" >

The colour is used for all following text until it is reset with another **<FONT COLOR = ... >** tag. You can use it to pick out words within normal text – though you can get strange results if you use the tags inside Headings.

Simple colour values

R	G	B	Colour
00	00	00	Black
80	80	80	Grey
FF	FF	FF	White
00	00	80	Navy Blue
00	00	FF	Blue
00	80	00	Green
00	FF	00	Lime
80	00	00	Maroon
FF	00	00	Red
00	80	80	Turquoise
80	00	80	Purple
80	80	00	Olive
00	FF	FF	Aqua
FF	00	FF	Fuchsia
FF	FF	00	Yellow

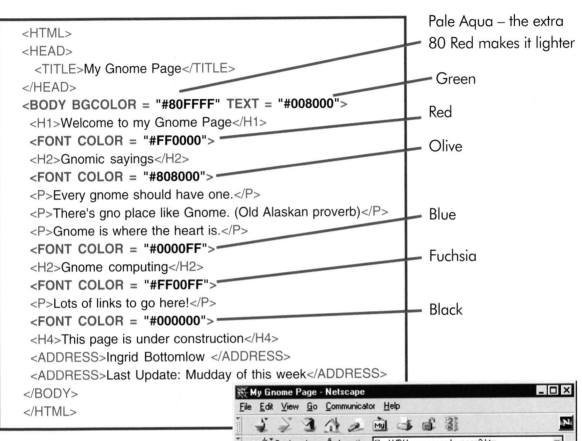

```
<HTML>
<HEAD>
  <TITLE>My Gnome Page</TITLE>
</HEAD>
<BODY BGCOLOR = "#80FFFF" TEXT = "#008000">
 <H1>Welcome to my Gnome Page</H1>
 <FONT COLOR = "#FF0000">
 <H2>Gnomic sayings</H2>
 <FONT COLOR = "#808000">
 <P>Every gnome should have one.</P>
 <P>There's gno place like Gnome. (Old Alaskan proverb)</P>
 <P>Gnome is where the heart is.</P>
 <FONT COLOR = "#0000FF">
 <H2>Gnome computing</H2>
 <FONT COLOR = "#FF00FF">
 <P>Lots of links to go here!</P>
 <FONT COLOR = "#000000">
 <H4>This page is under construction</H4>
 <ADDRESS>Ingrid Bottomlow </ADDRESS>
 <ADDRESS>Last Update: Mudday of this week</ADDRESS>
</BODY>
</HTML>
```

Pale Aqua – the extra 80 Red makes it lighter

Green

Red

Olive

Blue

Fuchsia

Black

Tip

You must have a good contrast in shade — as well as in hue — between your text colours and the background colour. These are too close together for easy reading.

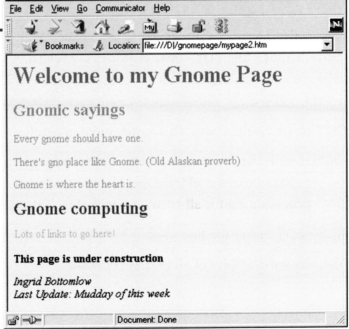

Lists and lines

Here are two more ways to enhance the appearance of your pages, without adding to download time.

Lists

These come in two varieties – bulleted and numbered. Both types are constructed in the same way.

- <OL> </OL>   (ordered/numbered) or <UL> </UL> (unordered/bulleted) enclose the whole list.

- Each item in the list is enclosed by <LI> </LI> tags,

e.g.

```
<UL>
   <LI> List item </LI>
   <LI> List item </LI>
   <LI> List item </LI>
</UL>
```

Lines

Also called Horizontal Rules, these are created with the tag <HR>. This is a single tag – there is no </HR> to end it. A simple <HR> produces a thin line with an indented effect. For variety, use the options:

SIZE to set the thickness. This is measured in pixels.

WIDTH can also be set in pixels, but is best given as a percentage of the width of the window – you don't know how wide your readers' windows will be.

NOSHADE makes the line solid.

You can see examples of all of these opposite.

Take note

Bullets are normally round. You can set the style to SQUARE, DISK or ROUND with the TYPE option, e.g.

<UL TYPE = DISK>

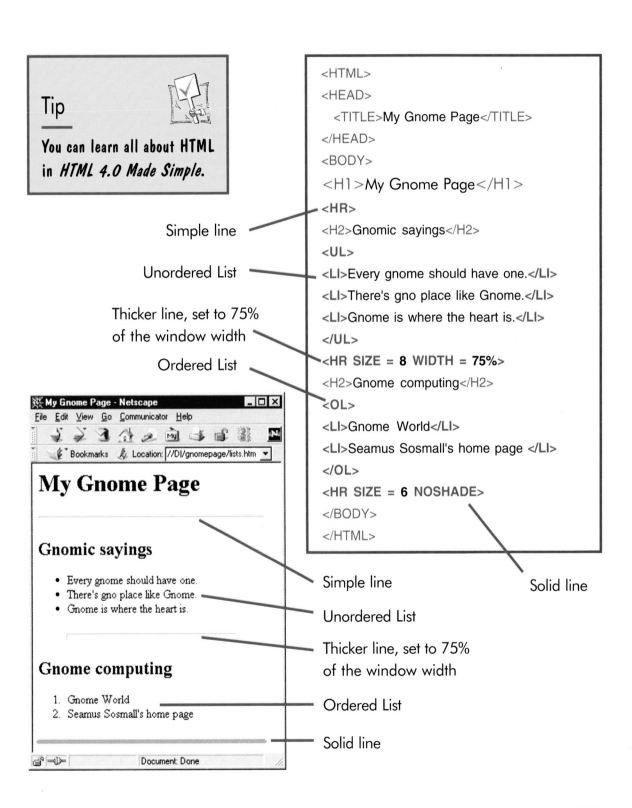

Tip
——
You can learn all about HTML in *HTML 4.0 Made Simple*.

Simple line

Unordered List

Thicker line, set to 75% of the window width

Ordered List

```
<HTML>
<HEAD>
  <TITLE>My Gnome Page</TITLE>
</HEAD>
<BODY>
<H1>My Gnome Page</H1>
<HR>
<H2>Gnomic sayings</H2>
<UL>
<LI>Every gnome should have one.</LI>
<LI>There's gno place like Gnome.</LI>
<LI>Gnome is where the heart is.</LI>
</UL>
<HR SIZE = 8 WIDTH = 75%>
<H2>Gnome computing</H2>
<OL>
<LI>Gnome World</LI>
<LI>Seamus Sosmall's home page </LI>
</OL>
<HR SIZE = 6 NOSHADE>
</BODY>
</HTML>
```

My Gnome Page - Netscape

File Edit View Go Communicator Help

Bookmarks Location: //DI/gnomepage/lists.htm

My Gnome Page

Gnomic sayings

- Every gnome should have one.
- There's gno place like Gnome.
- Gnome is where the heart is.

Gnome computing

1. Gnome World
2. Seamus Sosmall's home page

Document: Done

Simple line

Unordered List

Thicker line, set to 75% of the window width

Ordered List

Solid line

Solid line

219

Images

There's no doubt that images add greatly to a page, but there is a cost. Image files are very large compared to text files, and even small images will significantly increase the downloading time for a page. In the example opposite, the text takes 600 bytes – almost instant downloading – while the picture is over 26Kb and will take 10 seconds or more to come in. So, include images, but keep your visitors happy by following these rules:

● Keep the images as small as possible;

● If you want to display large images – perhaps your own photo gallery, put them on separate (linked) pages and tell your visitors how big they will be.

● Include text describing the image, for the benefit of those who browse with AutoLoad Images turned off.

The basic image tag is:

<IMG SRC = "filename">

You can also use these options:

ALIGN = "left/center/right"

ALT = "description"

ALIGN sets the position of the image across the page.

ALT is the text to display if the image is not loaded into a browser. In the example opposite, if image loading was turned off, you would see this: A picture of me

Background images

You can add an image with the **BACKGROUND** = "filename" option in the **<BODY>** tag. The image is automatically 'tiled' – repeated across and down to fill the window.

Tip

Images must be in GIF or JPG format for browsers to be able to display them. When you are preparing images, try both formats and use the smallest.

Take note

Window's Paint can only produce BMP images. To convert these to GIF or JPG you will need Paint Shop Pro or a similar graphics application.

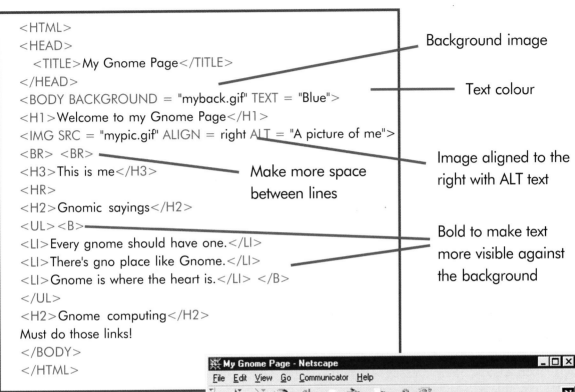

```
<HTML>
<HEAD>
   <TITLE>My Gnome Page</TITLE>
</HEAD>
<BODY BACKGROUND = "myback.gif" TEXT = "Blue">
<H1>Welcome to my Gnome Page</H1>
<IMG SRC = "mypic.gif" ALIGN = right ALT = "A picture of me">
<BR> <BR>
<H3>This is me</H3>
<HR>
<H2>Gnomic sayings</H2>
<UL><B>
<LI>Every gnome should have one.</LI>
<LI>There's gno place like Gnome.</LI>
<LI>Gnome is where the heart is.</LI> </B>
</UL>
<H2>Gnome computing</H2>
Must do those links!
</BODY>
</HTML>
```

Background image

Text colour

Make more space between lines

Image aligned to the right with ALT text

Bold to make text more visible against the background

The trick with background images is to use one which doesn't clash too much with the text. Very pale or bright images and black text work well. In this example, the background image is the same as the main picture, but smaller and with fewer, paler colours – and if it was even simpler and paler, the text would be more readable.

Links

A link is created with a pair of tags. The first contains the URL of the page or file to be linked, and takes the form:

<A HREF=*URL*>

The second is a simple closing tag </A>. The two enclose the image or text that becomes the clickable link, e.g.

<A HREF=http://www.gnomeworld.gn>Gnome World </A>

As you can see from the example opposite, the link can be embedded within a larger item of text – only '**here**' is clickable in the *IT's Made Simple* line. You can also use an image with, or instead of, text to make the link.

The example only has Web URLs, but you can equally well create links to FTP files and newsgroups. You can also add a link to give readers an easy way to contact you. This line:

<A HREF=mailto:me@my.e-mail.address> Mail me </A>

will open a new mail message window, with your e-mail address in the To: slot.

Links within the page

If you have a page that runs over several screens, you might want to include links within the page, so that your readers can jump from one part to another. The clickable link follows the same pattern as above, but you must first define a named place, or anchor, to jump to.

<A NAME = "Top">This is the start of something big </A>

The anchor tags can fit round any text or image, and you can even leave it blank in between if you like.

The HREF tag is slightly different for a jump.

<A HREF = #Top> Return to top of page </A>

Notice the # before the name. This is essential.

Take note

There's more to links than is shown here. In fact there is a lot more to HTML than can be covered in this book – we haven't touched Tables, Forms or Frames. If this has whetted your appetite and you want to know more, read *HTML 4.0 Made Simple*.

Tip

At some point, contact your access provider to find out what to call the home page file and where to store it and its images.

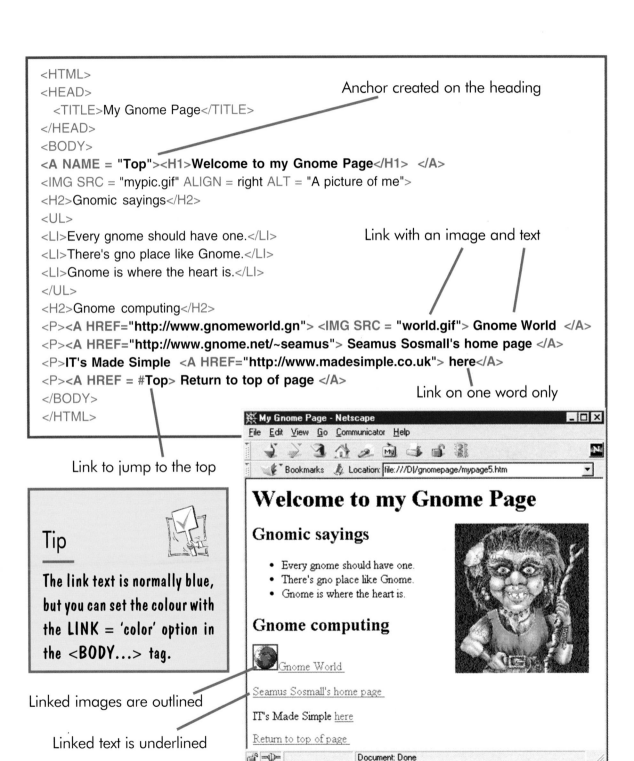

Anchor created on the heading

```
<HTML>
<HEAD>
   <TITLE>My Gnome Page</TITLE>
</HEAD>
<BODY>
<A NAME = "Top"><H1>Welcome to my Gnome Page</H1>  </A>
<IMG SRC = "mypic.gif" ALIGN = right ALT = "A picture of me">
<H2>Gnomic sayings</H2>
<UL>
<LI>Every gnome should have one.</LI>
<LI>There's gno place like Gnome.</LI>
<LI>Gnome is where the heart is.</LI>
</UL>
<H2>Gnome computing</H2>
<P><A HREF="http://www.gnomeworld.gn"> <IMG SRC = "world.gif"> Gnome World  </A>
<P><A HREF="http://www.gnome.net/~seamus"> Seamus Sosmall's home page </A>
<P>IT's Made Simple  <A HREF="http://www.madesimple.co.uk"> here</A>
<P><A HREF = #Top> Return to top of page </A>
</BODY>
</HTML>
```

Link with an image and text

Link on one word only

Link to jump to the top

Linked images are outlined

Linked text is underlined

My Gnome Page - Netscape

File   Edit   View   Go   Communicator   Help

Bookmarks   Location: file:///D|/gnomepage/mypage5.htm

Welcome to my Gnome Page

Gnomic sayings

- Every gnome should have one.
- There's gno place like Gnome.
- Gnome is where the heart is.

Gnome computing

Gnome World

Seamus Sosmall's home page

IT's Made Simple here

Return to top of page

Document: Done

Summary

- HTML stands for HyperText Markup Language, and is a set of tags and instructions that tells browsers how to display a page.

- Text can be formatted to appear as headings, bulletted or numbered lists, or in the *address* style.

- The background and the text can be set in the colours of your choice.

- Plain text pages can be improved by the use of bulleted or numbered lists and of lines.

- Images can be inserted anywhere on the page, and aligned to the left, centre or right of the display.

- Include ALT text in your image tags, for readers who have their image loading turned off.

- An image can be set to form a background, and will be repeated across and down to fill the window.

- You can add links to your other pages, to pages on remote sites or to a targeted point within a page.

13 Composer

Creating a Web page

HTML editors, such as Composer in the Communicator suite, take a lot of the hard work out of creating Web pages. Like many editors, it has no tools for creating forms or frames (sub-divided windows), but it is very good for handling text, images, links and tables. It also provides an easy way to upload files to your access provider's server when you are ready to publish your home page.

Basic steps

1 If you want to use a Template or Wizard, go online first.

2 Open the File menu, and point to New.

3 Select Blank to start from scratch.

or

4 Select Template or Wizard and follow its instructions.

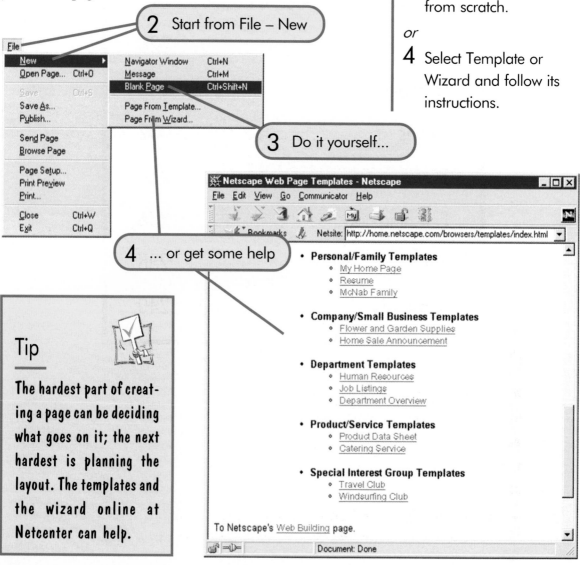

2 Start from File – New

File		
New ▶		
Open Page... Ctrl+O	Navigator Window Ctrl+N	
Save Ctrl+S	Message Ctrl+M	
	Blank Page Ctrl+Shift+N	
Save As...		
Publish...	Page From Template...	
	Page From Wizard...	
Send Page		
Browse Page		
Page Setup...		
Print Preview		
Print...		
Close Ctrl+W		
Exit Ctrl+Q		

3 Do it yourself...

4 ... or get some help

Netscape Web Page Templates - Netscape

File Edit View Go Communicator Help

Bookmarks Netsite: http://home.netscape.com/browsers/templates/index.html

- **Personal/Family Templates**
  - My Home Page
  - Resume
  - McNab Family

- **Company/Small Business Templates**
  - Flower and Garden Supplies
  - Home Sale Announcement

- **Department Templates**
  - Human Resources
  - Job Listings
  - Department Overview

- **Product/Service Templates**
  - Product Data Sheet
  - Catering Service

- **Special Interest Group Templates**
  - Travel Club
  - Windsurfing Club

To Netscape's Web Building page.

Document: Done

Tip

The hardest part of creating a page can be deciding what goes on it; the next hardest is planning the layout. The templates and the wizard online at Netcenter can help.

Composer toolbars

The editor has two sets of tools.

- The **Composition** toolbar is for file management and for inserting objects into the page.

- The **Formatting** toolbar is for setting style, alignment, indents, size, emphasis and colour – these will be familiar to anyone who has used a Windows word-processor.

Formatting toolbar
(see page 230)

New page · Open page · Publish · View in browser · Link · Target · Image · Line · Table · Spell check

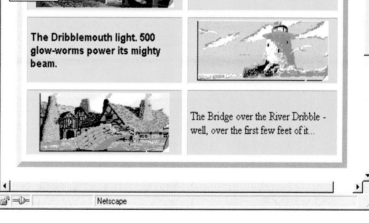

Text-only tables are easy to construct. Those containing images need some tweaking to make them work well.

Take note

Composer cannot handle frames. You can use it to create the pages within frames, but not the pages that set up the structure.

Take note

If you want to fine-tune the HTML or add tags that Composer cannot handle, you can open the page document in NotePad or WordPad and work on it there.

Editor Preferences

These can, of course, be set to changed at any time, but it is as well to get a few of the key ones sorted out at the very start. But before going to the panels, you should arm yourself with some information:

- If you may ever want to edit the HTML code directly – perhaps to add tags that the editor cannot handle – you will need to take the text into Notepad, WordPad or another word-processor. Decide which you will use, and locate its .EXE file in your folders. (NotePad and WordPad should be in the Windows folder.)

- If you want to be able to edit images, you should link in a graphics program such as Paint Shop Pro. Paint will not do, as images should be in JPG or GIF format.

- If you are creating your own home page, to be published on the Web, you need to know where the files should be stored on your access provider's site, and the URL of your page. Talk to your access provider.

1 Open the Edit menu and select Preferences.

2 Enter your name – this is written into the <HEAD> area of your pages (see page 236).

3 Turn Auto save on and set the timespan.

4 Click Choose and browse through your folders to locate text and image editors.

5 Set the Font size mode – stick to point size if you are used to word-processing.

6 On the Publish panel, leave the Maintain links and Keep images with documents options checked.

7 Enter the FTP URL of your space at your access provider's site.

8 Enter the HTTP URL for your home page.

9 Click OK.

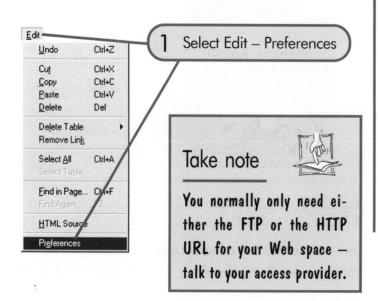

1 Select Edit – Preferences

Take note

You normally only need either the FTP or the HTTP URL for your Web space — talk to your access provider.

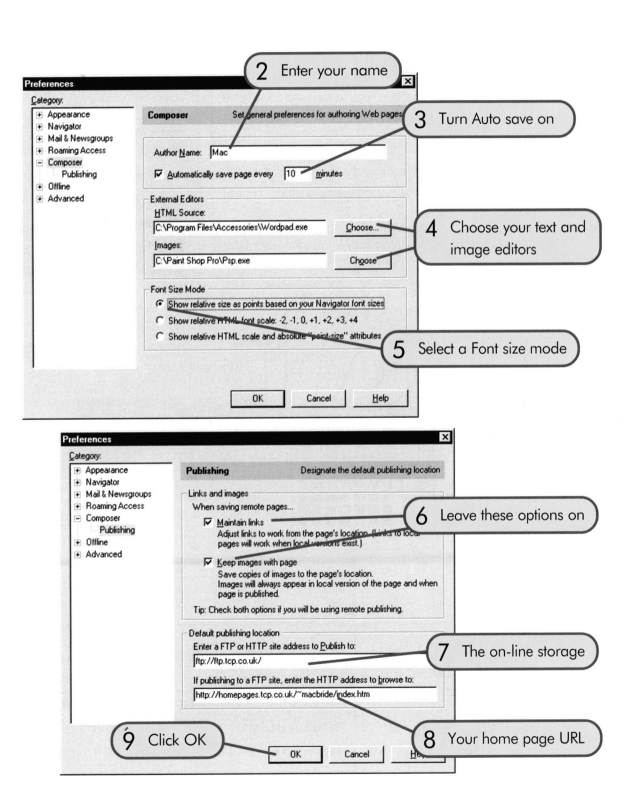

2 Enter your name

3 Turn Auto save on

Preferences ▣

Category:
⊞ Appearance
⊞ Navigator
⊞ Mail & Newsgroups
⊞ Roaming Access
⊟ Composer
    Publishing
⊞ Offline
⊞ Advanced

Composer   Set general preferences for authoring Web pages

Author Name: Mac

☑ Automatically save page every [10] minutes

External Editors
HTML Source:
C:\Program Files\Accessories\Wordpad.exe   [Choose...]

Images:
C:\Paint Shop Pro\Psp.exe   [Choose]

4 Choose your text and image editors

Font Size Mode
◉ Show relative size as points based on your Navigator font sizes
○ Show relative HTML font scale: -2, -1, 0, +1, +2, +3, +4
○ Show relative HTML scale and absolute "point-size" attributes

5 Select a Font size mode

[OK]   [Cancel]   [Help]

Preferences ▣

Category:
⊞ Appearance
⊞ Navigator
⊞ Mail & Newsgroups
⊞ Roaming Access
⊟ Composer
    Publishing
⊞ Offline
⊞ Advanced

Publishing   Designate the default publishing location

Links and images
When saving remote pages...

☑ Maintain links
Adjust links to work from the page's location. (Links to local pages will work when local versions exist.)

☑ Keep images with page
Save copies of images to the page's location.
Images will always appear in local version of the page and when page is published.

Tip: Check both options if you will be using remote publishing.

6 Leave these options on

Default publishing location
Enter a FTP or HTTP site address to Publish to:
ftp://ftp.tcp.co.uk/

If publishing to a FTP site, enter the HTTP address to browse to:
http://homepages.tcp.co.uk/~macbride/index.htm

7 The on-line storage

8 Your home page URL

9 Click OK

[OK]   [Cancel]   [He...]

Formatting text

The simplest way to to format text is to use the styles in the drop-down lists in the Formatting toolbar. These include a range of headings, lists and other styles, which should be enough to give variety and structure to a page.

You can set the font, size, colour or emphasis of any selected text – from a single letter to whole paragraphs – with the central set of tools.

The last five tools set the list style, indent level and alignment of selected paragraphs.

Tip

When planning the layout for a page, remember that people may view it from different sized windows in different sized screens. Simpler is often better.

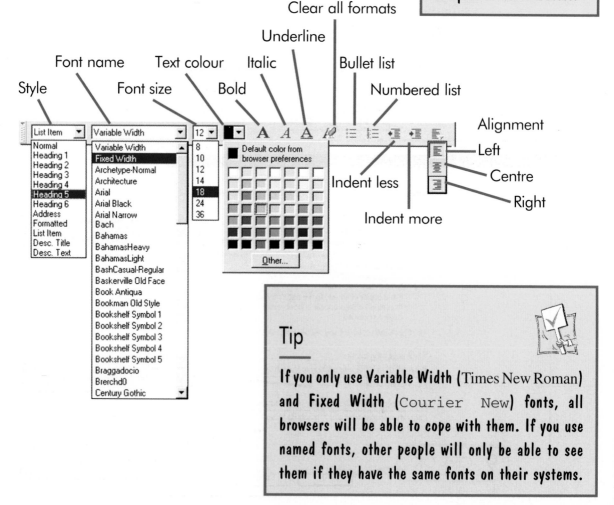

Tip

If you only use **Variable Width** (Times New Roman) and **Fixed Width** (Courier New) fonts, all browsers will be able to cope with them. If you use named fonts, other people will only be able to see them if they have the same fonts on their systems.

```
<!doctype html public "-//w3c//dtd html 4.0 transitional//en">
<html>
<head>
   <meta http-equiv="Content-Type" content="text/html; charset=iso-8859-1">
   <meta name="Author" content="Mac">
   <meta name="GENERATOR" content="Mozilla/4.5 [en] (Win98; I) [Netscape]">
   <title>Formatting in composer</title>
</head>
<body>
<center><h1>Composer</h1></center>
<div ALIGN=right><h2>in Netscape Communicator</h2></div>
<h3>makes formatting text so easy</h3>
<ul>
<li><b>Emphasise</b> text with a <i>click</i> of a <b><i>button</i></b></li>
<li>Vary the size - g<font size=+2>r</font><font size=+3>o</font><font size=+4>
w</font>and <font size=+4>s</font><font size=+3>h</font><font size=+2>r</font>
<font size=+1>i</font>n<font size=-1>k</font></li>
<li><b><font color="#FF0000">Splash</font> <font color="#FF9900">the</font>
<font color="#00CC00"></font><font color="#009900">COLOURS</font><font
color="#CC66CC"></font><font color="#3333FF">about</font>!</b></li>
</ul>
</body>
</html>
```

Except for the title, the text between the <HEAD> and </HEAD> tags is not displayed by browsers.

Fancy text effects take loads of code – far better to let Composer write it for you!

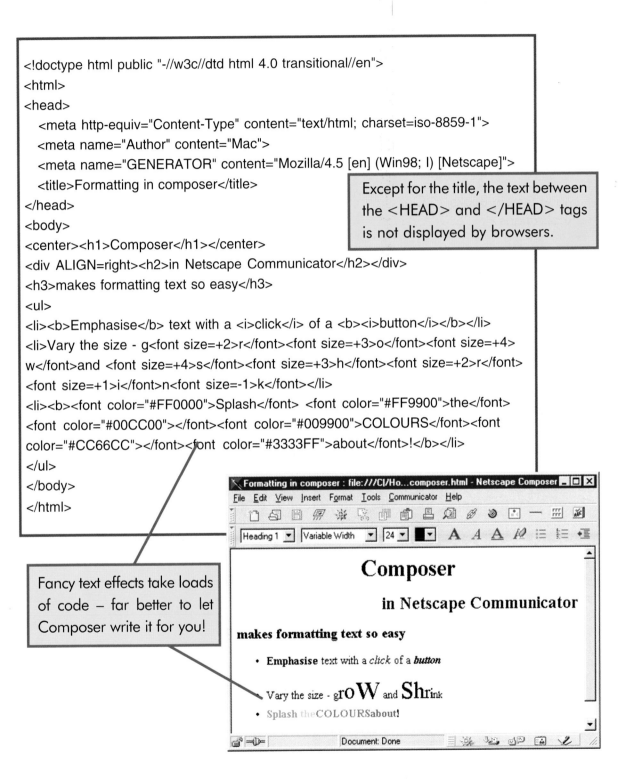

Tables

Tables are very fiddly things to construct when you are writing the HTML code by hand, but remarkably easy in Composer. If you don't believe me, view the Page Source after you have made a table!

Before you start, sketch out the table on paper to work out its size – it saves having to adjust it later.

Made Simple Books	Out Now	1999
Applications	27	12
Internet	9	7
Programming	10	3

This needs a table of 4 Rows and 3 Columns, giving us 12 cells. The overall size of the table can be fixed in pixels, or set as a percentage of the window. Percentages are better – you cannot know how large your readers' windows will be.

Basic steps

1 Use Insert – Table or click ▦ to open the New Table Properties.

2 Set the number of Rows and Columns.

3 Set the display options.

4 Click OK to create the blank table.

5 Move through the cells entering your text.

❑ Fine tuning

6 Select the cell(s) and right-click to open the shortcut menu.

7 Select Table Properties, switch to the Cell tab and adjust the settings.

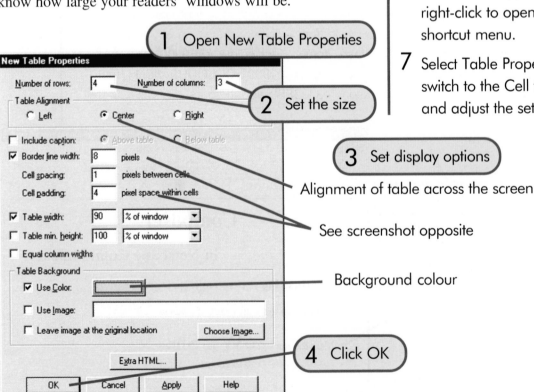

1 Open New Table Properties

New Table Properties

Number of rows: 4   Number of columns: 3

Table Alignment
○ Left   ⦿ Center   ○ Right

2 Set the size

☐ Include caption: ○ Above table   ○ Below table
☑ Border line width: 8   pixels
   Cell spacing: 1   pixels between cells
   Cell padding: 4   pixel space within cells

3 Set display options

☑ Table width: 90   % of window
☐ Table min. height: 100   % of window
☐ Equal column widths

Alignment of table across the screen

See screenshot opposite

Table Background
☑ Use Color: [ ]
☐ Use Image: [ ]
☐ Leave image at the original location   Choose Image...

Background colour

E_xtra HTML...

OK   Cancel   Apply   Help

4 Click OK

232

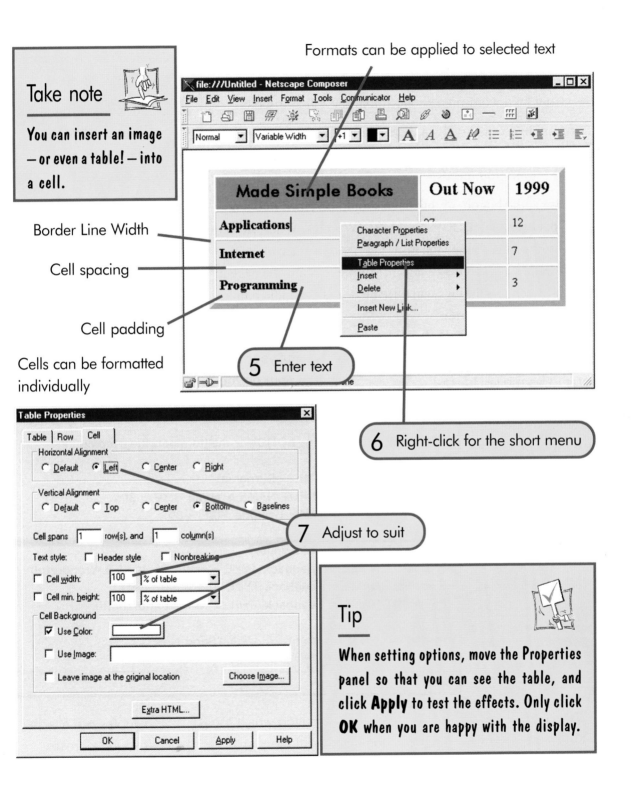

Formats can be applied to selected text

Border Line Width

Cell spacing

Cell padding

Cells can be formatted
individually

file:///Untitled - Netscape Composer

File Edit View Insert Format Tools Communicator Help

Normal   Variable Width   +1

Made Simple Books   Out Now   1999

Applications   12

Internet   7

Programming   3

Character Properties
Paragraph / List Properties
Table Properties
Insert
Delete
Insert New Link...
Paste

5 Enter text

6 Right-click for the short menu

Table Properties

Table | Row | Cell

Horizontal Alignment
○ Default   ● Left   ○ Center   ○ Right

Vertical Alignment
○ Default   ○ Top   ○ Center   ● Bottom   ○ Baselines

Cell spans [1] row(s), and [1] column(s)

Text style: ☐ Header style   ☐ Nonbreaking

☐ Cell width: [100] % of table

☐ Cell min. height: [100] % of table

Cell Background
☑ Use Color:
☐ Use Image:
☐ Leave image at the original location   Choose Image...

Extra HTML...

OK   Cancel   Apply   Help

7 Adjust to suit

Forms

Forms are an excellent way to get feedback from your visitors. Unfortunately Composer cannot handle them, though they can be written in a word-processor without too much trouble.

The simple example given here shows some of the main features of forms. You might like to copy it, then adapt it and extend it to fit your needs.

The text at the bottom of this page should be typed into a new page, between the **<BODY>** and **</BODY>** tags. When viewed in the editor you will see the torn 'tag' icon in place of each of the **<FORM>** and **<INPUT>** tags in your text. View the page in your browser, and the tags will turn into text slots, radio buttons and a 'Send Now' button.

Basic steps

1 Click ⬚ to start a new document.

2 Open the Edit menu and select HTML Source to take it into your word-processor.

3 Type in the code shown below.

4 Save the file and return to Composer.

5 Click ⬚ to view it in Navigator.

Sets up the form and arranges for it to be mailed to you

Put your e-mail address here – for more on mailto, see page 237

Creates a one-line text input box

```
<FORM METHOD = Post ACTION = mailto:macbride@tcp.co.uk>

<P>Name: <INPUT NAME = Surname>
<P>E-mail address: <INPUT NAME = email SIZE = 30>
<P>Tel No: <INPUT NAME = phone SIZE = 30>

<P>What do you think of my site?
<P><INPUT NAME = Feedback TYPE = radio CHECKED>Wonderful!
<P><INPUT NAME = Feedback TYPE = radio>Brilliant!!
<P><INPUT NAME = Feedback TYPE = radio>Fantastic!!!!

<P><INPUT TYPE = submit VALUE = "Send Now">

</FORM>
```

Start new line

Creates a set of radio buttons

End of the form area

Creates a button which mails the form's data to you

Quotes are needed around phrases

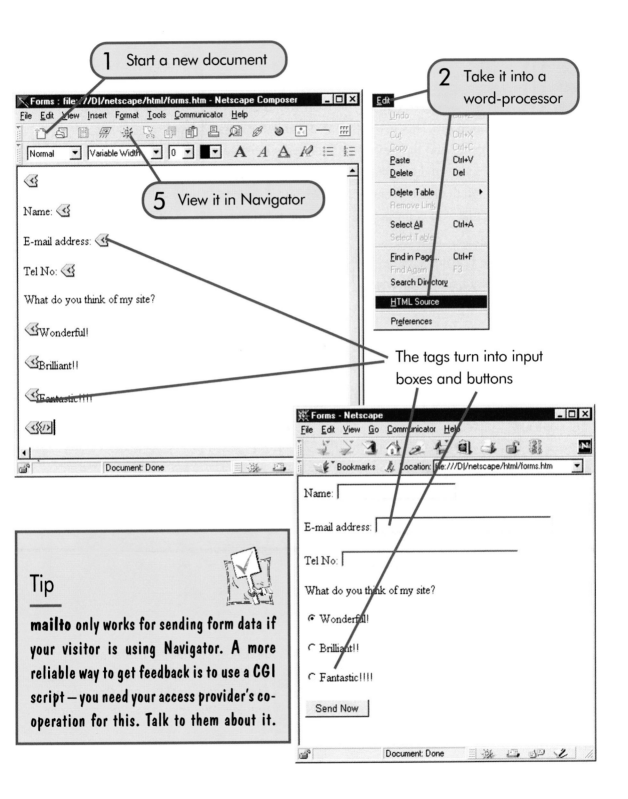

1 Start a new document

2 Take it into a word-processor

5 View it in Navigator

Forms : file:///D|/netscape/html/forms.htm - Netscape Composer

File Edit View Insert Format Tools Communicator Help

Normal ▾ Variable Width ▾ 0 ▾ ▮▾ A A A A ⋮≡ ⋮≡

Name:

E-mail address:

Tel No:

What do you think of my site?

Wonderful!

Brilliant!!

Fantastic!!!!

Document: Done

Edit

Undo
Cut   Ctrl+X
Copy   Ctrl+C
Paste   Ctrl+V
Delete   Del

Delete Table   ▸
Remove Link

Select All   Ctrl+A
Select Table

Find in Page... Ctrl+F
Find Again   F3
Search Directory

HTML Source

Preferences

The tags turn into input boxes and buttons

Forms - Netscape

File Edit View Go Communicator Help

Bookmarks   Location: file:///D|/netscape/html/forms.htm

Name:

E-mail address:

Tel No:

What do you think of my site?

⊙ Wonderful!

○ Brilliant!!

○ Fantastic!!!!

Send Now

Document: Done

Tip

mailto only works for sending form data if your visitor is using Navigator. A more reliable way to get feedback is to use a CGI script — you need your access provider's co-operation for this. Talk to them about it.

Finishing touches

Headers and keywords

The **<HEAD>** area is invisible unless you view the document source, but it is important. This is the part that holds the page title, its author's name, and the keywords that search engines will use for classifying – and for finding – the page. These can all be entered through the Page Properties panel, and should be done for any page that you want people to be able to find.

1 Open the Format menu and select Page Colors and Properties.

2 Enter the Title, Author and a Description.

3 Enter your Keywords and Classification text.

4 Click OK.

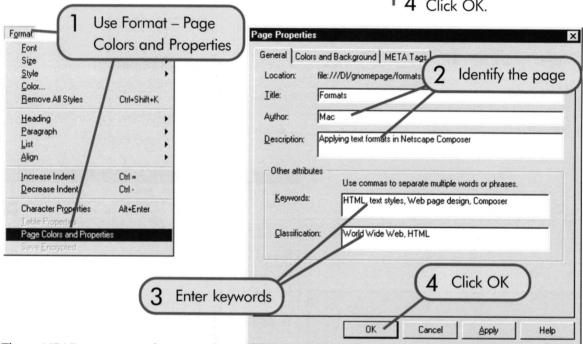

The <HEAD>, seen in the Page Source

```
<HEAD>
  <META NAME="Author" CONTENT="Mac">
  <META NAME="GENERATOR" CONTENT="Mozilla/4.5 [en] (Win98; I) [Netscape]">
  <META NAME="Classification" CONTENT="HTML, World Wide Web, Composer">
  <META NAME="Description" CONTENT="Applying text formats in Netscape Composer">
  <META NAME="KeyWords" CONTENT="HTML, text styles, Web page design, Composer">
  <TITLE>Formats</TITLE>
</HEAD>
```

Mail from the page

1 Type in some suitable text, such as *Mail to me* and select it.

2 Click 📎.

3 Enter *mailto:* followed by your e-mail address.

4 Click OK.

If you want readers to be able to get in touch with you, include a mailing link in your page. This should have *mailto:* followed by your e-mail address as the URL. When a reader clicks on this link, the New Message window will open, with your address already in the **Mail To:** slot.

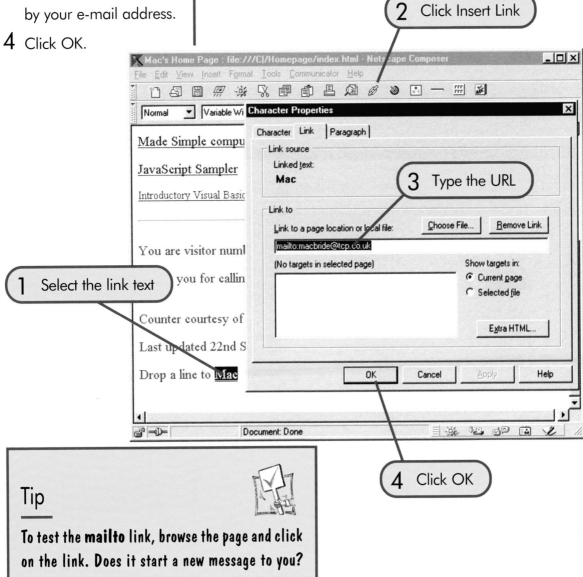

2 Click Insert Link

3 Type the URL

1 Select the link text

4 Click OK

Tip

To test the mailto link, browse the page and click on the link. Does it start a new message to you?

Publishing your page

To publish your page(s) on the World Wide Web, you must upload all the necessary files to the appropriate place at your access provider's site. Before doing this, check your files, and check your links.

Organising the files

When you upload your files to your access provider's site, they will be copied to one folder, with the links automatically adjusted to match their location. If they are not there already, move the files for your pages and images into one folder – then edit each page containing links and adjust the URLs if needed.

Take note

If the files are scattered throughout your system, the links will not work when they are uploaded unless you have the same directory structure at your access provider's site — and you won't have!

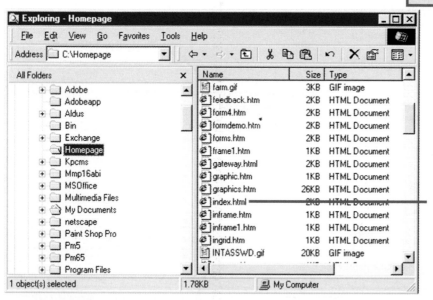

Normally, the first page must be called index.htm or index.html – check with your provider before uploading.

Final testing

Double-check the links by loading the home page (the top page of the set) into the Browser window. Visit every linked page and make sure that every image is displayed. If you have links to remote sites, go on-line and check those links.

Basic steps

Uploading

1 Connect to your access service.

2 Open your home page – or the topmost page if you have several – in Composer.

3 Select File – Publish or click 🖼.

4 If you did not write the location into the Preferences panel (page 228), type it now.

5 Enter your Password.

6 Set the All files option.

7 Click OK.

8 Wait while the files upload, then browse your new online pages, checking the display and the links.

If you are updating an exisiting set, just select the new ones

Composer's Publish routine makes uploading very simple. If you do have trouble, check the FTP address with your access provider – that is the most likely cause of problems.

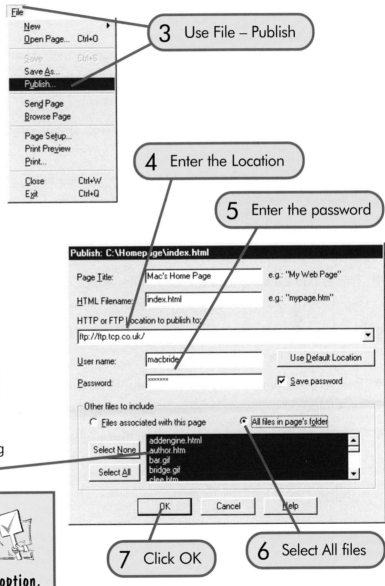

3 Use File – Publish

4 Enter the Location

5 Enter the password

7 Click OK

6 Select All files

Tip

If you tick the **Save password** option, you won't have to enter it next time.

Summary

- Composer makes Web page creation much easier. It is used just like a word-processor, and can handle text formatting, lines, images, links and tables.

- If you want to edit the source code directly, you should link a text editor in the Preferences panel.

- If you write your name into the Preferences panel, it will be automatically entered into your pages to identify you as the author.

- You must give the FTP address of your Web space, and the URL of your home page.

- Paragraphs can be formatted to appear as headings, bulleted or numbered list, or in the address style.

- Selected text may be made bold, italics, coloured or varied in size.

- Tables can be constructed easily in the editor, but if you want forms, you have to write the source code youself!

- If you add keywords, search engines will be able to index your site.

- Before uploading your pages, assemble all the files into one folder.

- After publishing your page, check it thoroughly.

14 FrontPage Express

Introducing FrontPage

FrontPage Express is supplied as part of the full Internet Explorer package. It is a cut-down version of FrontPage, a comprehensive Web page creation and site administration package (with graphics software). FrontPage Express lacks the administration and graphics software but has almost identical page editing facilities. The good set of tools, wizards and WebBots (embedded programs) greatly simplify page creation.

Basic steps

1 Open the File menu, and select New.

2 Select Normal Page to start from scratch.

or

3 Select a Wizard and follow its instructions.

4 Click OK.

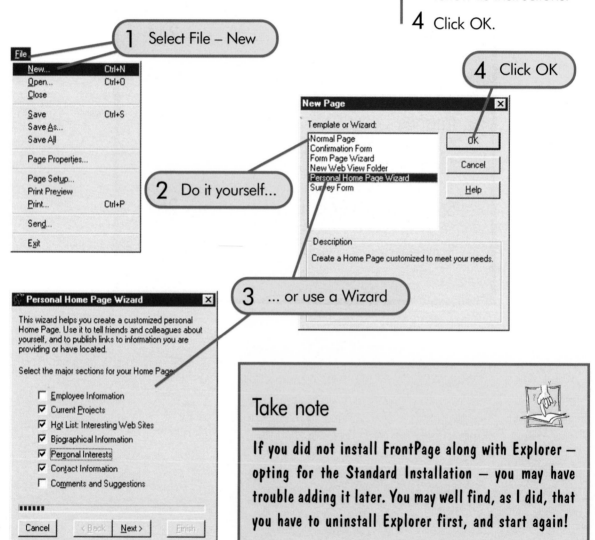

1 Select File – New

4 Click OK

2 Do it yourself...

3 ... or use a Wizard

Take note

If you did not install FrontPage along with Explorer – opting for the Standard Installation – you may have trouble adding it later. You may well find, as I did, that you have to uninstall Explorer first, and start again!

The editing tools

The main toolbar is identical to that of Word. Use these tools to set styles, fonts, alignment, bulleted or numbered lists, idents, emphasis and colour.

The second toolbar has the usual file and cut-and-paste facilities, plus tools for inserting tables, images, links, and WebBot components.

The Form Fields toolbar can be docked in the window frame or set to float anywhere on the window.

Take note

Text formatting is very easy — try it and see for yourself. We'll focus on the more interesting bits in this chapter.

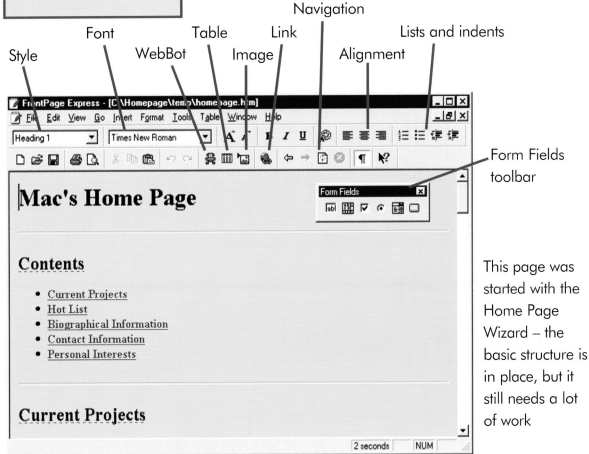

Style
Font
WebBot
Table
Image
Link
Navigation
Alignment
Lists and indents

Form Fields toolbar

This page was started with the Home Page Wizard – the basic structure is in place, but it still needs a lot of work

Tables

Like Netscape's editor, FrontPage makes light work of the chore of setting up tables. The Insert table tool will give you the basic structure. You can then work your way round the cells, inserting text, images – or even other tables. Formats can be applied to the whole table, or to selected rows, columns or individual cells. The overall size of the table can be fixed in pixels, or set as a percentage of the window.

Basic steps

1 Place the cursor where the table is to go.

2 Click 🔲.

3 Drag the highlight to set the size.

4 Enter and format your text and images.

5 Right-click on the table to get the short menu.

6 Select Table Properties

7 Adjust settings as required.

8 Click OK.

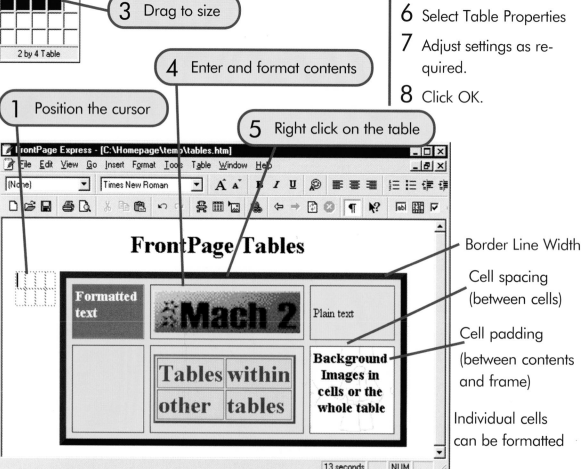

2 Click Insert Table

3 Drag to size

2 by 4 Table

4 Enter and format contents

1 Position the cursor

5 Right click on the table

Border Line Width

Cell spacing (between cells)

Cell padding (between contents and frame)

Individual cells can be formatted

244

6 Select Table Properties

Take note

Table width is best set as a percentage — you cannot know how large your readers' windows will be.

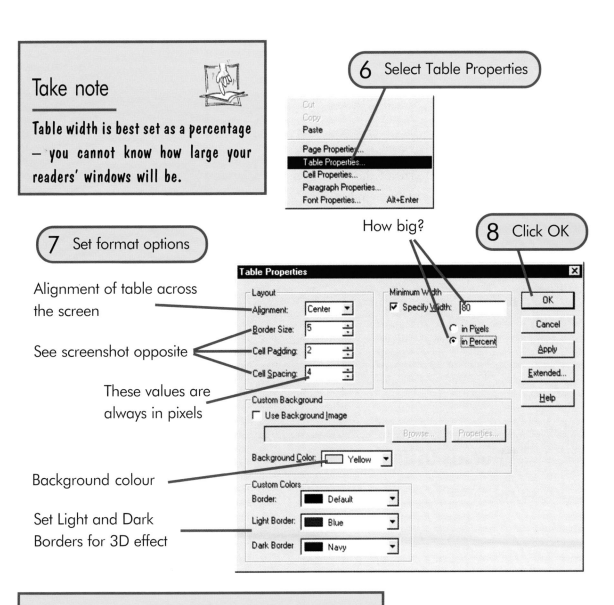

Cut
Copy
Paste

Page Properties...
Table Properties...
Cell Properties...
Paragraph Properties...
Font Properties...   Alt+Enter

How big?

8 Click OK

7 Set format options

Alignment of table across the screen

See screenshot opposite

These values are always in pixels

Background colour

Set Light and Dark Borders for 3D effect

Table Properties

Layout
Alignment: Center
Border Size: 5
Cell Padding: 2
Cell Spacing: 4

Minimum Width
☑ Specify Width: 80
○ in Pixels
● in Percent

OK
Cancel
Apply
Extended...
Help

Custom Background
☐ Use Background Image
Browse...   Properties...

Background Color: Yellow

Custom Colors
Border: Default
Light Border: Blue
Dark Border   Navy

Tip

When setting options, move the Properties panel so that you can see the table, and click Apply to test the effects. Only click OK when you are happy with the display.

Forms

Writing your own HTML code to create a form can take time. The Form Fields toolbar in FrontPage simplifies the job, though you still have to do some work to ensure that when the form is sent back to you, you can identify the items your visitors entered and the selections they made.

● Every Form Field must have a name.

● Text boxes can have sample text in them.

● Check boxes can be set on or off and need labels to tell the visitor what they're for.

● Radio buttons must have a Value (for feedback) and a text prompt.

● Drop-down menus need Choices (the items that are displayed on the menu) and Values (for feedback).

1 Place the cursor (type a label if needed) where you want the first field.

2 Select the field from the Form Field toolbar.

3 Right-click on the field and select Form Field Properties.

4 Set the Name and Value properties .

5 Click OK.

6 Repeat to add fields.

Keep all the fields within the outline – unless you want to have several separate forms on the page.

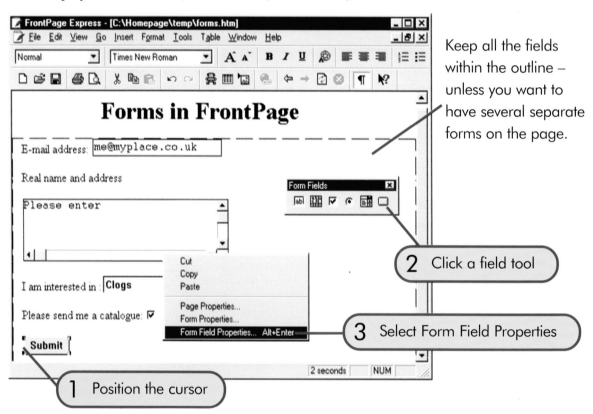

2 Click a field tool

3 Select Form Field Properties

1 Position the cursor

246

The Form Fields

Scrolling Text Box

Radio Button

Push Button

One-Line Text Box

Check Box

Drop-Down Menu

Buttons are simple – use Submit for one to send the form, or Reset to clear the values.

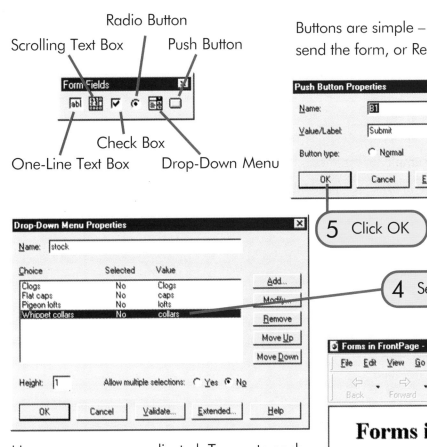

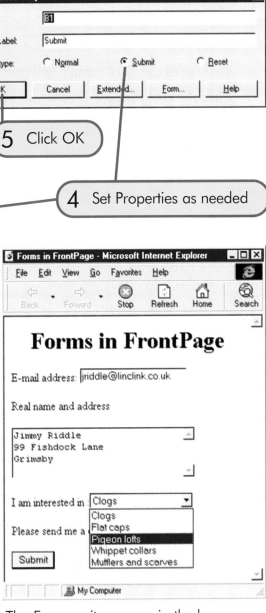

5 Click OK

4 Set Properties as needed

Menus are more complicated. To create each item, click Add and type in the Choice (which appears on the menu). This will also be used as the feedback Value, unless you select Specify Value and enter your own word.

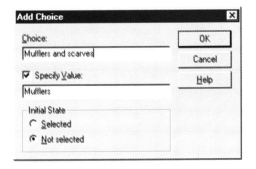

The Form as it appears in the browser

Images

Images are not difficult to manage in HTML, but FrontPage offers a few nice extra touches. It has a small, but well designed, set of Clip Art images – the Backgrounds and Lines are particularly good.

Basic steps

1 Place the cursor where the image is to go.

2 Open the Insert menu and select Image.

3 Switch to Clip Art.

4 Select a Category.

5 Pick an image and click OK.

6 Right-click on the image for its menu and select Image Properties.

7 Add a link if wanted.

8 Use the Appearance panel to set its size and position, if necessary.

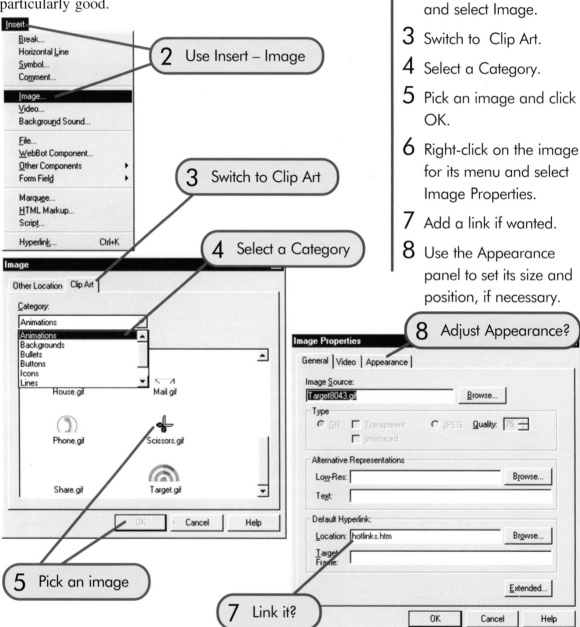

2 Use Insert – Image

3 Switch to Clip Art

4 Select a Category

8 Adjust Appearance?

5 Pick an image

7 Link it?

248

Basic steps

1 Open the Format menu and select Background.
2 Click Browse.
3 Select a background from the Insert Image dialog box.
4 Turn on Watermark if wanted.
5 Click OK.

You'll find this image in the Icons set

Backgrounds

A Background image can be easily added. If wanted, it can be set as a **Watermark**, so that when the screen is scrolled the background stays in place while the text and any other images move over it.

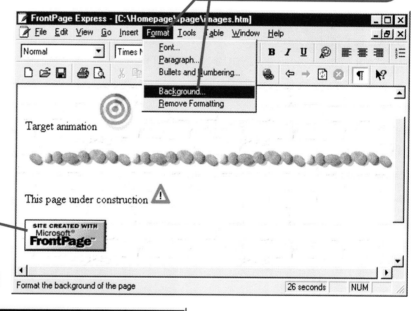

1 Use Format – Background

4 Set as Watermark?

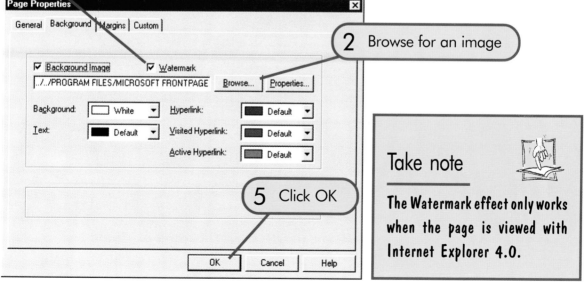

2 Browse for an image

5 Click OK

Take note

The Watermark effect only works when the page is viewed with Internet Explorer 4.0.

249

Marquees

If you want scrolling text on your page, you can do it two ways – write a program in Java, JavaScript or ActiveX (hard work), or use a marquee. This will let you scroll text in either direction at a chosen speed.

The background colour can be set from the Marquee Properties panel. To colour or format the text, use the standard tools.

● To select the marquee's text for formatting, click to the left – the whole text will be highlighted.

● To select the marquee itself (for moving or deleting), click anywhere within its border – the select handles will appear at the corners and mid-frame.

Key options

Delay   milliseconds between moves

Amount number of pixels to move

Scroll   the text moves across and off before repeating

Slide   the repeat starts once the last character has been brought into view

Basic steps

1 Place the cursor where you want the marquee.

2 Type in the Text.

3 Select the options to define how the text scrolls.

4 In Repeat, select Continuously or set the number of Times.

5 Set a Background Color if wanted.

6 Click OK.

7 Select the text.

8 Set font styles and colour as required.

9 Save the page and view it in Explorer.

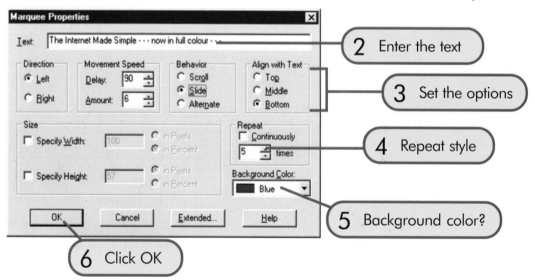

250

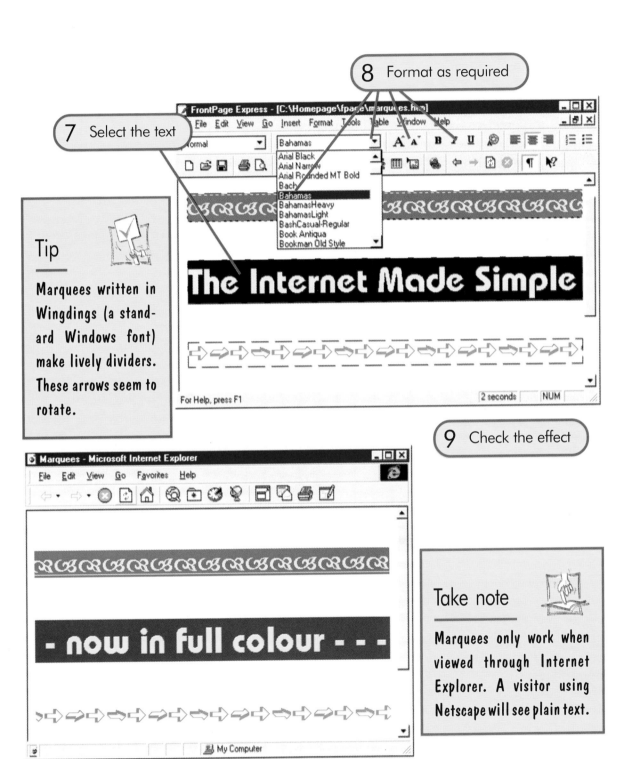

8 Format as required

7 Select the text

Tip

Marquees written in Wingdings (a standard Windows font) make lively dividers. These arrows seem to rotate.

9 Check the effect

Take note

Marquees only work when viewed through Internet Explorer. A visitor using Netscape will see plain text.

251

Saving and publishing

The full version of FrontPage contains site management facilities, and could be used for running an intranet (within an organisation) or an extensive Web site. Aspects of this show through in FrontPage Express – you'll notice it in the saving routines.

Saving

Where most applications assume that you will save your files onto your hard disk, FrontPage assumes that they will be saved – as pages – directly to your Web site. While you are still developing your pages, you are better saving them as files on your hard disk.

Basic steps

1 Open the File menu and select Save As...

2 Edit the Page Title if required.

3 Click As File...

4 Select the folder.

5 Edit the File name if required.

6 Click Save.

7 If the page contains images, you will be asked if you want to save them to the same folder – click Yes.

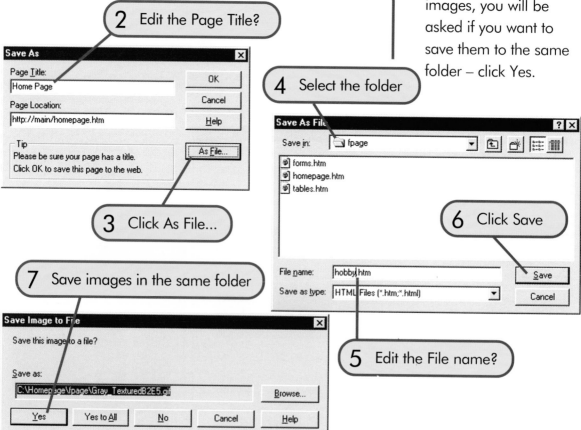

2 Edit the Page Title?

4 Select the folder

3 Click As File...

6 Click Save

7 Save images in the same folder

5 Edit the File name?

Basic steps

Publishing

1 Open the File menu and select Save As.

2 Click OK and save any images if asked.

❏ The Web Publishing Wizard will start. Get online now.

3 Browse for the folder containing your files.

4 Select your Web server if you have set one up.

otherwise

5 Click New and give the URL for your home page and path to the directory (folder) on your system.

6 Complete the Wizard.

The Web Publishing Wizard handles most of this. Before you run it, make sure that all the files – including any images and sounds – are all in one folder, and that this folder does not contain any other files.

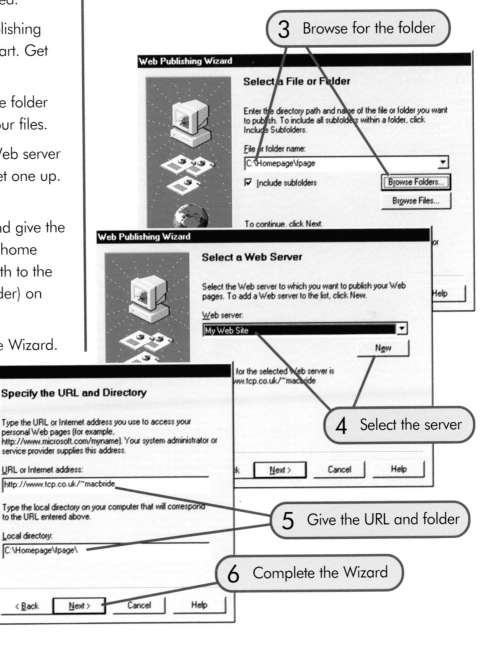

3 Browse for the folder

Web Publishing Wizard

Select a File or Folder

Enter the directory path and name of the file or folder you want to publish. To include all subfolders within a folder, click Include Subfolders.

File or folder name:
`C:\Homepage\fpage`

☑ Include subfolders

Browse Folders...

Browse Files...

To continue, click Next.

Web Publishing Wizard

Select a Web Server

Select the Web server to which you want to publish your Web pages. To add a Web server to the list, click New.

Web server:
`My Web Site`

New

for the selected Web server is
www.tcp.co.uk/~macbride

4 Select the server

Next >   Cancel   Help

Web Publishing Wizard

Specify the URL and Directory

Type the URL or Internet address you use to access your personal Web pages (for example, http://www.microsoft.com/myname). Your system administrator or service provider supplies this address.

URL or Internet address:
`http://www.tcp.co.uk/~macbride`

Type the local directory on your computer that will correspond to the URL entered above.

Local directory:
`C:\Homepage\fpage\`

5 Give the URL and folder

6 Complete the Wizard

< Back   Next >   Cancel   Help

Summary

- FrontPage Express is a cut-down version of Microsoft FrontPage. It has the same excellent HTML editor, but lacks the site management software.

- Tables are easily constructed. The table, selected cells or the contents of cells can be formatted separately.

- The Form Fields toolbar simplifies the creation of forms, but you will have to do some work – and you will need some understanding of forms – to set them up properly.

- There are sets of Clip Art images which can be incorporated into your pages.

- Backgrounds can be set as Watermarks to create an interesting effect.

- You can create scrolling text easily with a marquee, though these can only be enjoyed by visitors using Internet Explorer.

- Page files should be saved to your hard disk at first. When you want to upload them to your home page directory at your service provider's site, use the Web Publishing Wizard.

15 Hot lists

Selected Web sites

Directories and portals

Excite UK (page 88)
www.excite.co.uk

Lifestyle.uk (page 98)
www.lifestyleuk.co.uk

Lycos Top 5% (page 92)
point-uk.lycos.com

Magellan(page 110)
Focus on home users, family and children.
magellan.excite.com

MSN Web Directory (page 66)
home.microsoft.com/exploring

Netcenter (page 68)
home.netcenter.com

Starting Point (page 94)
www.stpt.com

UK directory (page 96)
www.ukdirectory.co.uk

Yahoo (page 82)
www.yahoo.com *or* www.yahoo.co.uk

Yahooligans (page 86)
www.yahooligans.com

Take note

There are millions of sites out there. The ones listed here are those covered in this book, plus a selection of those I've met on my travels and think are worth a visit.

Search engines

AltaVista (page 104)
www.altavista.com/

AOL Netfind (page 120)
www.aol.com/netfind

Ask Jeeves (page 112)
www.askjeeves.com

Dejanews
Search through the archives of the newsgroups
www.dejanews.com

Excite
If you can't find it at Excite, it probably isn't anywhere on the Web!
www.excite.co.uk

HotBot (page 108)
www.hotbot.com

Infoseek (page 106)
infoseek.go.com

UK Index (page 115)
www.ukindex.co.uk

UK Plus (page 124)
www.ukplus.co.uk

Web Crawler
Constantly crawling over the Web looking for new pages.
www.webcrawl.com

People finders

192.com
Look up anyone in the UK phone books.
www.192.com

Bigfoot
Another good people directory
www.bigfoot.com

Infospace (page 169)
www.infospace.com

Netscape Guide
Four of the best finders in one place.
guide.netscape.com

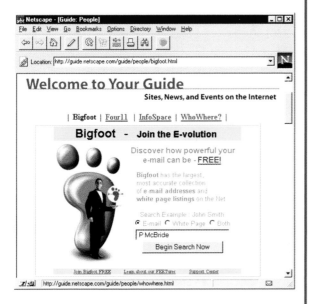

Yell (page 116)
www.yell.co.uk

Chat rooms and communities

Acme City (page 138)
www.acmecity.com

Excite (page 136)
www.excite.com/communities

Fortune City (page 139)
www2.fortunecity.com

Spurs fans
www.link-it.com/soccer/spurs.

Ultranet for chat software
www.ultranet.org.

Yahoo (page 136)
chat.yahoo.com

Web mail providers

All on page 166

MailCity
www.mailcity.com

Excite
mail.excite.co.uk *or* mail.excite.com

Netcenter
home.netcenter.com

Yahoo
mail.yahoo.co.uk *or* mail.yahoo.com

Free Internet access providers

BT ClickFree (Tel: 0906 802 0240)
Technical support 50p per min
www.btclickfree.com

FreeServe (Tel: 0990 500049)
Technical support 50p per min
www.freeserve.net

LineOne (Tel: 0800 111 210)
Technical support 50p per min
www.lineone.net

Telinco (Tel: 0800 542 0800)
Technical support free
www.telinco.co.uk

Tesco (Tel: 0906 602 0111)
Technical support 50p per min
www.tesco.net

Virgin (Tel: 0500 5588800)
Proper e-mail, but support at £1.00 per min
www.virgin.net

Browser and Web page resources

Apple, for QuickTime player
www.apple.com

Adobe (page 8)
For Acrobat Reader, and DTP/ design software.
www.adobe.com

Cosmo Galleries (page 78)
Demos of the leading VRML Language
www.cosmosoftware.com/galleries

Free Gifts & Animations
Animated GIFS, backgrounds and other goodies for Web builders.
www.fg-a.com

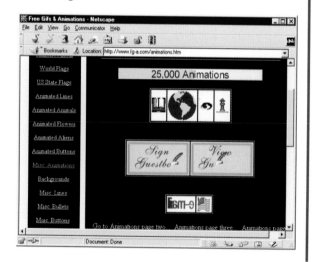

Ghostscript and Ghostview
www.cs.wisc.edu/~ghost/index.html

MapEdit (page 65)
http://www.boutell.com

Microsoft Tools & Samples Home Page
www.microsoft.com/gallery/default.asp

Netscape
For browser updates, plug-ins, advice and information
www.netscape.com

Netscape DevEdge Online
developer.netscape.com

NetNanny (page 35)
www.netnanny.com

Nexor, for Archie gateways
http://www.nexor.com/archie/

Paint Shop Pro
www.jasc.com. It

RealPlayer
www.real.com

Stuffit Expander
www.aladdinsys.com

WinZip
www.winzip.com

WS_FTP
http://www.ipswitch.com

Vzine (page 5, 146)
www.vzine.com

Computing

Babel
Dictionary of computer acronyms
www.access.digex.net/~ikind/babel.html

Computer Weekly
The computing professional's newspaper.
www.computerweekly.co.uk

Computer Buyer
News and reviews of hardware and software
www.comp-buyer.co.uk

Compaq
www.compaq.co.uk

Dan Technology (page 130)
www.dan.co.uk

Dell Computers
www.dell.co.uk/buydell

Elonex
www.elonex.co.uk

Gateway 2000 Europe
www.gateway2000.co.uk

Personal Computer World
www.pcw.co.uk

Viglen
www.viglen.co.uk

Entertainment

Dove
Child-friendly site, film reviews and more
www.dove.org

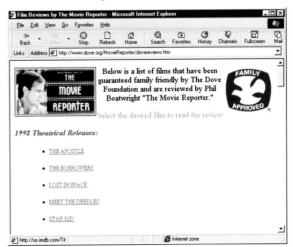

Future Games Network
www.fgnetwork.com

Games Domain (page 140)
www.gamesdomain.co.uk

Groucho Marx Quotes (page 76)
www.therightside.demon.co.uk/quotes/
groucho

Internet Movie Database (page 143)
www.imdb.com

Kids' Space (page 6)
Stories and activities for children.
www.kids-space.org

MSN Gaming Zone
zone.msn.com

The Oscars (page 9)
www.oscar.com

Wallace & Gromit fan page (page 7)
rummelplatz.uni-mannheim.de/~mfeld/
wallace&gromit.html

Walt Disney Pictures (page 7)
www2.disney.com/DisneyPictures

News and media

BBC Online (page 40)
www.bbc.co.uk

BBC News (page 71)
news.bbc.co.uk

Channel 4
www.channel4.com

Cosmopolitan (page 5)
www.designercity.com/cosmopolitan

Electronic Telegraph (page 144)
www.telegraph.co.uk

Financial Times (page 144)
www.ft.com

The Guardian (page 144)
www.guardian.co.uk

In-Box Direct
home.netscape.com/ibd

Le Monde
www.lemonde.fr

The Mirror (page 144)
Host to DomeWatch!
www.mirror.co.uk

Daily Mail, IT section (page 144)
www.dailymail.co.uk

New Scientist
www.newscientist.com

New York Times
www.nytimes.com

Private Eye
www.private-eye.co.uk

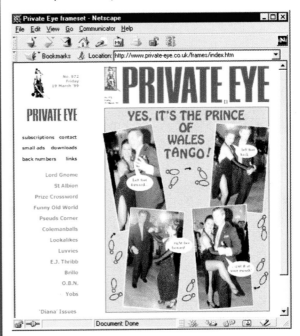

The Times (page 144)
and other News International papers
www.thetimes.co.uk

Washington Post
www.washingtonpost.com

Shopping

Buyers' Index (page 133)
Track down sellers of specific goods
www.buyersindex.com

Yahoo shopping (page 132)
Directory of online shops
shopping.uk.yahoo.com

Amazon
The Internet's leading bookstore.
www.amazon.com

Angler's Directory (page 6)
www.anglersdirectory.net

CD Now (page 129)
www.cdnow.com

The Early Music Shop (page 13)
Modern technology meets medieval music
www.e-m-s.com

Fortnum and Mason
Shop with the best!
www.fortnumandmason.co.uk

Gift Store UK (page 128)
www.giftstore.co.uk

HMV
www.hmv.co.uk

Internet Bookshop (page 131)
www.bookshop.co.uk

Internet Fraud Watch
Find out what to avoid!
http://www.fraud.org

Macdonald's smoked produce
Smoked haggis!
www.smokedproduce.co.uk/macdonalds

Sainsbury's (page 9)
www.sainsburys.co.uk

Tesco's
www.tesco.co.uk

Financial services

Abbey National (page 126)
www.abbeynational.co.uk

Barclays
www.barclays.co.uk

Royal Bank of Scotland (page 134)
www.rbs.co.uk

Virgin Direct and Virgin One (page 135)
www.virgin-direct.co.uk

Information sources

The CIA

Even secret services have Web sites! The CIA World Factbook is a good source of basic information about every country in the world.
www.odci.gov/cia

EDIS (page 142)

Index of encyclopedias on the Web.
edis.win.tue.nl/encyclop.html

Government Information Service (page 124)

UK government departments and agencies.
www.open.gov.uk

GCSE Answers

www.gcse.com

Global Classroom

www.global-classroom.com

The Herbal Encyclopedia (page 8)

Medicinal and magical uses of herbs.
www.wic.net/waltzark/herbenc.htm

Internet Language Dictionary

www.netlingo.com

Project Guternberg

Huge library of books in electronic format, available for free download or online reading
www.gutenberg.net/

Student UK

Information, news and lots more for students.
www.studentuk.com

WWW Virtual Library

High quality, academic information.
vlib.stanford.edu/Overview2.html

RAC Traffice reports (page 125)

www.rac.co.uk

Other sites worth visiting

Amanaka'a Amazon Network (page 3)

Amazonian indian rights campaign.
www.amanakaa.org

Appointments Plus (page 126)
www.appointments-plus.com

Britsh Monarchy
By royal appopintment.
www.royal.gov.uk

Mars Team Online
quest.arc.nasa.gov/mars/photos

NASA Photo Gallery
www.nasa.gov/gallery/photo/index.html

The National Trust (page 4)
www.nationaltrust.org.uk

Web Museum
Great paintings with excellent commentary
sunsite.doc.ic.ac.uk/wm/

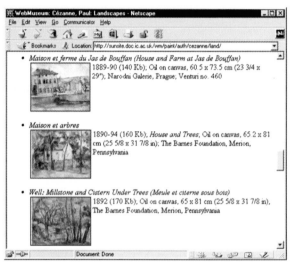

Take note

There's a regularly updated copy of these links online at the Made Simple site. Look for The Internet Made Simple at:

www.madesimple.co.uk

264

Shareware sites

Shareware can be tried out for free. If you want to use it after the trial period, you are asked to pay a fee to its authors. Fees typically are around £15, sometimes rising to £50 for the more comprehensive packages. The program's Help menu will tell you how to register your copy.

Some programs are **freeware** – and some of these are excellent!

Clicked
Offers the 'top 20 applications' in each of these areas: Internet applications, graphics, communications, multimedia, games and utilities.
www.clicked.com

Download.Net
Searchable archive for games, graphics, Internet, Winsock and desktop applications.
www.download.net

Internet Top 20
Quality, not quantity is the watchword here. The shareware listed at the Internet Top 20 is all reviewed and tested before inclusion.
home.pi.net/~tuur

Jumbo
This site has a different approach – it takes everything it can find. Jumbo had links to over 100,000 programs at the time of writing.
www.jumbo.com

Shareware Central
Interactive catalog, welcoming submissions from shareware authors.
www.q-d.com/wsc.htm

shareware.com
One of the largest stores of tested software, and links to other great clnet services.
www.shareware.com

The Software Site
Primarily for games enthusiasts. Its shareware is all tested and reviewed.
www.softsite.com

UK Shareware
Good range of Internet and other applications and utilities.
www.ukshareware.com

The Software Library
One of the Internet services run by ZD Net – and well worth a visit.
www.hotfiles.com/index.html

Tip

CNET (www.cnet.com), one of the most active Internet 'broadcasters' runs several excellent shareware sites at:

www.browsers.com/

www.gamecenter.com/

www.shareware.com/

Major FTP sites

ftp://ftp.demon.co.uk
Demon Internet hosts this comprehensive source of net tools and information – and while you're there you might look at what they have to offer as a service provider.

ftp://ftp.eff.org
The Electronic Frontier Foundation archives, source of much free software and a key centre for Linux enthusiasts.

ftp://ftp.uwp.edu
Its **/pub/msdos/games** directory is a major store of games – and it is frequently so crowded you can't get in.

ftp://ftp.microsoft.com
Microsoft's FTP base. Search it for information and software they have released into the public domain.

ftp://micros.hensa.ac.uk
Lots of Windows stuff in **/mirrors/cica/win3/ desktop**. This is a mirror (copy) of the main cica site in the States.

ftp://src.doc.ic.ac.uk (Sunsite UK)
– huge range of stuff, but a very busy site. Start from the **/pub** directory.

ftp://software.watson.ibm.com
IBM's public FTP site, an excellent source of software and documentation for business users and professional programmers.

Tip

Pick your time carefully and you can download files much faster. Avoid 7-11 in the evening, when you will be sharing your service provider's bandwidth with many other users. Avoid the working day at the FTP site, when you will be competing for the host's time with its local users – and remember that the host site may well be in a different time zone. The US is between 5 and 10 hours behind the UK.

Sunday morning is excellent – Europe is having a long lie-in or thinking about lunch and America is fast asleep!

Take note

This is a very limited selection of a huge number of FTP sites, with the focus on those in or closest to the UK. A full list can be found at:
http://hoohoo.ncsa.uiuc.edu/ftp

Index